‚ 1— talk about lotus, visicalc, Roth Pascal

☑ C0-DAC-723

COMPUTER
APPLICATIONS
GUIDE FOR
ACCOUNTANTS

408 - 970 - 9700
ext.
{ 7746
or
{ 7632

(1)

DSS - 440 Uls

1— each Group one chapter
2— each 2 one product
3— First 2 weeks overview
articles by Hossein

COMPUTER APPLICATIONS GUIDE FOR ACCOUNTANTS

Steven S. Weis

Reston Publishing Company, Inc.
A Prentice-Hall Company
Reston, Virginia

Library of Congress Cataloging in Publication Data

Weis, Steven S.
   Computer applications guide for accountants.

   Includes index.
   1. Accounting—Data processing.   I. Title.
HF5679.W44 1984   657'.028'54   83-19213
ISBN 0-8359-0851-8
ISBN 0-8359-0850-X (pbk.)

Editorial/production supervision and interior design
by Barbara J. Gardetto

© 1984 by
Reston Publishing Company, Inc.
A Prentice-Hall Company
Reston, Virginia 22090

*All rights reserved. No part of this book may be
reproduced in any way, or by any means, without
permission in writing from the publisher.*

10   9   8   7   6   5   4   3   2   1

Printed in the United States of America

about
the author

Steven S. Weis is a partner in the Los Angeles office of Ernst & Whinney, Certified Public Accountants. Steve's principal area of concentration is serving the needs of rapidly growing small- and medium-size businesses as an executive in the Privately Owned Business department. In this capacity, he assists clients in identifying operating problems and proposing solutions, many of which involve EDP. These solutions include selection of computer hardware and software, implementation planning, and more efficient and effective use of existing computer resources.

As Partner In Charge of Computer Auditing for 18 West Coast Ernst & Whinney offices, Steve is responsible for the use of computers as a tool to perform more efficient and effective audits and for the evaluation of computer controls.

He is a member of the Ernst & Whinney Los Angeles office EDP Steering Committee which is responsible for hardware and software selection for internal use and for priorities planning. He is also the codirector for the Western Region task force on the use of microcomputers and micronetworking.

Steve is a graduate of the University of California at Los Angeles where he earned his bachelor's degree in economics. In that school's Master of Science program in accounting, he received the Foundation's award for outstanding scholastic achievement. Steve is a Certified Public Accountant and a Certified Information Systems Auditor. In addition to being a frequent seminar leader, he has coauthored two audit guides published by the California Society of CPAs which provide "how to" guidance to CPAs regarding EDP controls.

I would like to thank all the people who provided encouragement and assistance along the way. Without their help, this book would never have been possible. Most of all, I would like to acknowledge a very special lady, Susan Renée Weis. She lived with my writing between 3 A.M. and 6 A.M., 7 P.M. to 10 P.M., and all day Saturday and Sunday from November 1982 through February 1983.

contents

preface   xiii

PART I _____
BACKGROUND   1

1 Technology: Understanding the EDP Environment   4
What You Need to Know About EDP   4
Understanding the Computer   5
Understanding the Black Box   5
Understanding Modern Peripheral Devices   6
Understanding the Software   10
Understanding Application Programming   11
Understanding the Hierarchy of Data   12
Understanding On-line Processing   13
Distinguishing Micros, Minis, and Mainframes   17
Understanding the Small Computer Boom   19

ix

Understanding Which Is More Important, Hardware or
    Software 21
Communicating with EDP Professionals and Vendors 22

2 What the Competition Is Up To 23
Why You Can't Afford to Sit Back and Watch 23
What Public Accountants Are Doing 24
What Accountants in Industry Are Doing 27
How Desktop Computers Are Being Used 33
Increasing Use of Graphics by Accountants 34

PART II
COMPUTERIZATION OPPORTUNITIES 37

3 Getting More Out of Basic Accounting Systems 39
General Ledger 39
Accounts Receivable 43
Accountants Payable 45
Payroll 48
Fixed Assests 50

4 Computerizing Services for Clients 53
Computerizing Accounting and Consulting Services for
    Clients 53
Using the Computer to Perform Tax Services for Clients 64

5 Computerizing Engagement and Practice Administration 69
Computerizing Time Accounting Functions 70
Computerizing Billing Functions 79

6 Using the Computer in Manufacturing Operations 89
Bill of Materials 91
Inventory Control 93
Material Requirements Planning 97
Master Production Scheduling 100
Cost Accounting 103
Warranty 105

7 Using the Computer in Distribution Operations 107
Order Entry 107
Sales Analysis 111
Inventory Management 113
Route Scheduling 117

8 Computerizing Finance Functions 120
Computerizing Budgeting Functions 120
Computerizing Projection Functions 125
Computerizing Economic Analyses 127

9 Computerizing Personnel Functions 130
Compensation 131
Continuing Professional Education 131
Personnel Evaluation Information 131
Recruiting 132
Requirements Planning 132
Scheduling 132
Skills Inventory 134

10 Using the Computer for Marketing Functions 136
Planning Marketing Activities 136
Monitoring Marketing Activities 139
Computerizing the Marketing Database 141

11 Using Graphics to Communicate Better 145
Understand Financial Graphics 145
Using Financial Graphics 148

12 Computerizing Your Office of the Future 152
Information Flow 153
Recurring Documents 158

13 Using Desktop Micros 161
Evolution of User Friendly General-Purpose Software 162
General-Purpose Application Software Packages and
    Application Opportunities 166

PART III
SELECTING COMPUTER HARDWARE AND SOFTWARE 181

14 Steps to Take Before Selecting a Vendor 183
Defining Computer Requirements 183
Selecting a Vendor 204

15 Purchasing Larger Micros and Minis 206
Communicating Requirements to Vendors 206
Selecting Vendors to Submit Proposals 211
Evaluating Vendor Proposals 212

Evaluating Final Candidates 221
Negotiating the Vendor Contract 224
Request for Proposal: A Case Study 226

16 Purchasing Desktop Micros 266
Characteristics of Desktop Micros Used in Business 266
Exploring the Reasons for Using a Different Approach 267
How to Purchase Desktop Micros 269
Select the Best Alternative 271

17 Implementing New Systems 278
Preparing the Implementation Plan 279
Monitoring Implementation Progress 287
Integrating Controls 288
Performing Postimplementation Evaluation 298

Appendices 301
Glossary 302
Checklists 317

Index 333

preface

If you are an accountant in public practice or private industry, this book is for you! If you are not presently using a computer or you feel like the computer you have isn't doing enough for you, read on. This book will illustrate what your competitors are doing with computers and help you to identify opportunities for computerization, to avoid hardware and software that won't meet your needs, and to compete in the marketplace more efficiently and effectively. A few of the benefits you will derive are listed next:

- Are you confused by the technical jargon used by data-processing professionals and vendors? This book will help you to understand their jargon and communicate with them more effectively. See Chapter 1.

- Are you falling behind in your work product? Are your competitors providing services you aren't? See what the competition is up to in Chapter 2.

- Have you computerized your basic accounting applications? Are you getting the most out of them? See Chapter 3.

- If you are an accountant in public practice or in a service industry:
  a. Are you using the computer for all your services to clients? See what more you can do in Chapter 4.
  b. Are you satisfied with your profitability on individual engagements and in total? If not, see how the computer can help you monitor and improve individual engagement and overall practice profitability in Chapter 5.
- If you are an accountant in private industry:
  a. Controlling production costs and obtaining timely and accurate information is critical to a manufacturing company. See how the computer can help you in Chapter 6.
  b. Minimizing inventory and stock-outs are key issues for distributing companies. See how the computer can help you in Chapter 7.
- Are you using pencil, paper, and typewriter to prepare budget drafts? Have you automated other finance functions? See how the computer can save you time and provide better information in Chapter 8.
- A small increase in employee productivity or utilization can result in large increases in your bottom line. Chapter 9 provides details for using the computer to help you accomplish this.
- Improving your market share is a constant battle. In Chapter 10, see how the computer can help you over the hurdles.
- Voluminous columns and tables divert attention away from important matters. Explore the exciting world of graphics in Chapter 11.
- Automating all your office needs can save you time and money. Explore the ways in Chapter 12.
- Why are desktop microcomputers proliferating? How can you use them in your every day business life? See Chapter 13.
- What size computer do you need? What can you do if you already use a computer and it isn't meeting your needs? We explore these topics in Chapter 14.
- Communicating needs and evaluating vendors are critical steps toward capitalizing on your opportunities. Practical techniques are provided in Chapter 15.
- Some desktop micros may not meet your needs. Chapter 16 will help you avoid the pitfalls.
- The best system in the world can fail if you don't consider two more things—people and controls. Chapter 17 will help you avoid the pitfalls in both areas.

How To Use This Book

Specific Challenges. If you are interested in a specific problem, such as "What are the opportunities for automating your office?" turn to the Contents to locate the chapter which discusses that topic (in this case, Chapter 12). Each chapter includes a discussion of the various issues. Pitfalls are pointed out and recommended strategies are presented. Use them for effective problem solving.

General Challenges. If you can relate your challenge to one of the following general areas, direct your initial reading toward the related relevant chapters:

General area	Chapter
Understanding modern EDP technology and communicating with EDP professionals and vendors	1
Determining what the competition is up to	2
Application opportunities for all accountants	3, 8 through 12
Additional opportunities for public accountants	4 and 5
Additional opportunities for accountants in industry	6 and 7
Desktop microcomputer applications	13
Determining information requirements and purchasing computer systems	14 through 17

For across-the-board types of problems in one of these major areas, go to the indicated chapters. Study the points of each chapter one at a time until you are comfortable that you understand the issues. Use the "How to's" and recommended strategies to problem solve in that particular area.

The Accounting and Finance Perspective

This book emphasizes problems and solutions from the perspective of the accountant in public practice and industry. Other members of management (e.g., marketing, sales, production, and administration) and financial analysts, consultants, and investment bankers will also find this book invaluable for identifying opportunities to computerize and for dealing more effectively with computer selection and implementation issues. Turn to the chapters containing topics that relate to your needs and areas of responsibility. Take the time to understand the issues. Next, review the recommended techniques or strategies and use them for effective problem solving.

PART **I**

background

In Chapter 1 we will look at the concepts underlying computers, including what they are, how they work, and the characteristics that distinguish smaller computers from larger computers. At this point you may be asking yourself why you need to understand how computers work. After all, we use many electrical and electronic devices everyday without needing a detailed understanding of how they work to make intelligent decisions as to which one to purchase. When we want to buy a new refrigerator, for example, we don't need to know much more than how much it costs and whether certain options are available (slightly larger storage capabilities, automatic icemaker, extended warranty, color, etc.). We certainly don't need to know about motors, coils, and the like, to make a decision as to which refrigerator to buy. The same is true for typewriters, automobiles, stoves, power tools, and many other electronic devices.

Why then do we need to understand computers? To answer this question, we need to focus on the following two points:

1. Price
2. Intended use

Price

The price for today's computers ranges from less than a thousand dollars to several million dollars. The chances are slight that the former will meet your business needs. At the other end of the scale, unless you are a multibillion dollar company, you don't need to spend several million dollars for a computer system. This leaves you in the intolerable position of being in an unidentified spot somewhere in between these two extremes. It is precisely for this reason that you need to have a basic understanding of computers to help ensure that:

1. You don't spend a lot of money buying what you don't need.
2. What you do buy will work and satisfy your needs.

Intended Use

The second point we need to focus on is intended use. It is truly unfortunate, but also a stark reality, that EDP is not yet a mature industry. There are hundreds of computer hardware manufacturers collectively pumping thousands of computers into the marketplace each and every business day. Substantially all of them have absolutely no idea of how they are going to be used! Contrast this with our earlier refrigerator example. The manufacturer knows exactly what you are going to do with your refrigerator—store perishable food. Simply plug it in and use it.

Our computer hardware manufacturers dutifully crank out computers in varying sizes, shapes, capabilities, and capacities. They do have one very important thing in common, however. They are all functionally useless! Without software, the hardware can't solve any of our problems. It's like producing a television or radio for which there is little or no programming. Yet that's exactly what the computer hardware industry has historically done—the sign of an immature industry. Perhaps by the end of this decade that will change. As we'll see in Chapter 2, you can't afford to sit back and wait that long. For now, a basic understanding of computers will help ensure that the hardware you ultimately purchase will in fact function according to your intended use.

1 technology: understanding the EDP environment

WHAT YOU NEED TO KNOW ABOUT EDP

If you are concerned that you will need in-depth technical knowledge of electronic data processing (EDP) in order to get the most out of your computer, set your concern aside. You don't need to understand how electrical impulses travel through logic circuitry or where programs are stored in memory. You won't need to know how to program the computer unless you are specifically interested in doing that. What you will need is a basic understanding of computer fundamentals and concepts. You'll need to know what the basic hardware components are and the primary functions of software. At that point we'll be prepared to forge ahead (use the Glossary in Appendix A to review technical terms). The technical and conceptual material in this chapter and throughout this book is equally applicable to microcomputers, minicomputers, and large-scale computers. This is also true as to your opportunities and pitfalls. However, if you are going to purchase a large-scale computer (we'll define the term shortly),

Files
Input
Output
Processing

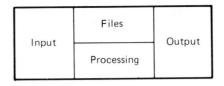

FIGURE 1.1
Computer activities.

you will need qualified EDP professionals on your staff to resolve the technical issues.

UNDERSTANDING THE COMPUTER

From the accountant's perspective, the computer consists of four types of functional devices associated with the four major activities depicted in Figure 1.1. Input devices facilitate the conversion of data into machine-readable form for transfer to the processing device (the *black box*). Once data are transferred to the processing device, either from an input device or file (*secondary storage*) or both, they can be acted upon and the results transferred to an output device or to a file for further processing.

UNDERSTANDING THE BLACK BOX

The term "black box" was originally coined because one cannot see inside the heart of the computer system, the central processing unit (CPU). Without being able to see inside the CPU, what took place there seemed to be very mysterious. While the CPU is certainly a complex device and varies from manufacturer to manufacturer, it has three components whose functions are quite straightforward (see Figure 1.2).

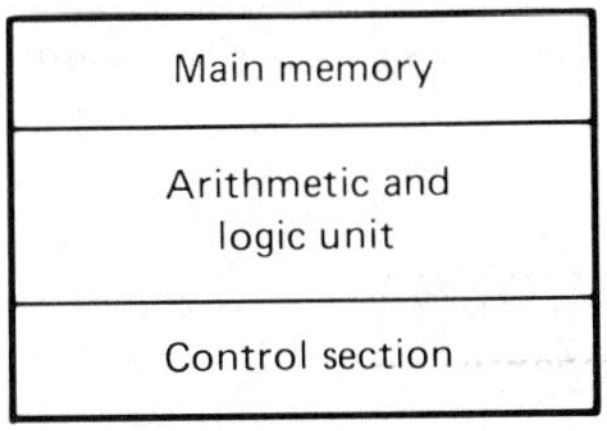

Main memory
Arithmetic and
logic unit
Control section

FIGURE 1.2
Central processing unit.

Main Memory

Main memory simply functions as a repository. For data to be processed, two conditions must be met. First, the data must be physically resident in main memory. Second, the instructions as to what type of processing is to take place must also be in main memory. Of particular importance to you is the fact that, in large quantities, memory is relatively expensive, so you don't want to buy more than you need. Recognizing this, many vendors offer expandable memory capabilities. If more is needed at a later date, it is simply added. However, once you reach the upper limit, you'll have to buy a new computer for any further growth.

One term you'll need to be familiar with is the *byte*, which represents a single storage position in main memory. Each byte is capable of storing a single character (e.g., the alphabet letter A or a punctuation character such as the exclamation point, !) or a numeric digit (e.g., the number 9), although in larger systems, two numeric digits may be represented. The unit of measure most commonly used is the *kilobyte*, abbreviated as K and representing 1000 bytes (actually, for the purists it's 1024). So, a main memory consisting of approximately 128,000 storage positions or bytes would be referred to as 128K. At the 1000K level, the unit of measure becomes the *megabyte* (1 million bytes).

Arithmetic and Logic Unit

The arithmetic and logic unit performs all the mathematical functions such as addition, subtraction, multiplication, and division. It is also the unit that performs all the logical functions, such as testing for certain conditions (greater than, less than, and equal to).

Control Section

The control section coordinates the operations of the computer system, including input and output devices, the arithmetic and logic unit, and transferring data and instructions to and from main memory. It retrieves instructions stored in memory, interprets them, and issues commands to other system components for execution.

UNDERSTANDING MODERN PERIPHERAL DEVICES

As an accountant, what you need to know about peripheral devices consists of the functions they perform and where the technology is leading us.

Input Devices

Before data can be processed by the CPU, they must be converted into machine-readable form and transferred into the CPU. Earlier technology required separate devices (keypunch machines and card readers) to handle these two tasks; and, typically, they were placed within the EDP department. Today's technology combines these two tasks within one device and places it (typewriter keyboard with CRT display) directly in the user department. Frequently referred to as workstations or data-entry terminals, these devices dramatically expedite the data-entry process.

Output Devices

Today's technology provides us with two primary types of output: screen (CRT) display or hard-copy printed reports. Large volumes of data in printed reports are time consuming and cumbersome to work with to resolve specific questions. In addition, the reports themselves may not reflect the most current information. CRT display devices lend themselves to dealing with these types of inquiry and retrieval issues. Questions such as "What are the details of XYZ Company's accounts receivable balance?" and "How many widgets do we have in stock?" can be answered in a fraction of a second.

The other primary device for output is the printer. Selecting the right printer today would seem to be a straightforward task. Unfortunately, that's not the case! However, the task of selecting the right printer can be greatly simplified if you focus on three key considerations: quality, speed, and cost.

Quality. The quality of the printed output depends primarily on whether the printer uses *fully formed* or *dot matrix* technology. Fully formed character printers produce letter-quality output. Their print heads are similar to the print ball used in typewriters. All the characters are contained on the ball, and it is simply rotated to the correct character

Fully formed   Dot matrix

FIGURE 1.3
Impact and dot matrix fonts.

position and pressed against the ribbon and paper to create the printed character. Dot matrix printers print a series of dots to "resemble" a character. The larger the size of the matrix and the closer together the dots are printed, the better the quality of the resembled character. Samples of fully formed and dot matrix characters are shown in Figure 1.3.

Speed. The most important consideration regarding printer speed is that the output reports must be printed within the business' work period, however that is defined (e.g., a single eight-hour shift). Accordingly, the two key factors to be considered are the volume of data to be printed and the speed of the printer itself. As to the latter, there are yet again two types of printers to be considered. Single-character printers generally print at speeds ranging from 12 to 200 characters per second, with letter-quality printers being the slowest. Simple mathematical calculations indicate that these printers require as much as a full minute to print a single page. Contrast this with the speed of line printers (which print an entire line at one time) with common speeds of 300 to 3000 lines per minute (approximately 3 to 500 times faster). For the largest of businesses, there are printers that will achieve thousands of lines of printing per minute.

Cost. Printers range in cost from several hundred dollars to tens and even hundreds of thousands of dollars. As a practical matter, it is not uncommon to use a letter-quality printer for important word-processing applications (outside correspondence and the like) and a faster dot matrix printer for internal high-volume applications (accounts receivable and the like).

File Storage Devices

File storage devices serve two essential functions: storing data and programs for backup and for further application processing.

Backup Storage Devices. The importance of adequate backup is well known to accountants. In the event of accidental (or sometimes purposeful) destruction of files, we need to be able to continue processing capabilities by reconstructing the destroyed data. Since these are usually infrequent occurrences, it is more cost effective to use less expensive, slower access devices to create the backup files. Common devices include magnetic tape drives and floppy disk drives. In larger EDP installations with large volumes of data, disk drives with removable hard disks for backup are frequently used. In the mini- and microcomputer systems, recent technology has provided high-speed, low-cost cartridge tape devices as a very efficient and cost-effective alternative.

(handwritten at top: high resolution = high clarity)

Files for Further Processing. Since main memory cannot contain all the data and programs necessary for processing, secondary or auxiliary storage devices are necessary to store them so that portions of the data and programs can be stored there until needed for processing. Recent technological advances in disk storage devices are quickly making tape drives obsolete as secondary storage devices (the drawback of tape is that information cannot be accessed directly; the entire tape must be read until the desired information is found). While floppy disk drives were used extensively in mini and micro systems, they are giving way to *Winchester-type* fixed or removable disk devices previously found only in the larger computer systems. In addition to providing much faster data access time, these Winchester-type hard disks are capable of storing mammoth amounts of data. For example, if a floppy diskette can store 140,000 characters, a 5-megabyte (5 million bytes) disk is the equivalent of approximately 35 floppy diskettes.

(handwritten: 5 MB = 35 Floppy; 20 MB = 140 Floppy)

Graphics

Graphics consist of shapes such as lines or circles and objects such as drawings. There are three primary techniques for producing graphics representations. The devices that produce them and the techniques employed are illustrated in the following matrix:

	CRT	Printer	Plotter
Lines			X
Dots	X	X	
Characters		X	

Lines. Plotters create graphics representations by plotting two or more points and drawing a line to connect them. Drawings are created by connecting a series of lines.

Dots. CRTs and printers create shapes and drawings by using dots. The closer together are the dots, the greater the resolution (clarity) of the graphics. The specific capabilities of a CRT or printer to create graphics representations are a function of both the hardware and the application software.

Characters. If defined as a part of the printer's character set, dot matrix printers can produce predefined characters in the same fashion as they do other characters such as letters.

With our discussion of hardware now complete, let's move on to the other key ingredient—software.

UNDERSTANDING THE SOFTWARE

The entire collection of software necessary to make the hardware useful and produce work can simply be referred to as the *operating system*. The operating system in turn can be subdivided into two groups as illustrated in Figure 1.4.

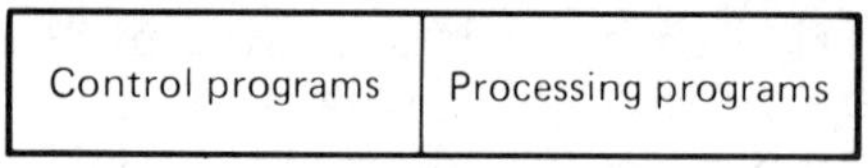

Control programs	Processing programs

FIGURE 1.4
Operating system.

Control Programs

As their name indicates, control programs are responsible for controlling computer operations. Their tasks include scheduling processing programs for execution based on user-defined priorities, moving data in and out of main storage, and supervising the execution of processing programs. Control programs are purchased with the computer hardware. From your standpoint, you don't need to know anything more about them other than the fact that they consume memory (they must be present in main memory when needed to perform their functions). Thus, the amount of memory available to processing programs is the gross amount of main storage less the storage required by the control programs (this may vary since portions of control programs can be brought into main memory only when they are needed).

Processing Programs

Processing programs can be subdivided into three groups as illustrated in Figure 1.5.

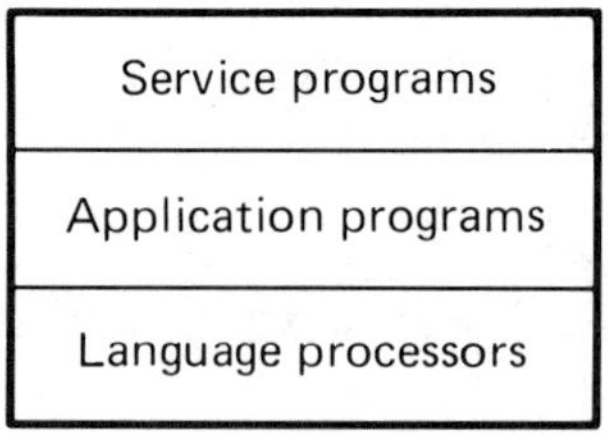

Service programs
Application programs
Language processors

FIGURE 1.5
Processing programs.

Service Programs.   Service programs are provided by vendors and perform frequently used functions such as sorting and merging data and copying data files and programs from one storage device to another.

Application Programs.   Application programs process data and are the sole purpose for which computer systems exist. After being translated into machine language, they perform the work that we find useful (prepare billings and update accounts receivable, maintain perpetual inventories, etc.).

Language Processors.   Language processors translate the application program into machine-language instructions that can be executed by the computer. They also are provided by vendors.

UNDERSTANDING APPLICATION PROGRAMMING

Do we accountants need to be intimately familiar with programming languages and the characteristics that distinguish them? Frankly, I don't think so. It is true that some programming languages are easy to learn and use (e.g., BASIC). On the other hand, complex application programming is best left to those who are highly skilled at it. With your accounting expertise, you can perform a critical function—challenging whether or not the application meets the needs of your organization.

What you need to know about languages and programs is simply some fundamentals:

1. Application programs can be written in a variety of programming languages such as COBAL, FORTRAN, RPG, and BASIC.
2. Programming languages vary as to complexity and, therefore, skill requirements.
3. All computer programs have to be translated into machine language (instructions that the machine can understand) by a language processor. Machine language, in terms of what it looks like to us, consists of zeros and ones representing binary states.
4. Each sentence ("line of programming code") equates to one or more computer instructions. Programming languages that, when translated, produce a single computer instruction for each line of programming code (low-level languages) are less Englishlike and require a greater degree of skill.
5. All application programs, whether developed by a vendor or an employee, need to be thoroughly tested:

- During the implementation process
- Whenever programming changes are made

UNDERSTANDING THE HIERARCHY OF DATA

As an accountant, you don't need to understand the technical details of how data are stored. However, a conceptual understanding of the hierarchy of data will be useful to you for purposes of planning requirements and

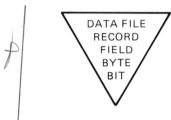

FIGURE 1.6
Hierarchy of data.

communicating with EDP people. The pyramid diagram in Figure 1.6 illustrates this hierarchy, the elements of which are defined as follows:

- **Bit.** A bit is an acronym for BInary digiT. Based on the binary numbering system, it is the smallest unit of data and may take on the values zero or one.

- **Byte.** A group of eight adjacent bits. Since each bit in the group can take on two values, the entire group, or byte, may take on 256 different values. A single byte then is sufficient to represent any of the 26 letters in the English language or the decimal digits 0 through 9, with room left over to represent special characters such as semicolons and commas.

- **Field.** An item of information such as customer name.

- **Record.** A collection of related fields (e.g., all the fields pertaining to a given customer).

- **Data File.** A collection of related records, such as accounts receivable.

In a manual system, we tend to approach the data hierarchy much more informally. For example, consider a sales invoice. If the customer's address won't fit in the field (allowable space) designed for it, we can simply let it flop over into the field for city. Or if all the sales invoices won't fit in the filing cabinet, some of them can be put on top of the cabinet or on the floor. In the world of computers, a lack of adequate planning could easily result in fields being overwritten so that the information is incomprehensible or whole records being lost because there is insufficient space to store them. We'll explore the importance of planning and how to go about it in subsequent chapters. For now, let's move on to recent techniques for speeding up the processing and retrieving of information in the data hierarchy.

UNDERSTANDING ON-LINE PROCESSING

The term *on-line* is frequently used to describe any computer system in which a terminal is involved. This vagueness only leads to confusion as to the nature of the on-line activities taking place. We can eliminate this confusion by (1) contrasting single-transaction systems with batch-oriented systems and (2) reviewing the types of on-line processing.

The table in Figure 1.7 illustrates that batch-oriented systems are EDP oriented, while transaction-oriented systems are user oriented. In transaction-oriented systems, the user can process a transaction immediately and completely as opposed to batch systems, which focus on processing a group or groups of accumulated transactions. Accordingly, batch systems are program oriented in that the program asks for the data as needed; in transaction-oriented systems, the transaction asks for the program it needs (the transaction type determines which programs to use). Batch systems facilitate smoothing out of the workload; applications can be processed when it is most convenient and efficient to do so. Not so with transaction-oriented systems; processing takes place now when the user demands it. Batch systems also lend themselves to slower sequential-type masterfile storage, since many transactions of the same type (shipments and the like) will be processed at the same time. In transaction-oriented systems, a single masterfile record must be accessed very quickly, which requires direct-access storage devices. Finally, batch systems lend themselves to using a

Batch	Single-transaction
Transactions grouped in batches	Transactions processed as entered
Program driven	Transaction driven
Scheduled operations	On-demand operations
Sequential files	Direct-access storage devices
Run-by-run processing	Fast-response processing

FIGURE 1.7
Characteristics of batch and single-transaction systems.

series of programs to accomplish specific tasks (edit, status checking, sort, update, etc.), one task at a time, while transaction-oriented systems require all the tasks to be performed prior to moving on to the next transaction.

While the table in Figure 1.7 illustrates the differences between batch and on-line systems, it should be noted that not all on-line systems are alike. In fact, there are several types of on-line activities or capabilities:

1. Inquiry
2. Edit
3. Update
4. Remote processing
   - Remote batch
   - Remote job
   - Distributed processing

On-Line Inquiry

On-line inquiry capability permits a user to retrieve information from a file and display it on the screen. This type of activity is useful for researching problems (reviewing cash receipts applied to customer invoices) and determining availability (inventory stock status).

On-Line Edit

The purpose of on-line edit is prompt detection and correction of input errors. Examples include:

- Checking customer number, inventory part number, and vendor number against the master file for validity.
- Range and limit checks such as comparing payroll hours input against a predetermined limit (e.g., 40 hours) or customer order amount against a predetermined credit limit.

Transactions that pass the edit checks are then accumulated on a file for further processing in groups (similar to batch processing).

On-Line File Update

Frequently referred to as *transaction* or *item* oriented systems, on-line file update systems are the most sophisticated. After the edit checks described previously are performed, the affected account balances are updated immediately. For example, after editing a shipment for valid customer and part numbers, the inventory and accounts receivable balances would be immediately updated. You may also hear the terms *real time* and *fast response* used to describe these systems. Properly used, these terms refer to systems for which the results of processing are available fast enough to affect the environment. The classic example is the airlines reservation system. Within a few seconds, a reservation agent can retrieve the flight availability status. If a reservation is booked, the status is updated quickly enough so that the next inquiry as to availability on that flight reflects the new booking.

On-Line Programming

If you are not going to be doing any programming in-house (either original development or modifications), you may skip this section. The primary purpose of on-line programming is to improve programmer productivity. In a punched card/batch-oriented environment, programs are written in longhand, converted to machine-readable form via punched cards, read into the computer, and compiled. During the compiling process, the program is checked for conformity with the particular rules (*syntax*) of the programming language being used. If there are syntax errors, the related punched cards must be corrected and the revised deck of cards resubmitted and compiled until all syntax errors are corrected. At that point, the program can be run against test data to ascertain that it performs the required editing tasks and that the logic produces the intended results. Detected errors (*bugs*) must be corrected and the process repeated. From the time the programmer submits the program for compilation or running against test data until the programmer receives the results, he or she is idle and devotes attention to changing another program (which entails getting up to speed on that program again). On-line programming solves these inefficiencies. Using a terminal, the programmer can change the program lines on the screen and compile and run. Errors can be corrected on-line and the program rerun immediately. The program can be stored in a test file at the end of the day and retrieved immediately the following day. The inefficiencies of punched card/batch-oriented programming are eliminated.

Remote Processing

For businesses for which transactions take place at more than one location (multiple offices, plants, etc.), EDP facilities can be installed at each location. There are essentially three types of on-line remote processing:

1. **Remote batch.** Transactions are entered and temporarily stored at the remote site. Periodically (hourly, daily, etc.), the central site requests

the remote sites to transmit accumulated transactions (using telephone lines or the like). After the transactions are received at the central site, they can either be processed immediately or stored for later processing. Of particular importance is the fact that the central site is controlling the activities and computer resources (more on this aspect later).

2. **Remote job.** Remote job technology transfers utilization of the central site's resources to the user. Processing of transactions is performed when requested and can be either batch or transaction oriented, both as to editing and file updating.

3. **Distributed processing.** While there are many definitions of distributed processing, there are two concepts involved. First, application development, acquisition, and modification functions are performed at the central site. Second, some or all of the processing takes place at the remote sites using small computers and programs developed by the central site. Thus, the remote sites might be responsible for receivables, inventory, and payables; the results of processing would then be forwarded to the central site for consolidation and analysis.

As you can see, there are many types of on-line processing. As an accountant, there are two prime considerations that you will want to address—controls and cost.

Controls. The primary purpose of on-line systems is to speed up activities by bringing computer resources out of the computer room and into the hands of users. This is accomplished by using terminals that provide access to data files, application and service programs, and to the CPU itself. Access then is the key issue and our concern is unauthorized changes to programs or data files and unauthorized processing. Furthermore, in transaction-oriented systems, traditional control techniques (batch totals and the like) are not applicable.

How then do we know that all authorized transactions have been processed correctly and that unauthorized transactions have not been added? We will address these types of concerns in detail in Chapter 12. For now, suffice it to say that the extent and quality of controls provided by the vendor should be an important factor in selecting a vendor.

Costs. From the cost standpoint, greater on-line activity costs more. To handle multiple users and more on-line activities requires (1) larger, more sophisticated control programs and application programs, as well as more main memory to accommodate them, and (2) larger or more direct access auxiliary storage devices since more files and programs will be on-line. The issue then becomes whether the benefits (increased cash flow from faster processing, better service, and/or more timely and better information) outweigh the cost.

At this point, our review of basic technology is complete and prepares us for the remaining topics of this chapter: distinguishing the various sizes of computers, the small computer boom, hardware versus software, and communication with EDP types.

DISTINGUISHING MICROS, MINIS AND MAINFRAMES

Vendors frequently distinguish size by reference to whether it is a microcomputer (micro), minicomputer (mini), or large-scale computer (mainframe). Within each of these general classifications there is a relatively wide range of capabilities. You may also hear the terms "supermicro" and "supermini" used; these terms simply mean that the vendor indicates that it is a model toward the upper end of the range in its category and may rival the low end of the next higher category. The table in Figure 1.8 illustrates the range of commonly used criteria for distinguishing micros, minis, and mainframes, described as follows:

1. Instruction word length (or just word length) represents the typical length of the computer instruction and, accordingly, places limitations on the power (or completeness) of the computer's instruction repertoire. The larger the word length, the more powerful the instruction set is.

2. The dollar amounts include the CPU and frequently purchased peripheral devices and exclude application software.

3. Speed represents the approximate number of computer instructions that can be executed in 1 second (smaller computers may require many instructions to accomplish a single task; however, the table does provide a means for relative comparison).

4. The low end of the range represents the minimum amount of main memory frequently offered by vendors. The high end of the range represents the theoretical maximum amount of main memory that can

CRITERIA	MICRO	MINI	MAIN FRAME
Word length (1)	8–16 Bits	16–32 Bits	32–64 Bits
Cost—000's (2)	1–40	25–300	250–10,000
Speed—000's (3)	10–35	20–400	250–2,500
Main memory (4)	4K–64K	32K–4,000K	512K–32,000K

FIGURE 1.8
Distinguishing micros, minis, and mainframes.

be addressed, based upon the address word length of each category; see item (1) of Figure 1.8. New techniques have been developed to extend these maximums. For example, extended addressing, memory bank switching, and virtual storage techniques enable computers to utilize many times the theoretical maximum amount of main memory.

As Figure 1.8 illustrates, there isn't any clear dividing line between categories. In fact, large micros are becoming indistinguishable from small minis and large minis from mainframes. However, the table is useful for relative comparisons. Other criteria that may be used include:

- The number of users the system can accommodate at one time.

FIGURE 1.9
Miniaturization. (Courtesy of International Business Machines Corporation)

2. • The number and size of auxiliary storage and output devices that can be attached.

3. • The extent of EDP personnel necessary to utilize the computer:

   a. Micros: none

   b. Minis: one computer operator (other personnel as well if programming is to be done in house)

   c. Mainframes: generally extensive

UNDERSTANDING THE SMALL COMPUTER BOOM

To understand the small computer boom, you need only be familiar with a single concept, which is illustrated in Figure 1.9—miniaturization. The first computers used in the late 1940s and 1950s utilized vacuum tubes (see Figure 1.9) as their basic component, required thousands of them to function, and filled a very large room with their bulky architecture. By the late 1950s, these bulky vacuum-tube machines began to be replaced by smaller (and more reliable) solid-state transistors. But it wasn't until the mid 1960s that small computers became commercially viable. What made that possible was the ability to fabricate many component parts (transistors, diodes, etc.) in a single process on a tiny piece of silicon—the integrated circuit. From that point on it's been a process of expanding the miniaturization concept—packing more and more data into the same space in disk storage devices and main memory and putting more and more components together on a single chip. In the early 1970s, a complete CPU

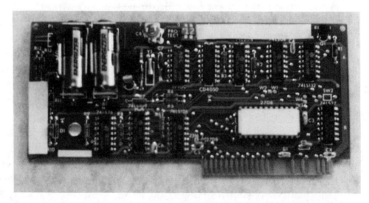

FIGURE 1.10
Expansion boards.

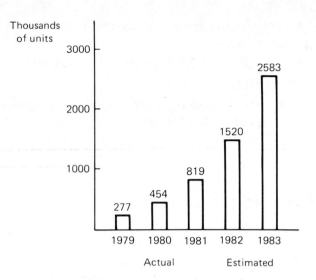

FIGURE 1.11
Number of microcomputers sold. (Courtesy of International Data Corporation)

(microprocessor) was placed on a single chip smaller than your fingernail. These early microprocessors were single-task-oriented (running appliances and the like), and their stored instructions could not be easily changed. Shortly thereafter, main memory and input/output interfaces were added, all on a single circuit board (*motherboard*), and the microcomputer was born.

Many of today's microcomputers provide expansion capabilities. More main memory can be obtained by replacing a chip in the motherboard. Another widely used technique is the expansion *slot* in the motherboard into which additional boards (see Figure 1.10) can be inserted. Expansion boards provide the ability to communicate with other computers, to connect additional input and output devices, and even to add a second microprocessor to run application software developed for that microprocessor. Miniaturization and other technological developments have brought the cost of small computers down to the level where they are an attractive alternative for both small businesses and home use.

While microcomputers were initially used for home entertainment (games) and personal finance, they are proliferating in the business environment as well. Figure 1.11 illustrates the dramatic growth of microcomputers. The number of microcomputers sold increased 80% in 1981, with projected increases of 86% for 1982 and 67% for 1983. Clearly, microcomputers are big business. The dollar value of projected 1982 sales exceeds $5 billion, and that's just for hardware.

UNDERSTANDING WHICH IS
MORE IMPORTANT, HARDWARE
OR SOFTWARE

The technical material in this chapter was presented to provide you with a basic understanding of computer fundamentals and concepts. Much of that technology dealt with hardware and system software, rather than application software. This does not mean that application software should be de-emphasized—as we are about to see, it shouldn't!

When commercial computers were in their infancy, only the largest of businesses could afford them. Often a multimillion dollar expenditure was made just to obtain the hardware and system software. If application software had to be developed, the cost of several man-years of programming effort was only a small fraction of the hardware cost. Accordingly, the emphasis was on the hardware. Find the biggest and fastest computer and then worry about the software.

The emphasis today is on application software, not hardware, and there are several reasons for this. First, the cost of computing power has decreased substantially. Today's microcomputer has the power of the earliest computers at less than one-hundredth of the cost. On the other hand, salaries of application programmers have continually risen, not only as a result of inflation in general but also because there is an industry shortage of qualified personnel. Accordingly, the cost of developing application software in-house is extremely expensive. In recent years there

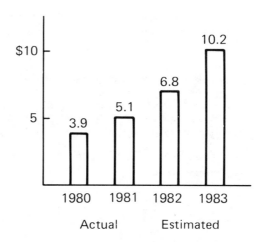

FIGURE 1.12
Billions of dollars of packaged software sales.
(Courtesy of International Data Corporation)

has been a substantial increase in the development of application software packages by independent third parties. Figure 1.12 illustrates a recent survey regarding the market for packaged software (micros, minis, and mainframes).

While the packaged software business is far from being mature, there are some very fine software houses with high-quality products that may meet your needs. If after reading this book you remember only one thing, it should be, *Find the application software that meets your needs; then find the hardware that it will run on!*

COMMUNICATING WITH EDP PROFESSIONALS AND VENDORS

After many discussions with EDP professionals and vendors, I am still amazed at how wrapped up they are in the technology. Programmers talk to you in terms of how efficient their programming techniques are and how efficiently they utilize computer resources. EDP managers talk about having the latest machines. Hardware vendors dwell on machine cycles, access speeds, and the sophistication of their operating systems. Software vendors tell you all about what their programs do (not what they won't do). In later chapters we'll explore specific strategies and techniques for evaluating vendors. For now, you'll need to store away some pointers to keep in mind as we progress through subsequent chapters:

1. Stay away from discussions on technology. You're concerned with results, not how they are achieved.

2. Don't permit computerese in your conversations. If you initiate it, you have given an open invitation for them to do the same, and they do it better than you. If they initiate it, ask them to explain it in English. If they know what they are talking about, they will easily be able to translate it into terms you understand.

3. After you are told what it does do, ask about what it doesn't do. After all, they are salespersons trying to sell you something. Reputable EDP personnel will respond to you.

Keep these suggestions in mind as we progress through each chapter. They will serve you well.

2 what the competition is up to

Chapter 1 provided conceptual materials to understand better the black box, why computers are proliferating, and how to communicate with EDP personnel. In this chapter, we will review the results of taking a "wait and see" attitude and what our counterparts and others are doing to gain a competitive advantage.

WHY YOU CAN'T AFFORD TO SIT BACK AND WATCH

How tempting it is sometimes to sit back and bathe in the luxury of our past successes. The business is profitable and why exert ourselves further? The chances are that you have felt like this at sometime in your career (after all, you're only human)! If you are not presently using a computer or if you are not getting the most you can out of the computer you have, then:

1. If you are in public accounting, you may be on your way to losing profitable clients.

2. If you are an executive in industry, you may be wasting valuable company resources and being noticed as not being innovative.

Sitting back and watching doesn't work, because customers and clients search for more cost-effective alternatives. Innovative competitors are eager to provide these alternatives. Given the rapidly expanding EDP technology, the computer is playing an ever-increasing role in providing more efficient and effective solutions. What then is the competition up to?

WHAT PUBLIC ACCOUNTANTS ARE DOING

As professionals in a service industry, our profitability is a function of:

- The fee we collect for services rendered.
- The direct costs to render those services.
- Indirect costs, including administration overhead.

If your goal is to maintain your present level of profitability without adding new clients and without improving cost performance (i.e., maintain the status quo), then your competitors are probably closing in on you (please reread the introductory section of this chapter).

If your goal is to increase your profitability, then focus on the following primary objectives to accomplish your goal:

- Increasing the fee for services rendered.
- Adding new clients.
- Performing new services.
- Reducing the cost of present services rendered.
- Reducing administrative costs.
- Obtaining more and better information for decision making.

The first objective is beyond the scope of this book, to which the author would only add that, in periods of financial difficulty, many of your clients are experiencing declining cash flow and profitability and expect that you not increase your fees (some of them will even expect that you will reduce fees).

But look at the remaining objectives. Their scope includes the majority of your practice! If you would like to improve your success in any or all of these areas, EDP can be a major factor. Let's take a look at what your competitors are doing.

Computerizing "Write-up" Services and Internal Accounting

For many decades accountants have been helping their clients with their internal bookkeeping function. We write up their cash receipts and cash disbursements journals, post their subsidiary accounts receivable and accounts payable subledgers, and, finally, post their general ledger. Then we take off a trial balance, locate and correct posting errors, and then and only then we prepare financial statements. In light of some of our clients' preferences, we will probably continue to perform write-up services for decades to come, if we are cost effective.

Given the decreasing cost of computer hardware and software, the method of delivering these services, as well as performing our own internal accounting function, is changing. Some examples are:

- Performing data-entry and processing services on in-house computers.
- Using terminals at client locations where data are entered and transmitted to the accountant's office for further processing on an in-house computer.
- Entering data in tne accountant's office and transmitting it to time-sharing service centers for further processing.

If you are performing write-up services manually, the chances are that you are not cost effective. If you are using service centers, explore turnkey systems as a potential more cost-effective solution (guidance on analyzing alternatives will be provided in Chapter 14). If you are not automated for internal accounting functions, you may be incurring excessive administrative costs or not receiving important and timely information for decision-making purposes.

Assisting Clients with Computerized Forecasts, Budgets, and the Like

Your client may not have the internal capability or inclination to prepare and use meaningful cash and profit forecasts and budgets or perform modeling functions to analyze operating challenges. If this is the case and you are not helping in these areas, you may be missing opportunities to perform important and valued services. One historical inhibitor to performing these types of services has been the cost. Varying the assumptions requires extensive time-consuming recalculations. Many public accounting firms have computerized these functions, which enables them to:

- Reduce the time required of senior-level personnel.

- Eliminate totally the significant clerical effort associated with the numerous recalculations.

Adding New Clients

If you feel secure because you believe that other firms aren't actively pursuing your privately owned clients, then read on! The reality is that competitors are using computers to identify your clients as potential clients of theirs ("target companies").

Several entities, including the *Standard & Poors* reporting service, maintain a large database on businesses. Thus, accounting firms (and others) can and do receive this information. The type of information they are presently obtaining is typified as follows:

- Name of company
- Address
- Key company executives and ownership percentages
- Principal products or services
- Number of employees
- Annual sales volume
- Professionals serving this company

Given the potential volume of companies on these lists, the ability to utilize this information effectively on a manual basis is questionable. Contrast this with the ability, using a computer, to sort this information quickly and print reports. Armed with this information and the ability to manipulate it on a computer, competitors are using it to develop a target list of companies to add to their practice. We'll explore these types of activities in Chapter 10.

Obtaining More and Better
Information for Decision Making

If you are (1) devoting a lot of time to sorting through and analyzing data or (2) you don't have the time to do so, you are probably missing opportunities to:

- Expand your practice
- Implement cost efficiencies
- Qualitize your practice

Let's examine what the competition is doing in the area of computerized practice management.

A major by-product of computerizing accounting systems (time-keeping, billings and collections, etc.) is the ability to obtain management reports. By retaining the basic data on file, it is then available for further processing such as sorting (collections by service code and the like), exception reporting (e.g., percent of standard less than desired), calculations (e.g., collected rate per hour), and trending (e.g., comparisons to prior periods). This in turn enables accountants to:

1. Reduce time devoted to collecting and analyzing data and devote more time to managing the practice and developing new business.

2. Identify engagements on which inefficiencies have occurred and take corrective action.

3. Eliminate substandard engagements and substitute more profitable work.

Having looked at some examples of what public accountants are doing, we'll move on to what industry is doing, and then conclude this chapter with a discussion of how desktop micros are being used.

WHAT ACCOUNTANTS IN INDUSTRY ARE DOING

As a business advisor to privately held companies I am frequently asked questions such as:

- Should I computerize?
- What more should we be doing with our computer?
- How can we use the computer to produce more management information?
- How can we speed up our processing time?
- How can we use the computer to make decisions for us?

These questions are best answered by looking at your competitors who are in the process of implementing solutions to the issues raised by these questions.

Smaller Businesses Are Computerizing

A few years ago it was primarily businesses with annual revenues of more than $10 million that were computerizing for the first time. The technological advances of the past few years have changed that. Today, more and more smaller businesses are using computers. Some are purchasing turnkey systems; others are using service centers, including using time-sharing services (we'll explore these alternatives in Chapter 12). If you are still manually processing all your business applications, chances are that others are gaining a competitive edge.

Next let's look at a sample application, followed by some techniques being used to increase operating efficiency and obtain better information.

Computerizing Order Entry

In a manual system, order entry wins first prize for generating sheer volume of paper work. No other function has a more pervasive effect throughout the business. Businesses are computerizing order-entry functions because of the opportunities to obtain new or more timely information to manage more effectively, as illustrated by the following:

1. Sales and marketing
   - Product analysis
   - Salesmen/representative performance
   - Backlog
   - Lost sales
   - Changes in customer buying patterns
   - Analyze "what if" scenarios
2. Inventory and production control
   - Scheduling production
   - Reducing stock-outs
   - Increasing inventory turnover
3. Credit granting
   - Reviewing credit history
   - Retrieving up-to-date balances (receivables plus on order)

We'll explore these and other specific opportunities in Part II. For now, let's look at some techniques being used.

Putting Terminals into User Departments

The traditional centralized data-entry methodology placed the data-entry function directly under the control and supervision of the EDP or accounting departments. Source documents (shippers, purchasing requests, etc.) were grouped and forwarded (interoffice mail and so on) to data entry. Given that many of today's minicomputers and microcomputers can support multiple terminals, companies are putting the terminals in the user departments. This trend is totally consistent with the overall trend toward user-oriented data-processing services. The underlying reasons make a lot of sense. Look at the implications of forwarding source documents from one department to another:

- A source document (or worse yet, an entire batch) is lost or misplaced. There should be sufficient controls to detect this, but consider the time involved to investigate and identify the missing documents, locate them, and, finally, resubmit them.

- The documents find their way to data entry, but an edit error occurs, causing the source document (or worse yet, the entire batch) to be rejected and returned to the user department. Consider the time involved to return the transactions to the user department and the time lost, after the user has made corrections, to return corrected items to data entry.

From a business perspective consider:

- The lost cash flow if these were shipping documents.

- The lost sales if these were purchase request documents that, after processing, generated purchase orders to fill stock-outs.

The solution to these types of problems is to locate the terminals in the user department. In this example, consider putting terminals in the shipping and purchasing departments. Naturally, you'll have to look at the cost and personnel side of the issue, too (which we'll be doing in subsequent chapters).

Putting Terminals in Remote Locations

Suppose you have two locations providing services or shipping and receiving goods. The second location is sufficiently far away that the source documents it generates cannot be hand delivered to the corporate data-entry office. Accordingly, they are mailed to the central location for further processing. Assume the following facts:

1. The second location generates $10 million in annual revenues.

2. Time delay (mail and so on) is 2 days.

3. You are currently borrowing from a bank at the prime rate of 16% plus 2% = 18%.

4. Expediting billings accelerates cash receipts.

The result is that the processing delay costs you $13,846 per year (each and every year) as follows:

Daily sales ($10,000,000)/52 weeks/5 days per week =	$38,462
Days collections delayed	2
Dollars delayed	76,923
Interest rate	18%
Annual pretax dollars lost	$13,846

A potential solution to this problem would be to install a terminal at the second location. Let's do a quick break-even analysis by looking at the present value of the annual dollars lost (potential savings):

Annual pretax dollars lost	$13,846
Present value of these pretax dollars using a period of five years and the 18% interest rate	$43,299
Tax effect, say 50%	21,650
Net of tax effect	$21,649

What this analysis tells us is that, if the after-tax cost of installing a terminal and revising the software to permit processing from a remote site is less than $21,649, but more than $13,846, then we would be money ahead by doing it.

Understanding Integrated Systems

As we climb up the ladder of computer sophistication, as we are about to, be aware that we are also moving toward more expensive systems. Whether or not these systems make sense for you will depend on your specific needs and your cost–benefit evaluation.

To begin with, let's clarify the phraseology that vendors will likely want to use with you. The phrase *integrated systems* connotes some sort of "togetherness," but, without further specificity, is totally useless. Consider the statement, "Our accounts receivable system is integrated." That doesn't tell you very much, does it? We also need to know "with what." For example, the statement might simply mean that there is an "automatic interface" between the accounts receivable and general ledger applications. In other words, the accounts receivable application automatically creates entries for and posts to the general ledger.

On the other hand, the phrase "Our accounts receivable system is

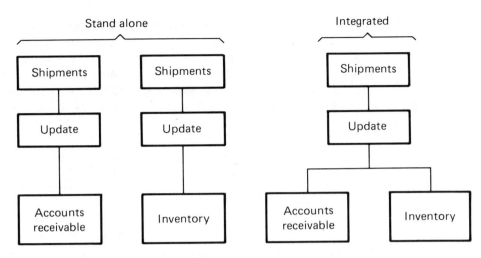

FIGURE 2.1
Understanding integrated systems.

integrated" might mean that it is integrated with another subsystem application such as perpetual inventory. Consider the diagram in Figure 2.1. On the left side of the diagram are *stand alone* applications (they are so called because the data that are input update only that application). The accounts receivable application is run, shipping information (customer name and number, part description and number, quantity shipped, etc.) is input, and the accounts receivable balance is updated. Then the inventory application is run. Inventory-related information (part descriptions, numbers, and quantities) is input again to update the quantities on hand.

On the right side is an example of an integrated application. The application program that processes the shipping information "knows" that the information is used to update both accounts receivable and inventory. This eliminates duplication of data input and permits expediting file updates. Now this is starting to make some sense.

When selecting a system, you would want to know more about the masterfile update process (is the masterfile updated after each transaction is entered or are the transactions collected in a history file for updating at a later time); we'll cover these considerations in subsequent chapters. For now, let's move on and see how we might use integrated systems.

Using Integrated Systems

Although manufacturing companies are frequent users of integrated systems, there are opportunities for many other types of businesses to use them. Let's look at a cross section of businesses to see how integrated systems are being used.

1. A single-location electronics manufacturer has been experiencing difficulty with production scheduling, pinpointing cost overruns, producing timely financial statements, and growing inventories. Although many applications are computerized, systems are not integrated and frequently produce conflicting information. New systems are installed that integrate order entry/accounts receivable, manufacturing, and inventory control. The order-entry system interfaces with the finished goods perpetual inventory and the shop scheduling systems to help ensure that what is manufactured is needed, and vice versa. Work order and shop status reporting by cost center enable labor inefficiencies to be isolated and facilitate timely correction. The material requirements planning system interfaces with order entry, purchasing, and raw materials perpetual inventory systems to eliminate excessive raw materials buildup.

2. A single-location distribution company is experiencing stock-outs along with growing inventories. The present computer systems have not been significantly revised in over five years. The hardware is upgraded and new integrated packaged software is installed that (1) expedites processing and (2) provides new or improved reports on slow moving goods and product line/customer profitability analyses.

3. A rapidly growing multilocation equipment rental company is experiencing difficulty with maintaining manual equipment availability records, stock-outs, and obtaining equipment utilization reports. Billing and accounts receivable, although presently computerized, could be improved. New hardware is installed, including terminals at each location, together with new application software integrating order entry, accounts receivable, and rental equipment inventory. As a result, equipment availability is automated, billing is processed more timely, and information is available to make decisions regarding purchase of new rental equipment.

4. A rapidly growing privately held magazine publisher uses a service center for subscription fulfillment (new subscribers, magazine delivery, accounts receivable, and revenue recognition). An in-house computer is used to process accounts payable, general ledger, and financial analysis (statistics, trends, and forecasting). The owner is unhappy with the service center's performance, and the company has outgrown the in-house computer. New hardware is purchased and terminals are placed in user departments. Packaged software is purchased for accounts payable and general ledger. New systems are developed in-house to integrate subscription fulfillment and financial analysis.

5. A single-location seasonal garment manufacturer was computerized as to accounts receivable, accounts payable, and general ledger. Order-

entry functions were performed manually, but the company had been using its cardex system for years, felt comfortable with it, and had been reluctant to revise it. A decline in sales caused the company to reexamine its cost structure, which, in turn, led to reexamining order entry. A software house was engaged to modify their existing order-entry system to interface with the company's present accounts receivable system. The result of this action a net reduction of four personnel.

These examples illustrate some of the benefits to be derived from using integrated systems. However, they do generally cost more for some very good reasons:

- They are more complex and require more expertise to design and program.
- Since they interact with more data files, more data files must be on line requiring larger auxiliary storage to house them.
- Being more complex, the programs are longer, which may require:
    a. More main memory for executing them
    b. Larger auxiliary storage to store them

These types of cost/benefit trade-offs will be examined in Chapter 14. For now, let's take a look at the recent phenomenon, desktop computers.

HOW DESKTOP COMPUTERS ARE BEING USED

Some applications do not warrant the purchase of a larger computer but have a very quick payback period when implemented on a low-cost desktop computer. Recognizing this, accountants are using desktop computers (1) on their desktops, (2) in the field, and (3) in some cases, to process all accounting applications. Examples of the types of things being done with desktop computers follow:

- **Database management software:** Define, maintain, and produce sorted reports and mailing labels based on user-defined fields and criteria. Examples include detailed client and customer files and key executives by company and industry.

- **Economic and statistical software:** Calculate present values, amortization tables, the internal rate of return, and the lease/purchase alternatives.

- **Text editing/word processing software:** Form letters, proposals, financial statements, and other standard documents, nonstandard documents including letters, articles, and, you may have guessed it, books (this entire book was drafted, edited, and revised for final typesetting on a personal computer).

- **Financial planning software:** Projections, forecasts, project monitoring, budgeting, and requirements planning.
- **Communications:** Between computers within the business, time-sharing applications, and accessing commercial database systems.

The examples listed above do not represent a "wish list" or what may be done in the future. They are examples of what innovative people are doing today. In Chapter 13, we'll explore desktop computers in detail.

Increasing Use of Graphics by Accountants

The use of graphics is certainly not new. Just pick up the daily newspaper and turn to the business section. Bar diagrams are used to indicate relative market shares for companies in a given industry. Pie charts are used to display a company's lines of business. We see graphics used in annual reports to shareholders to depict sales growth over time and the like. So there is certainly nothing new about using graphics. What is new is who is using graphics—your competitors.

Today's modern accountant is using graphics to gain a competitive edge. We have traditionally either prepared or reviewed pages of numbers with neat little columns placed side by side. We've been used to doing it and don't often stop to think much about it. But ask someone outside the accounting profession what they think about all our little columns of numbers. The response you're likely to get is—borrrinnng! And rightfully so; just consider the disadvantages of a voluminous presentation of columnar figures. From a reader's standpoint, they are:

- Time consuming to:
  - a. Read and digest the information
  - b. Determine the relevance
- Difficult to:
  - a. Interpret
  - b. Identify trends or significant changes

The lengthier they are, the more they encourage reader boredom. Contrast this with a presentation that includes graphics. As the old saying goes, "One picture is worth a thousand words," because graphic data are easier to interpret and trends are clearly identifiable. Instead of being intensely studied, the numeric data can be scanned in general, with specific emphasis devoted to trends, changes, and significant items. Whether you are in public accounting or industry, the potential uses of and audiences for graphics are essentially the same. They are limited only by your imagination. We'll explore the uses of graphics in Chapter 11. For now, suffice it to say that competitors are using them and gaining a competitive edge.

In Chapter 1 we looked at technology and in this chapter got some ideas about what our competitors are doing. Now we are ready to move into the meat of the book—specific applications.

PART II

computerization opportunities

The materials in Part II (Chapters 3 through 13) present computerization opportunities. Based on personal experience, discussions with others, and industry statistics, it is apparent that:

- Existing computer users are not using them to the fullest extent. In this regard:

  a. Computerized applications frequently do not contain features necessary to get the maximum benefits of computerization.

  b. Additional computerized applications (presently performed manually or not at all) could be implemented.

- Many firms make little or no use of computers.

Before we get into specific applications, a few words are in order as to how Part II is organized and how to determine which chapters to read.

Organization

The materials on application opportunities are organized as follows:

- **Narrative overview:** Each application area begins with a brief discussion of the overall application purpose and the value of automation.

- **Features:** The value of a computerized application is dependent on what the underlying software has been designed to do. In this regard, a detailed listing of features has been provided.

- **Reports:** In addition to the list of features, a detailed list of report types has also been provided. This list includes reports to support accountability as well as provide management information for decision-making purposes.

Determining Which Chapters to Read

At first glance, it may be tempting for you to pick and choose among those chapters that appear to directly affect you. In this regard, I have the following suggestion—read all the chapters! If you read selectively, you may miss some of the not so obvious opportunities. For example, if you are an accountant in public practice, you may be able to help your clients solve manufacturing or distribution problems, or recognize opportunities for clients to use desktop micros, and so on. If you are an accountant in private industry, you may likewise identify additional opportunities by reference to chapters other than those that directly affect you. With that in mind, let's get into the specifics.

3 getting more out of basic accounting systems

Poorly designed or archaic application software can rob you of many of the significant benefits of computerization. The basic accounting systems represent the building blocks of your accounting and information systems. Accordingly, we will begin our review of opportunities with the following basic accounting systems:

- General ledger
- Accounts receivable
- Accounts payable
- Payroll
- Fixed assets

GENERAL LEDGER

In the increasingly complex and competitive world we live in, survival itself can frequently be a function of the timing, extent, and quality of basic information. While traditional manual systems often cannot meet the ever-growing need for more and better information, an automated general ledger system can.

A properly designed automated general ledger system is much more than simply a general ledger trial balance. It is a fully integrated management information system that produces reports in a useful format. Reporting is sufficiently timely to utilize the information before it becomes stale.

Features

1. Provide transaction entry and editing in an on-line interactive mode.

2. Process journal entries for subsystems for which automation isn't required.

3. Provide thorough editing regarding journal entries and batch balancing. Optional capabilities include reversal of accruals and suspense processing for entries not passing editing criteria.

4. Accepting valid transactions within a group of transactions and resubmitting only the transactions with errors (contrasted with rejection of entire groups of transactions).

5. Perform double-entry balancing.

6. Permit transaction entry for more than one period. In this regard, permit entries to be posted to a prior period while also permitting entries to the current period.

7. Perform on-line inquiry as to user-specified accounts, including budget, actual, current period, prior period, details, and the balances.

8. Permit on-line maintenance to the general ledger masterfile for additions, deletions, or changes to the following elements:

   Account number   Budgetary information
   Account description   Cost allocation
   Actual balances   Relationship information

9. Calculate and compare totals to control totals submitted by users for the number and amount of debit and credit entries.

10. Identify all errors that exist in each entry prior to rejecting transactions based upon initial error detection.

11. Provide user-specified automatic interfaces with other systems.

12. Capacity for at least x number of general ledger accounts.

13. Provide for validation of account numbers.

14. Provide capability to process multiple ledgers with unique charts of accounts.

15. Perform automatic backup of all general ledger files before posting to facilitate recovery to preposting conditions.

16. Provide multiple levels of subsidiary accounts and facilitate listing and summarization at any level in the financial statements.

17. Automatically generate multiple entries from a single entry such as those required for intercompany transactions.

18. Generate recurring journal entries.

19. Automatically reverse accruals.

20. Compare budget to actual.

21. Provide details of variances from budget based upon user-submitted criteria.

22. Provide budget comparisons consistent with periods for which actual figures are reported.

23. Provide trend analyses using current period, prior periods, and budgets. In this regard, the reports themselves should be capable of being used as turnaround documents to be facilitate budget refinement.

24. Capacity to provide flexible or variable budgeting based on rates, standards, or projected volumes.

25. Provide for cost allocations among related accounts.

26. Produce account analyses at any level of the general ledger reporting.

27. Post general ledger accounts after the initial reports have been run or error lists have been generated (e.g., multiple closings).

28. Validate zero balances prior to deleting general ledger accounts at any level.

29. Report exceptions based on criteria such as:
    - Transactions in excess of predefined limits
    - Account balances in excess of predefined limits
    - Accounts with transactions or balances contrary to their nature (debit/credit)
    - Accounts for which expected entries were not received

30. Perform editing prior to account updates.

31. Update prior periods when adjustments are made.

32. Provide for the following minimum information:

Account number (multiple levels)	Year to date actual
Description	Current period budget
Company/entity	Year to date budget
Account type	Prior month balance forward
Cost center	Variances (amount and
Current period actual	percentage)

33. Provide full details of general ledger postings including:

Account number	Date
Nature of entry	Amount
Source reference	

34. Capacity to handle:

- Fiscal year ends other than December
- Thirteen-week quarters (5-5-4 reporting periods)

Reports

1. Chart of accounts with user-defined levels of combinations.

2. Exception reports and/or earmarked items with exceptions.

3. Preliminary trial balance to be used as a turnaround document for further journal entries.

4. General ledger reports listing all transactions for the current month, balance forward amounts, prior period adjustments, and closing balances.

5. Financial statements:

- Nature
  a. Balance sheets
  b. Income statements
  c. Changes in financial position (cash or working capital)
  d. Cost-center reports

- Period
  a. Weekly
  b. Monthly
  c. Quarterly
  d. Semiannual
  e. Annual
  f. Year to date

ACCOUNTS RECEIVABLE

Extending credit to customers is a necessity for most businesses. Controlling your accounts receivable balances manually can be a time consuming and error-prone process. Consider also the timeliness of being able to compute the present balance both as to shipped and on-order amounts.

If clerical accounting procedures do not result in complete and timely reporting, consider automating accounts receivable. An automated system can also improve the accuracy of information provided, as well as assist you in projecting cash flow.

Features

1. Apply cash on-line.

2. Apply cash based on individual open items as contrasted with a balance-forward technique.

3. Apply cash based on user-specified criteria [oldest invoice, specific matching, and suspense (unapplied cash)].

4. Apply cash on a partial invoice basis.

5. Enter adjustments to open items such as payments, invoices, credits, and unapplied cash.

6. Preclude deletion of customer master accounts for customers with nonzero balances.

7. Handle payments for which customer master accounts have not been established (suspense accounts with specific identification of remittances).

8. Capacity to override, with exception reporting, masterfile control information such as shipping instructions, billing addresses, discounts, and so on.

9. Verify all semipermanent data (customer name, customer number, etc.) prior to transaction processing.

10. Facilitate customer balance reporting (accounts receivable balances) for the following levels of detail:
    - Summary totals by customer (balance forward, purchases, payments, adjustments, ending balance); optional capabilities include year to date transaction information (balance forward, purchases, payments, adjustments, ending balance) and comparable information for the prior year.
    - Summary totals for all customers (balance forward, purchases,

payments, adjustments, ending balance); in addition, the system should provide prior year comparable information.

11. Accommodate x customers in total and y active customers.

12. Provide flexible billing such as cycle billing.

13. Capacity to add automatic interest charges for user-specified accounts and accounts for which user-specified criteria are met within the current month.

14. Interface directly with the general ledger system for sales, cash receipts, freight, sales tax, discounts, returns, credits, interest charges, and other adjustments.

15. Support 13-period fiscal year.

16. Accommodate discount terms based on:
    - Cumulative dollar purchases in total
    - Cumulative dollar purchases for a specific product
    - Timeliness of payment

17. Maintain customer masterfile information, which, as a minimum, would include:

Customer number	Customer name	Customer address
Bill to address	Contact	Account type
Billing code	Credit limit	Salesman code
Current balance	Aged past due	Period to date payments
Terms	Discount %	Period to date sales
On-order balance		

Reports

1. Aged accounts receivable reports (detail/summary/aging).

2. Mailing labels (user-defined sequence: alpha, numeric, selective).

3. Invoices with account details and user-defined messages.

4. Statements for predefined intervals.

5. Statements with dunning messages (based on user-defined criteria).

6. Registers (cash, sales, adjustments, etc.) detailing monthly transactions and that provide all posting references and other information.

7. Batch balancing and control information (detail listings, control totals, etc.).

8. Customer lists based on user-defined criteria (alpha, numeric, industry dependent, selective).

9. Sales tax reports (collected, due, etc.).

10. Daily business reports (gross sales, discounts, net sales, cash receipts, beginning accounts receivable balance, and ending accounts receivable balance).

11. Sales analysis reports (by salesman, customer, territory).

12. Exception reports (credit limits, unusual volume, days outstanding, adjustments, etc.).

13. Cash receipts forecast (by day, specific period, etc.).

ACCOUNTS PAYABLE

There are several reasons why it is important to maintain an adequate accounts payable system. First, obligations need to be recorded on a timely basis to facilitate preparation of accurate accounting and management information. Second, the timing of cash disbursements is critical for managing cash flow. In this regard, some companies simply pay all vendor invoices upon receipt. By delaying payment until the contractual due date, the related cash can be used to finance inventory growth, reduce bank borrowings, made temporary investments, and so on. Other cash flow considerations include taking advantage of cash discounts when it is advantageous to do so. Finally, there is the overall credit reputation of the business. A poor credit rating may result in disadvantageous credit terms or, worse yet, vendors refusing to do business with you.

Manual accounts payable systems require extensive clerical effort to support an adequate management information system. If your needs are not being met, automation may be an effective solution for you.

Features

1. Enter new purchase orders on-line and update quantities on order.

2. Override debit and credit account distributions when entering invoices.

3. Enter vendor credit memos and apply them against balances due.

4. Retain the following information: invoice date, discount date, payment date, distribution date, quantity, PO numbers, and vendor names through on-line maintenance transactions.

5. Select open items to be paid and, on a turnaround document basis, indicate which vouchers are to be paid, which are to be retained on file, and specify partial payments to be made.

6. Ascertain that a vendor has a zero balance prior to deleting a vendor from the vendor masterfile.

7. Edit entries for which the amounts exceed user-defined limits.

8. Override, with appropriate exception reporting, a discount that would otherwise be taken.

9. Match receiving documents with vendor invoices and report discrepancies for quantities, descriptions, and unit of measure.

10. Print checks based on vouchers to be paid.

11. Print checks based on recurring payments (user-specified).

12. Process x number of vouchers and y number of vendors.

13. Provide for manual checks.

14. Interface with the general ledger system.

15. Maintain month to date and year to date dollar amounts and detailed information by vendor.

16. Allow for partial payment.

17. Edit, by vendor, for duplicate invoice numbers and reject duplicates.

18. System calculation of standard discounts.

19. Proration of sales tax and/or freight charges among specific line items.

20. Accommodate various formats for combination checks/remittance advices.

21. Automatic interface to check reconciliation subsystem.

22. System reversal of distribution entries for canceled checks.

23. System-performed housekeeping for end of period processing, including zeroing month to date totals and accumulating year to date figures.

24. Comprehensive editing capabilities for vendor number, company number, division number, department number, account number, and product number.

25. Process x detailed distribution lines associated with a single invoice.

26. Maintain x years of vendor information regarding total payments, discounts taken, and discounts lost.

27. Maintain details and report in accordance with tax requirements regarding Forms 1099 and similar requirements.

28. Maintain a vendor masterfile containing, as a minimum, the following:

Vendor number	Vendor name	Vendor address
Telephone number	Current balance	Year to date purchases
Last payment amount	Last payment date	Year to date payments

29. Maintain the following elements of detailed information for vendor invoices and checks.

Invoices	Checks
Invoice number	Check number
Payment date	Invoice number
Payment amount	Check amount
Balance due	Discount
Invoice date	Bank number
Invoice amount	Check date
Discount	

30. Maintain a voucher file containing, at a minimum, the following:

Voucher number	Amount due	Discount date
Check amount	Discount amount	General ledger
Check number	Discount percent	distribution
Date due	Invoice number	(amount and account)

Reports

1. Alphabetical lists of vendors based on user-specified criteria, including vendor groups or ranges.

2. Accounts payable open item report including invoice date, due date, pay date, purchase order number, invoice amount, and related discounts.

3. Check register.

4. Daily purchases register, by vendor invoice.

5. Daily distribution register detailing the distribution of vendor invoices.

6. Outstanding check listing (checks issued but not returned by the bank).

7. Aged summary accounts payable report, by vendor, containing the following:

   • Aging categories of current, 30, 60, and 90 days and advance payments.

   • For each vendor, year to date amounts invoiced, discounts taken, and the year to date highest balance due at any point.

8. Aged accounts payable trial balance with details supporting the summary totals listed in the preceding report.

9. Check reconciliation report listing the details of checks that cleared the bank.

10. Remittance advices with capability of printing x lines of detail.

11. Prelisting of checks scheduled for payment to be used as a turnaround document for suppressing check preparation.

12. Cash requirements report listing, by vendor and due date, vendor summary totals for all open vendor invoices.

13. Open purchase order report in purchase order number sequence, vendor number sequence, and article number sequence.

14. Daily voucher detail register.

15. Voucher distribution register.

16. Hard-copy and inquiry capability regarding details, by account number, of accounts payable and cash disbursements distribution to the general ledger.

17. Vendor masterfile change report (before and after change information).

18. Vendor masterfile details (all information on file) with control totals for number of vendors and hash totals.

PAYROLL

If the payroll function was simply a matter of writing checks, only the larger companies would have an incentive to automate payroll. However, given the requirements of taxing authorities, vacation and sick pay plans, savings and other contributory plans, and variable compensation arrangements, small- and medium-sized businesses can also benefit from an automated payroll system.

Features

1. On-line entry of employee masterfile information (adds, deletes, and changes) with edit, prior to deletion, for employees with balances due or other unsettled accounts.

2. Process hourly, incentive based (piecework, commissions, etc.), and salaried employees, with or without time cards.

3. Process user-specified deduction categories, rates, and algorithms.

4. Process expense advances and credits for expense reports.

5. Automated check reconciliation.

6. Accommodate changes in withholding tax rates.

7. Automated tax calculations for employer and employee amounts for federal, state, and local taxes.

8. Automated calculation of miscellaneous deductions, including health and other insurance, donations, and so on.

9. Override system tax withholding calculations to accommodate exempt situations.

10. Process payroll based on a variable payroll cycle.

11. Calculate overtime and other differential pay rates.

12. Automated year-end closing.

13. Distribute payroll expense based on user-specified criteria.

14. System calculations of, and accounting for, vacation, holiday, and sick pay, including hours and dollars.

15. Handling direct-deposit arrangements such as wire transfers and employee notification.

16. Accommodate multicompany situations.

17. Accommodate credit union situations and union benefit calculations.

18. Automatic interface with the general ledger.

19. Automatic end-of-period housekeeping such as zeroing month to date totals and accumulating year to date figures.

20. Edit checks during maintenance and update for social security account number, company number, division number, department number, and so on.

21. Edit checks, based upon user-defined criteria, for range and reasonableness (hours in excess of x, wages in excess of x, number of units, etc.).

22. Accumulate and prepare reports to taxing and other authorities.

23. Maintain an employee masterfile with, as a minimum, the following fields:

Employee number	Social security number	Employee name
Employee address	Year to date	Current pay rate
Type (hourly, etc.)	compensation	
	Year to date deductions	

24. Interface with, where applicable, personnel systems.

Reports

1. Payroll checks with year to date and current deductions detail.

2. Check register for manual and computer checks.

3. Masterfile maintenance report with before and after information reported.

4. Masterfile report listing the entire contents of the file (with control totals for total employees and hash totals).

5. Reports for taxing and other authorities:
   - Federal, state, and local taxing authorities
   - Workman's compensation
   - Others as required
   - Equal employment opportunities report

6. Labor distribution reports based upon user-specified criteria such as:
   - General ledger account number
   - Work order project (direct/indirect, chargeable/nonchargeable)
   - Department/division

7. Deduction summary report by deduction type.

8. Overtime and similar exceptions report based on user-specified criteria.

9. Personnel reports:
   - Number of employees by classification/department with comparable data for the prior period (current period and year to date).
   - Employee turnover information compared to the prior periods (current period and year to date).
   - Job class by hire date information.
   - Absence monitoring based upon user-specified criteria.

10. Mailing labels.

FIXED ASSETS

A few years ago, life was very simple when it came to depreciation calculations. In the worst case, you had to make two calculations, one for tax purposes (an accelerated method) and another for financial reporting purposes (straight-line method). Then came ACRS (Accelerated Cost Recovery System), with the result of different tax methods for federal and state income tax purposes. That was bad enough! Add to that the recent requirements to reduce the depreciable base for a percentage of the investment tax credit and the whole depreciation area begins to get extremely complex. Finally, consider the benefits of maintaining detailed fixed asset cost records for insurance and property tax purposes. If your present manual systems are not adequate to keep up with continually increasing demands, automation should be considered.

Features

1. System edit for completeness (cost, life and depreciation method, etc.).

2. Masterfile editing, including, as a minimum, the following fields:

Vendor	Description	Methods
New or used	Useful life	Equipment type
Cost	Equipment number	Salvage value
Manufacturer	Date purchased	

3. Accommodate multiple depreciation methods, including book, tax (federal and state), basis for depreciation for each method (e.g., reductions for tax regarding investment tax credits).

4. Process on-line masterfile changes.

5. Depreciation calculations based on user-defined periods (monthly, quarterly, semiannual, or annual).

6. System-calculated investment tax credits based upon current regulations.

7. Depreciation forecasts, by quarter and in total, for the current year and a user-specified number of years.

8. Maintain category balances for cost, accumulated depreciation, and net book value (net depreciated cost) based on user-specified groupings.

9. Maintain masterfile information for, as a minimum, the following fields:

Asset cost center	Asset location	Vendor name
Manufacturer	Equipment number	Depreciation group
Useful life	Description	Purchase date
Original cost	Salvage value	Investment tax credit
Depreciation method	Addition first year depreciation	Year to date depreciation
Accumulated depreciation		

10. Accommodate fixed asset control requirements of up to x digits.

11. System purging of sold assets, including current period and year to date information of assets deleted (identification, original cost, accumulated depreciation, etc.) and reconciliation to profit and loss accounts to which the asset was charged (sales proceeds, cost, accumulated depreciation, net carrying amount, and net gain or loss).

Reports

1. Masterfile change report (before and after changes).
2. Masterfile contents report with control totals (total items and hash totals):

Asset cost center	Asset location	Vendor name
Manufacturer	Equipment number	Depreciation group
Useful life	Description	Purchase date
Original cost	Salvage value	Investment tax credit
Depreciation method	Addition first year depreciation	Year to date depreciation
Accumulated depreciation	Insured amount	Replacement cost

3. Depreciation reports for each method of depreciation as follows:
   - By asset and in total
   - Contents (by category, by asset, and in total):
     a. Cost:
        (1) Original cost
        (2) Current period additions
        (3) Transfers (between cost categories and the like)
        (4) Current period deletions
        (5) Ending balance
     b. Accumulated depreciation:
        (1) Beginning balance
        (2) Current period depreciation
        (3) Transfers (between cost categories and the like)
        (4) Current period deletions (accumulated depreciation)
        (5) Ending balance

4 computerizing services for clients

Historically, accountants have relied heavily on their own labor to perform services for clients. Being the "keeper" of debits and credits, they dutifully helped clients with preparing journals, posting ledgers, reconciling control accounts, and preparing income tax returns. Although there were tools such as adding machines and calculators to help, still it was manual labor that got the job done. Unfortunately, this labor-intensive approach is becoming less and less viable because it simply costs too much.

As an accountant in public practice, the computer presents you with a golden opportunity to perform new services for clients or to perform existing services on a more cost-effective basis. In this regard, let's explore our computerization opportunities in each of the various practice areas:

- Computerizing accounting and consulting services for clients.
- Using the computer to perform tax services for clients.

COMPUTERIZING ACCOUNTING AND CONSULTING SERVICES FOR CLIENTS

While it makes sense for industry giants such as IBM, General Motors, and Exxon to maintain large accounting staffs, many small- and medium-sized businesses simply cannot afford to maintain any accounting expertise whatsoever. Given the fact that the vast majority of the private sector in the United States is comprised of small- and medium-sized businesses, we can continue to expect that, in the near term, these companies will look to outsiders for cost-effective solutions to their needs. Opportunities for computerized accounting and consulting services include:

- Write-up services
- Forecasts, budgets, and projections
- Economic and financial analysis
- Compiling statistics
- Work-paper preparation

Write-up Services

Traditionally, write-up services have been the bread and butter of single practitioners and local firms. On a computerized basis, this service area has attracted even the giant national accounting firms. What makes this service area so attractive is (1) the size of the marketplace, (2) the level of personnel required, and (3) the degree of standardization that can be employed.

1. **Size of marketplace:** For computerization to be effective from a cost standpoint, some reasonable level of volume must be achieved. In this regard, the potential for computerized write-up services is enormous. Potential clients include those in professional industries (doctors, dentists, lawyers, engineers, architects, entertainers, etc.), as well as numerous other small commercial enterprises (retail stores, maintenance and repair service companies, wholesalers, etc.).

2. **Level of personnel:** It used to take an experienced accountant to find and locate subsidiary posting errors and balance the general ledger. A major benefit of automation is the incorporation of extensive editing capability to eliminate posting errors before they occur. Accordingly, you can use paraprofessional/clerical personnel to perform the work, thus driving down the cost of services. Additionally, this will enable you to devote your attention to the results of processing (e.g., financial trends) and help your clients in an advisory capacity.

3. **Degree of standardization:** A common drawback of the manual approach is the tendency toward lack of uniformity, including forms, records, and different approaches. All these lead to inefficiencies, including excessive start-up time and relearning time regarding dealing with different systems. Computerization, when properly designed and implemented, eliminates these inefficiencies by standardizing data-entry procedures and utilizing uniform reporting.

The extent of write-up services that can be computerized is almost as varied as the marketplace itself. In addition to considering the specific needs of your present and prospective clientele, also consider the fact that computerization may permit you to provide additional or more extensive services. Opportunities include:

1. Accounts receivable
   - Billings
   - Sales register
   - Cash receipts journal
   - Accounts receivable ledger and agings
   - Sales analysis
2. Accounts payable
   - Purchase journal
   - Cash disbursements journal
   - Accounts payable ledger and aging
   - Purchases analysis
3. Payroll
   - Payroll checks
   - Payroll journal
   - Labor distribution
   - Payroll tax returns
   - Vacation and sick pay records
   - Personnel statistics
4. Fixed assets
   - Fixed asset register
   - Depreciation
5. General ledger
   - Trial balance
   - Financial statements

The specific software features and reports for these write-up opportunities are identical to those for basic accounting applications and are included in Chapter 3. Assistance in inventory functions (physical inventory pricing, missing tag reports, cost accounting, etc.) might also represent an opportunity, in which case refer also to the chapters on distribution and manufacturing. In addition, further software features and reports applicable to write-up services should be considered.

Features.

1. Ability to process and update files for each client independent of other client files.

2. Ability to print reports (control information and client reports) individually for selected clients on a group basis or all clients as a combined group.

3. Ability to interface directly with an automated work-in-process/billing system.

4. Ability to produce standard accountants' letters (compilation, review, etc.).

5. Ability to interface with a job accounting system for client billing purposes (or provide equivalent information directly).

Reports.

1. Daily resource utilization report in sufficient detail to facilitate scheduling changes (to eliminate bottlenecks, overtime, etc.).

2. Client billing information.

3. Client reports and transaction recaps (for control purposes).

4. Clients not processed report (for follow-up).

Forecasts, Budgets, and Projections

A primary reason for the absence of success or even failure of small businesses is the lack of planning, particularly financial planning. What a tremendous opportunity this presents! Can you think of anyone more qualified than yourself to help your clients assemble information based on accounting concepts? And yet our profession as a whole has not been aggressive in pursuing opportunities in this area for, in my opinion, two reasons—risk and cost.

Risk.   Admittedly, there is a certain amount of risk involved in being associated with a document pertaining to future events. However, the risk isn't that the events won't take place; rather, the risk is that we will be sued because someone relied on the document and was hurt financially. In this regard, it is important to *minimize and manage your risk!* Accept only engagements for which the risk is tolerable. For example, contrast the following two scenarios. In the first, a total stranger walks into your office and wants you to prepare a five-year "projection" for an entity to be formed and for which successful operations are dependent upon research and development effort that has not yet started. The primary purpose of the projection is to solicit limited partnership investments from the public. In the second scenario, you are requested by an existing client to assist in the preparation of a forecast for the following year. The user of the forecast is a banker with whom you will discuss the forecast in detail. The first situation should certainly be avoided, whereas you should be eager and enthusiastic to accept the second.

Cost.   Cost used to be a major obstacle. In this regard, not only did it require heavy involvement by senior personnel in the preparation stage itself, each iteration was a time-consuming process. Changing just one little assumption often meant erasing and recalculating results from beginning to end. Therein lies the beauty of the computer. Good software will make all the calculations and recalculations in a small fraction of the time it would take you, and, unlike you and me, the computer doesn't make mistakes!

In Part III, we'll examine costs and alternatives from the computerization standpoint. At this point, let's define some specific opportunities and review common software approaches.

Opportunities.   For purposes of our discussion, we'll use the following definitions:

- **Budget**—desired financial results
- **Forecast**—most likely financial results
- **Projection**—financial impact of changing factors or assumptions

Smaller businesses frequently do not have the internal capabilities to prepare budgets at any meaningful level of detail. Often it requires someone from the outside to help them establish the discipline necessary for proper planning. In this regard, you can help them with the budgeting process. Examples include revenue planning (new customers and how they will be obtained, additional business from existing customers and what needs to be done to make that happen), and cost planning (determining variable and fixed cost relationships, establishing details supporting budgeted figures, etc.). Once the discipline itself has been established, the computer can be used to calculate and store the results. After discussion with management, revisions will be necessary (the initial results may come as a shock); enter the revised input and let the computer do the rest. Once acceptable profit and loss results are achieved, the computer can also be used to forecast cash flow for highlighting cash flow deficiencies (permitting the much needed lead time to contact the bankers and arrange adequate financing) or surpluses for temporary investment purposes.

TABLE 4.1
Projection Model Using Generalized Software

Category	Total	Number of days	Average daily rental	Average quantity	Daily rental rate — Achieved	Daily rental rate — Standard	Daily rental rate — Utilization	Forecast of percent increase — Daily rental rate	Forecast of percent increase — Quantity	Forecast of percent increase — Utilization
A	540,000	365	1,479	540	2.74	3.00	91.32%	3	10	1
B	1,240,000	365	3,397	980	3.47	3.60	96.29%	4	8	0
C	430,000	365	1,178	345	3.41	4.00	85.37%	2	2	2
D	1,200,000	365	3,288	125	26.30	35.00	75.15%	1	0	5
E	565,000	365	1,548	101	15.33	23.50	65.22%	1	0	8
Totals	3,975,000		10,890							

REVENUE

Category	Actual 19 × 1	Forecast 19 × 2	19 × 3	19 × 4	19 × 5	19 × 6
A	540,000	617,938	707,124	809,183	925,972	1,059,617
B	1,240,000	1,392,768	1,564,357	1,757,085	1,973,557	2,216,699
C	430,000	456,319	484,249	513,888	545,342	578,721
D	1,200,000	1,272,600	1,349,592	1,431,242	1,517,832	1,609,660
E	565,000	616,302	672,262	733,303	799,886	872,515
Totals	3,975,000	4,355,927	4,777,584	5,244,701	5,762,589	6,337,212

Additional opportunities include computer-assisted analysis of cost relationships at various revenue levels and monitoring of performance by comparing budget to actual and analyzing variances.

Bankers frequently recommend that external accountants be involved when credit is granted. Opportunities include assisting with preparation of the forecasts to demonstrate the company's ability to meet debt service requirements.

Another opportunity to assist smaller businesses is in the area of projections for internal management use. Essentially, you can take advantage of the computer's ability to quickly perform "what if" calculations such as:

- What if revenues increase/decrease by x percent a year?
- What if the cost of revenues increases/decreases by x percent a year?
- What if other costs increase/decrease by x percent a year?
- What if collections increase/decrease to x days outstanding?
- What if payments to vendors are accelerated/delayed for x days?

In this regard, the computer can be used to make projections by month, year, product category, and so on.

Common Software Approaches. While there are many variations, there are two general approaches to packaged software for these types of practice opportunities. The first software approach is the *general-purpose* type of software. Its virtue is flexibility of use. In this regard, it is not application dependent and, accordingly, can be used for a variety of applications based upon the user's needs. Its drawback is that the user must design the specific use (define the rules for input and calculations, specify the output format, etc.). A frequently encountered derivation is the *template* for which the author (vendor or third party) has, using the generalized capabilities of the package, constructed specific application uses. You might visualize the template as an overlay upon the general-purpose application. In this regard, the overlay may or may not be flexible (if it is not, it isn't much different than the second software approach).

The second software approach is the *specific-purpose* type of software. Its virtue is that it is designed to accomplish specific tasks and eliminate user involvement in the design process. Its drawback is that it tends to be rigid in terms of input requirements and output design.

Examples. To illustrate what can be done with each of the two types of software, let's look at an example of each.

Table 4.1 is an example of a projection model developed using a generalized software package (in this case, an electronic spreadsheet). The company for which the projection model was developed is in the equipment rental business and has several categories of equipment. The purpose of the

TABLE 4.2
Cash Flow Analysis Model Using Specific-Purpose Software

		January	February	March	April	May	June	July	August	September	October	November	December	Total
SALES		1,150,000	690,000	920,000	1,150,000	1,610,000	3,220,000	2,760,000	2,990,000	2,760,000	2,300,000	1,840,000	1,610,000	23,000,000
Collections:														
Month 1 – 20%		230,000	138,000	184,000	230,000	322,000	644,000	552,000	598,000	552,000	460,000	368,000	322,000	4,600,000
Month 2 – 65%		715,000	747,500	448,500	598,000	747,500	1,046,500	2,093,000	1,794,000	1,943,500	1,794,000	1,495,000	1,196,000	14,618,500
Month 3 – 15%		225,000	165,000	172,500	103,500	138,000	172,500	241,500	483,000	414,000	448,500	414,000	345,000	3,322,500
Totals		1,170,000	1,050,500	805,000	931,500	1,207,500	1,863,000	2,886,500	2,875,000	2,909,500	2,702,500	2,277,000	1,863,000	22,541,000
PURCHASES	47% of next month's sales	324,300	432,400	540,500	756,700	1,513,400	1,297,200	1,405,300	1,297,200	1,081,000	864,800	756,700	658,000	10,927,500
Payments:	42 days outstanding													
Month 1		0	0	0	0	0	0	0	0	0	0	0	0	0
Month 2		399,740	237,819	317,093	396,366	554,913	1,109,826	951,279	1,030,553	951,279	792,733	634,186	554,913	7,930,700
Month 3		189,600	145,360	86,479	115,306	144,133	201,786	403,573	345,919	374,746	345,919	288,266	230,613	2,871,700
Totals		589,340	383,179	403,572	511,672	699,046	1,311,612	1,354,852	1,376,472	1,326,025	1,138,652	922,452	785,527	10,802,401
LABOR	20% of this month's sales	230,000	138,000	184,000	230,000	322,000	644,000	552,000	598,000	552,000	460,000	368,000	322,000	4,600,000
Payments:														
Month 1 – 50%		115,000	69,000	92,000	115,000	161,000	322,000	276,000	299,000	276,000	230,000	184,000	161,000	2,300,000
Month 2 – 50%		107,745	115,000	69,000	92,000	115,000	161,000	322,000	276,000	299,000	276,000	230,000	184,000	2,246,745
Totals		222,745	184,000	161,000	207,000	276,000	483,000	598,000	575,000	575,000	506,000	414,000	345,000	4,546,745
SELLING EXP	23% of this month's sales	264,500	158,700	211,600	264,500	370,300	740,600	634,800	687,700	634,800	529,000	423,200	370,300	5,290,000
Payments:														
Month 1 – 30%		79,350	47,610	63,480	79,350	111,090	222,180	190,440	206,310	190,440	158,700	126,960	111,090	1,587,000
Month 2 – 70%		177,100	185,150	111,090	148,120	185,150	259,210	518,420	444,360	481,390	444,360	370,300	296,240	3,620,890
Totals		256,450	232,760	174,570	227,470	296,240	481,390	708,860	650,670	671,830	603,060	497,260	407,330	5,207,890
G&A EXPENSES		96,667	96,667	96,667	96,667	96,667	96,667	96,667	96,667	96,667	96,667	96,667	96,667	1,160,004
OPERATING CASH FLOW:														
Receipts		1,170,000	1,050,500	805,000	931,500	1,207,500	1,863,000	2,886,500	2,875,000	2,090,500	2,702,500	2,227,000	1,863,000	22,541,000
Disbursements		1,165,202	896,606	835,809	1,042,809	1,367,953	2,372,669	2,758,379	2,698,809	2,669,522	2,344,379	1,930,379	1,634,524	21,717,040
Totals		4,798	153,894	–30,809	–111,309	–160,453	–509,669	128,121	176,191	239,978	358,121	346,621	228,476	823,960
BORROWINGS:														
Beginning balance		50,000	52,202	0	0	38,542	198,452	724,710	661,210	582,033	429,082	141,739	0	50,000
Additions:														
Principal		0	0	0	38,542	157,213	509,669	0	0	0	0	0	0	705,424
Interest – 14% (1)		7,000	7,154	3,654	0	2,697	16,589	64,621	97,014	87,027	70,778	39,957	9,921	406,412
Repayments		4,798	59,356	3,654	0	0	0	128,121	176,191	239,978	358,121	181,696	9,921	1,161,836
Ending balance		52,202	0	0	38,542	198,452	724,710	661,210	582,033	429,082	141,739	0	0	0
INVESTMENTS:														
Beginning balance		0	0	94,538	64,801	0	0	0	0	0	0	0	164,925	0
Deposits:														
Interest – 10% (1)		0	0	4,726	7,966	3,240	0	0	0	0	0	0	8,246	24,178
Principal		0	94,538	0	0	0	0	0	0	0	0	164,925	218,555	478,018
Withdrawals		0	0	34,463	72,767	3,240	0	0	0	0	0	0	0	110,470
Ending balance		0	94,538	64,801	0	0	0	0	0	0	0	164,925	391,726	391,726
Net interest income/<–expense>		–7,000	–7,154	1,072	7,966	543	–16,589	–64,621	–97,014	–87,027	–70,778	–39,957	–1,675	–832,234

(1) Based on average of prior month's balances and charged or credited in next month.

model is to (1) calculate the historical equipment utilization percentages and the historical profit and loss relationships and (2) prepare income statement projections using varying assumptions (what if utilization increases by x percent while operating costs remain a constant percentage or changes to y percent, and so on). The model required approximately one hour of set-up time! When the assumptions are changed, it takes 2 to 3 *seconds* to display the recalculated results, which, if the user desires, can then be printed.

Table 4.2 is an example of a cash flow model using specific-purpose software. The model demonstrates the impact of acceleration/delaying receivable collections and vendor payments as they relate to the level of borrowings required and the profit and loss impact thereof. All the mathematical calculations and output formats are part of the packaged software. The user need only enter the input data.

Economic and Financial Analysis

In the ordinary course of conducting their business, our clients are faced with making economic decisions. In the absence of any internal capability, these decisions are frequently made without the benefit of proper analysis. Examples of the types of decisions that must be made include whether to lease or purchase an asset, which type of financing is most advantageous, and does this investment have a positive rate of return. Economic decisions all center around the time value of money. Computerized practice opportunities include:

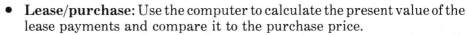

- **Lease/purchase:** Use the computer to calculate the present value of the lease payments and compare it to the purchase price.

- **Feasibility:** Use the computer to calculate the net present value of cash inflows and outflows and determine whether the result is positive or negative. Vary the assumptions (interest rates, timing, and/or amount of payments) and determine the most advantageous terms.

- **Financing alternatives:** Use the computer to discount the various payment streams to determine which alternative is most advantageous.

- **Loan amortization:** Use the computer to determine the periodic payments necessary to amortize a loan.

- **Pro forma effects:** Use the computer to prepare financial statements or analyses to give effect to contemplated transactions.

It is true that these types of calculations can be made on some calculators (if they are capable of storing computer programs and have memory, they are really computers, not calculators). However, the calculator cannot compete with the computer when it comes to (1) formatting the output so that it can be easily understood by others and prepared in a professional manner, (2) handling large volumes of data or assumptions, and (3) multiple iterations.

Compiling Statistics

Many organizations look to outsiders to assist with compiling statistics because they don't have the internal capabilities. Examples of these organizations include trade associations, local chapters of unions, medical service organizations, and charitable organizations. Still others look to outsiders to compile statistics because the information is highly confidential. Using the computer makes sense for these types of services whenever (1) the volume of data is large or (2) numerous calculations are required.

Let's use an example to illustrate the opportunities in this area. One of my clients is a trade association comprised of a number of commercial entities. Revenue information is highly confidential. In addition to assuring confidentiality, the service we provide is a monthly market share and statistics report, a portion of which is shown in Table 4.3.

TABLE 4.3
Statistics Report

	CURRENT YEAR				PRIOR YEAR			
	Month		Year to date		Month		Year to date	
	All entities	Your rank	All entities	Your rank	All entities	Your rank	All entities	Your rank
Revenue category A								
B								
etc.								
TOTAL REVENUE								

Each month we receive a report from each entity listing their revenues by category and in total. Revenues are then totaled and rankings are calculated. In addition, other market share data (not illustrated) are also calculated. Each entity receives a report containing total revenues for all entities (the total market) and their respective market shares. Thus, each entity is able to determine total market growth and how it individually is doing in terms of maintaining market share and so on.

This service was originally performed manually, an accountant's nightmare! All of the information had to be listed on work sheets. Then some *400* calculations had to be made and rechecked for accuracy. Next, the individual reports had to be typed. After that came proofreading to check for typographical errors. Then the application was computerized. Now the computer makes all the calculations, which are internally balanced for accuracy. The computer also prints the individual reports together with a control report for audit trail purposes. Gone are the work sheets and professional staff involvement. Gone also is the typewriter. Finally, gone is the frustration (mine and my secretary's).

Work Paper Preparation

No area of accounting practice consumes more time than the preparation of work papers. Given the computer's ability to calculate, manipulate, store, and retrieve information much more rapidly than we can (also without error or lapse of memory), let the computer take over as much of the burden as possible. Whether you are doing compilations, reviews, or audits, here are some opportunities:

- Client preparation packages
- Footing trial balances
- Calculating general ledger variances (amounts and percentages; store the prior period amounts on the computer)
- Pro forma schedules with prior period balances
- Carry-forward schedules
- Depreciation calculations
- Prepaid expense calculations
- Accrued expense calculations
- Inventory extensions and footings
- Accounts receivable footings and agings
- Accounts payable footings and agings
- Overhead calculations
- Earnings per share calculations
- Debt convenant compliance
- Footnote information:
  a. Inventory classification

    b. Fixed assets categories

    c. Lease classification (operating/capital)

    d. Operating and capital lease commitments

    e. Stock options

Now that we've reviewed the accounting and consulting opportunities, let's move on to the other key area of your practice—taxes.

USING THE COMPUTER TO PERFORM TAX SERVICES FOR CLIENTS

My first job in public accounting was working part-time for an individual practitioner ("Barney"). I was a junior in college at the time and eager to get some "hands-on" experience and earn some much needed money. Barney had an enormous income tax return practice and, during busy tax season, worked at least 10 to 12 hours per day (sometimes more) for all seven days a week. Notwithstanding all those hours he worked, there wasn't any way for him to prepare all those tax returns without help. So Barney employed me to help him during that 1968 tax season. My job was to prepare the pro formas. With the prior year's tax returns on my left and blank forms on my right, I would transfer the carry-forward information (names, addresses, captions, etc.) to the blank forms. This I did from December to April. Three things remain vivid in my mind:

1. I quickly began to hate the monotony of the "straightforward" 1040s, which added next to nothing to my professional skills. But there were the complex 1040s and occasional 1041s and 1120s from which I could learn more!

2. I also quickly noticed that an intense pain was building up on the side of my middle finger where the pencil lay. After a couple of weeks, the pain began to subside and I was well on my way to developing the familiar "accountant's callus".

3. The third thing I recall was asking, "Isn't there a better way?"

Fortunately, there are many better ways to do things on the tax side of the practice. Let's explore the details for each of the tax practice areas:

- Economic and financial analysis
- Year-end tax planning
- Return preparation
- Work-paper preparation
- Research

Economic and Financial Analysis

The nature of the opportunities we looked at on the accounting side apply to the tax side and then some. Consider the following scenarios. Client A is considering investing in a real estate limited partinership and wants you to analyze the deal. Client B is considering buying a business for which the seller wants to (1) achieve installment sales treatment and (2) allocate a significant portion of the selling price to intangibles. Your mission is to analyze the contemplated terms and provide alternative suggestions for structuring the transaction. Client C wants to form a research and development partnership that will contract with a corporate entity to perform the work. The agreement should provide for (1) an option to purchase the technology after x years and (2) royalty payments in the event the option isn't exercised. The client wants you to analyze the economics and tax ramifications. You respond and two days later the client says, "We changed the terms based on your analysis. Here are the changes. Please rerun the numbers"!

Using the computer to help you analyze the economics and tax ramifications of proposed or completed transactions may save you a significant amount of time.

Year-end Tax Planning

The clerical aspect of complete year-end tax planning involves a top-to-bottom income tax calculation. In this regard, opportunities for computerized year-end tax planning are fourfold:

1. The process itself is error prone in terms of mathematical accuracy. On a manual basis your alternatives are (a) total recalculation, which is inefficient, or (b) take shortcuts and run the risk of inaccurate results. Neither of these alternatives is desirable. Using a computerized approach will save you time or grief.

2. The process itself is error prone in terms of using wrong tax rates or not considering all alternatives, such as maximum tax, alternative tax, and minimum tax. Good computer software eliminates these types of manual errors.

3. Effective year-end tax planning is an iterative process. That is, once the initial calculation is made, additional benefits are derived from "what-if" analyses. On a computerized basis, the rerun time is really negligible.

4. Whether you are running a manual tax projection or using the computer, the captions themselves, together with prior year data, have to be entered on a work sheet or screen. Additional time can be saved

using an integrated system. In this regard, prior year captions and data already on file can be retrieved, resulting in further time savings.

Return Preparation

On the accounting side, clients tend for the most part to be forgiving of occasional simple errors (a footnote mistake or a typographical error). This isn't the case when it comes to their personal affairs. All the many good things you have done for a client can be eradicated in your client's mind by a simple mistake in their individual tax return. In their mind, there isn't any excuse for omitting a deduction or making mistakes in their tax calculations or payments. Couple the mistake with their fear of a revenue examination and you incur the wrath of an unrelenting client.

Although extremely important, clerical accuracy is not the only benefit to be derived from computerization of income tax returns. Other benefits include:

- Reduction in clerical time to make mathematical calculations.

- A more professional looking work product (computer printed versus pencil prepared).

- Pro forma information for next near, further eliminating clerical effort.

- Error messages warning you of missing data or further opportunities.

- Integration with year-end tax planning. In this regard, integrated systems permit you to view the information accumulated during the year-end planning phase and revise only the data that have changed, thus reducing both clerical and review time.

The primary processing alternatives available to you consist of:

1. **Service center processing:**
   - **Batch processing:** Input documents are mailed or sent by messenger to the service center. After the returns are prepared, they are mailed or returned by messenger to you together with the input documents. If errors are noted, corrections must be sent back to the service center for reprocessing of the returns.

   - **On-line processing:** Input data are keyed in by your personnel using a terminal in your office. If errors are detected (either when the data are entered or after completed returns are received), the errors can be corrected on-line and the returns reprocessed.

2. **In-house processing:** The entire return preparation process is completed in your office.

Whether you use a service center or an in-house computer, consider the following features (as they relate to your practice needs) and reports:

Features.

1. Ability to provide comprehensive editing of input data (e.g., missing data).
2. Ability to check for alternative strategies (e.g., income averaging).
3. Ability to process all schedules for a given form (e.g., schedule A).
4. Ability to process all entity types (individuals, corporations, estates, etc.).
5. Ability to process x states and x cities.

Reports.

1. Federal, state, and local tax returns
2. Estimated income tax payments
3. Pro forma returns for the next year
4. Complete error diagnostics

Work-Paper Preparation

In addition to using the computer for documenting planning and analysis calculations, consider computerizing other work papers as well. Examples follow:

- Carry-forward schedules, such as timing differences and related tax effects
- Cash to accrual conversions (and vice versa)
- Loss carry-back calculations
- Client preparation guides
- Pro forma work papers

Research

Life would be a lot simpler if all tax issues were black or white. Unfortunately, that's not the case. Resolving tax issues may require referring to regulations, revenue rulings, case law, and the like. Trying to find a situation with similar facts can be a time-consuming process. Here is yet another instance in which computerization can be of help to you. Time-sharing services such as the American Institute of Certified Public Accountants' Lexis system offer research aids. Using a keyword search technique, you can enter a keyword for the subject area you are researching (such as "goodwill"), and the screen will display all references in the literature to that keyword. Then you can scan the display to see if there is anything on point to your issue. If the list is too large or includes matters not pertinent to your issue, you can narrow the list down by entering a more specific keyword phrase (such as "purchased goodwill"). Then, refer to the specific citations. In this fashion, you can avoid inefficient manual searching. In addition, you may find a citation on point that might not otherwise have been found.

5 computerizing engagement and practice administration

As an accountant in public practice, time is your most valuable asset. How you use that time and the amount you bill and collect for it represent the core of your practice. Questions that arise include:

- How many hours were devoted to nonchargeable activities such as professional society meetings? What percentage of change does that represent compared to the prior year?

- How many hours were chargeable to clients? Did that figure increase or decrease compared to the prior year?

- How did your planned hourly billing rate compare to your actual billing rate? How much did your write-offs amount to? Did that figure increase or decrease? How much of your write-offs were attributable to start-up time on new clients?

- How much do you plan to charge per hour next year? How many hours will be chargeable to clients? What gross income figure does that represent? What would the impact be of an x percent increase in efficiency?

If you don't have the information to answer these types of questions, you may not be getting the information you need to manage your practice. In that regard, computerization can help you to obtain more and better information while, at the same time, provide you with better control. Accordingly, in this chapter we will explore computerizing time accounting and billing functions.

COMPUTERIZING TIME ACCOUNTING FUNCTIONS

Your computerized time accounting system is comprised of:

- Timesheets
- Billing rates
- Accounting reports
- Time management reports
- Engagement management reports
- Practice management reports

Timesheets

Timesheets are a convenient means for gathering and inputting the information necessary to produce your accounting and management reports. Let's explore the various elements, together with the system design and philosophical issues that arise.

Timesheet Period. The first issue you need to deal with is the period to be covered by a timesheet. Considerations include (1) the amount of administrative time to prepare them, (2) smoothing the input workload, and (3) breaking up the calendar month into even parts. In this regard, a semimonthly period seems to be a good compromise.

Employee Number. Make sure the number of characters is large enough to accommodate growth. In addition, consider using a numbering scheme that will facilitate distinguishing staff classifications (e.g., partner-1××, staff accountants-9××, etc.). The purpose of this is to permit sorting historical transactions by employee classification for planning and analysis purposes.

Employee Name. Necessary for error correction (data entry errors and the like).

Client Number.   As with the employee number, make sure the number of characters is large enough to accommodate growth. In addition, provide for predesignated nonchargeable activities. In this regard, you should capture all time related to business activities, including compensated absences. Consider the following types of nonchargeable activities:

Administration	Professional societies
Education	Special projects
Holidays	Time off
Illness	Unassigned
New client development	Vacation

Client Name.   Necessary for error correction.

Service Code.   Give a lot of thought to this item. Considerations include:

1. **Billing:** Whether or not the computer will be used to generate billing invoices, there must be sufficient information captured to describe the nature of the services rendered.

2. **Management reporting:** The extent of information you get regarding the nature of your practice (for profitability analysis and planning purposes) is directly dependent on the service code scheme.

Examples of service code descriptions include:

* Accounting and auditing:

Audit	Review	Compilation
Acquisition	Accounting	SEC filings
analysis	assistance	Bookkeeping

* Tax:

Corporate returns	Individual returns	Fiduciary returns
Revenue examinations	Tax planning	

* Consulting:

Projections	EDP	Executive
EDP	requirements	search
implementation	Feasibility	EDP selection
Budgets	studies	

Service Code Description (optional).   Consider providing for the capability of entering a description of services rendered (telephone call to attorney, March financial statements, etc.).

Hours.   Consider the minimum amount you want to keep track of and whether the system will accommodate it.

TABLE 5.1
Unbilled Work in Process

CLIENT A

Unbilled work in process
For the month ended May 31, 19xx

Employee	Billing rate	Service code	Beginning balance				Additions					Billings				Ending Balance			
			Hours	Standard time	Expense	Total	Hours	Standard time	Expense	Total	Invoice number	Hours	Standard time	Expense	Total	Hours	Standard time	Expense	Total
Totals																			
Advance billings																			
Net unbilled																			

Out-of-Pocket Expenses. Consider a dual purpose timesheet/expense report to facilitate timely recording of expenses.

Employee Discipline (optional). Larger firms may want to track performance by discipline (audit, tax, and consulting).

Billing Rates

Notwithstanding the fact that actual fees are frequently determined by factors other than standard billing rates (perceived value, fixed fees, etc.), the use of standard billing rates is vital to a well-managed practice for the following reason. The use of standard billing rates facilitates planning and establishing accountability. Revenue goals can be established using forecasted chargeable hours (extended by billing rates). Performance can then be monitored (overall, by employee, by client, etc.).

Accounting Reports

For discussion purposes, let's assume that your general ledger is maintained on an accrual basis during the year and converted to a cash basis at year-end for income tax purposes. After processing masterfile maintenance activity, hours chargeable to clients are key entered and extended by the computer at standard billing rates. The results, together with out-of-pocket expenses, are added to "unbilled work in process" (with a corresponding credit to revenue). The unbilled work in process account is reduced by billings to clients processed during the period (discussed later in this chapter). In addition to the necessary control reports (masterfile changes and unbilled work in process activity), the primary accounting report is the detail, by client, of all unbilled work in process (see Table 5.1).

Time Management Reports

Time management reports are designed to enable the individual to plan the work year and monitor progress. Table 5.2 illustrates the planning report.

To minimize the amount of time required to prepare the forecast, use the computer's capability to retain, retrieve, and manipulate data. For example, forecasted time could be a computer model that would be used as follows:

1. **First iteration:** The computer retrieves the prior year data and inserts it in *both* the forecast period columns and the prior year actual column.

2. **Second iteration:** The user modifies the forecast data to conform to current estimates, and the computer performs all the calculations.

TABLE 5.2
Forecasted Time by Employee

| | EMPLOYEE A | | | | |
| | Hours forecasted for 19XX | | | | |
Client	January	December	Total	Prior year actual	Increase/ (decrease)
Chargeable:					
Client A	_____	_____	_____	_____	_____
•	_____	_____	_____	_____	_____
•	_____	_____	_____	_____	_____
•	_____	_____	_____	_____	_____
TOTAL	_____	_____	_____	_____	_____
Nonchargeable:					
Administration	_____	_____	_____	_____	_____
Education	_____	_____	_____	_____	_____
Holidays	_____	_____	_____	_____	_____
Illness	_____	_____	_____	_____	_____
New client development	_____	_____	_____	_____	_____
Professional societies	_____	_____	_____	_____	_____
Special projects	_____	_____	_____	_____	_____
Time off	_____	_____	_____	_____	_____
Unassigned	_____	_____	_____	_____	_____
Vacation	_____	_____	_____	_____	_____
TOTAL	_____	_____	_____	_____	_____
GRAND TOTAL	_____	_____	_____	_____	_____

3. **Third and succeeding iterations:** The user modifies the forecast data until an acceptable plan is achieved.

With the planning cycle completed, the computer can then be used to provide progress reports as illustrated in Table 5.3.

Engagement Management Reports

Engagement management reports are intended for the partners (or other personnel) responsible for a group of clients. In this regard, the reports should be designed to facilitate both planning and monitoring. The majority of the function relates to billing types of activities, which will be covered in the next section. At this point, for engagements that span more

TABLE 5.3
Time Utilization Report

EMPLOYEE A

| | Prior year | | Current year | | | | Percent variance from prior year | |
| | | | Actual | | Forecast | | | |
	Hours	Percent	Hours	Percent	Hours	Percent	Actual	Forecast
CHARGEABLE:								
Nonchargeable:								
Administration								
Education								
Holidays								
Illness								
New client development								
Professional societies								
Special projects								
Time off								
Unassigned								
Vacation								
TOTAL								
GRAND TOTAL								

than one calendar month and/or require more than one employee, consider using the computer to assist in the timing of services function. Table 5.4 illustrates this function.

TABLE 5.4
Employee Hours by Month

	Client A		
Personnel:	January	December	Total
Employee A	_____	_____	_____
•	_____	_____	_____
•	_____	_____	_____
•	_____	_____	_____
•	_____	_____	_____
•	_____	_____	_____
•	_____	_____	_____
•	_____	_____	_____
•	_____	_____	_____
TOTAL	_____	_____	_____

The underlying computer model for client time planning works the same way as the model for individual time forecasting. The computer retrieves the data for the prior year and prints the report illustrated in Table 5.4. The user then makes changes based on the current year's facts and circumstances (services to be performed, personnel changes, etc.). A revised printout is then obtained and becomes the current year plan or the basis for a staffing request. In addition, if the personnel scheduling function is computerized, the data can then be manipulated from the scheduling standpoint (assignments, conflicts, etc.).

Practice Management Reports

After the time management planning has been completed at the individual level, use the computer to summarize the details for the entire practice. Table 5.5 illustrates the first of the practice management reports.

Armed with the current year forecast based on the individual forecasts, you can determine whether the overall results are acceptable. If not, what corrective action needs to be taken? Consider:

1. Is the relationship between chargeable and nonchargeable time appropriate?

2. Are there specific areas within the nonchargeable category to which additional time should be devoted?

TABLE 5.5
Forecasted Time for All Personnel

| | ALL EMPLOYEES | | | | |
| | Hours forecasted for 19XX | | | | |
Category	January	December	Total	Prior year actual	Increase/ (decrease)
CHARGEABLE:	_____	_____	_____	_____	_____
Nonchargeable:					
Administration	_____	_____	_____	_____	_____
Education	_____	_____	_____	_____	_____
Holidays	_____	_____	_____	_____	_____
Illness	_____	_____	_____	_____	_____
New client development	_____	_____	_____	_____	_____
Professional societies	_____	_____	_____	_____	_____
Special projects	_____	_____	_____	_____	_____
Time off	_____	_____	_____	_____	_____
Unassigned	_____	_____	_____	_____	_____
Vacation	_____	_____	_____	_____	_____
TOTAL	_____	_____	_____	_____	_____
GRAND TOTAL	_____	_____	_____	_____	_____

3. Do the total hours indicate an unreasonable level of overtime? Not enough?

4. Which months indicate insufficient chargeable time? What development effort should be undertaken to obtain additional clients? Who should perform the development activity?

Use the power of the computer to model "what if" calculations to assist you in determining what needs to be done. When you are completely satisfied with the results, commit the action plan to writing so that progress can be measured.

After your overall plan is developed, the next step is to monitor results. Table 5.6 on the following page illustrates your monitoring report.

Actual utilization statistics such as those illustrated in Table 5.6 will help you monitor overall progress. In addition, the same information could be obtained by (1) staff classification, (2) practice area (audit, tax, etc.), and/or (3) service code.

TABLE 5.6
Time Utilization Report for All Employees

| | Prior year | | Current year | | | | Percent variance from prior year | |
| | | | Actual | | Forecast | | | |
	Hours	Percent	Hours	Percent	Hours	Percent	Actual	Forecast
CHARGEABLE:	—	—	—	—	—	—	—	—
Nonchargeable:								
Administration	—	—	—	—	—	—	—	—
Education	—	—	—	—	—	—	—	—
Holidays	—	—	—	—	—	—	—	—
Illness	—	—	—	—	—	—	—	—
New client development	—	—	—	—	—	—	—	—
Professional societies	—	—	—	—	—	—	—	—
Special projects	—	—	—	—	—	—	—	—
Time off	—	—	—	—	—	—	—	—
Unassigned	—	—	—	—	—	—	—	—
Vacation	—	—	—	—	—	—	—	—
TOTAL	—	—	—	—	—	—	—	—
GRAND TOTAL	—	—	—	—	—	—	—	—

COMPUTERIZING BILLING
FUNCTIONS

The mechanics of accounts receivable functions and accounting reports are discussed in Chapter 3. What we will focus on in this section is the billing function and related overall practice management. Our topics are:

- Billing system capabilities
- Accounting reports
- Engagement management reports
- Practice management reports

Billing System Capabilities

Given the various billing arrangements with clients, your computerized billing system should be able to:

- Accommodate billings that do not result in a relief of unbilled work in process but that are tracked by client ("advance billings").
- Interface with the accounts receivable system to provide information regarding collections applicable to advance billings.
- Accommodate partial billings (relieve only a portion of unbilled work in process: hours, expenses, service codes, etc.).
- Apply advance billings to unbilled work in process when the work is complete.
- Accommodate billing adjustments (in whole or in part) to previously recorded invoices (accounts receivable write-offs/write-ups), including related billing statistics.
- Accommodate computer-prepared invoicing.
- Accommodate computer-generated invoices (e.g., standard monthly billings).
- Accommodate manual invoices.
- Code and categorize clients by relationship (new clients, lost clients, continuing clients, etc.).
- Categorize billing adjustments by nature and amount.
- Code and categorize fee arrangements (minimum fee, fixed fee, per diem rates, etc.).
- Accommodate budgeted amounts.

In addition, the billing system should interface directly with the time accounting system to reduce clerical time for relief of unbilled work in

TABLE 5.7
Example of a Completed Turnaround Document

CLIENT A

Unbilled work in process
For the month ended May 31, 19xx

Employee	Billing rate	Service code	Beginning balance Hours	Standard time	Expense	Total	Additions Hours	Standard time	Expense	Total	Invoice number	Billings Hours	Standard time	Expense	Total	Ending balance Hours	Standard time	Expense	Total	Bill this period — Work in process reduction (1) Hours	Expense	(2) All	(3) Bill Amount
A	35	10	1	35	0	35										1	35	0	35				35
B	50	10	1	50	0	50	2	100	0	100						3	150	0	150				150
C	60	10	1	60	25	85										1	60	25	85				85
D	75	20	5	375	25	400	5	375	25	400						10	750	50	800				800
Totals			8	520	50	570	7	475	25	500						15	995	75	1070			1070	1070

Advance billings   0   (3)

Net unbilled   1070

(1) For partial billings to be closed out to receivables:
   a. If an entire line item is to be billed, place a checkmark in the "all" column.
   b. If only a portion of a line item is to be billed, indicate the number of hours and expenses to be billed.

(2) If total balance is to be billed and closed out to receivables, enter total unbilled balance on last line of "all" column.

(3) If billing is an additional advance billing, enter the amount here.

process. In this regard, during the billing cycle the unbilled work in process details are displayed on the screen. The user is then prompted to indicate which line items are to be billed and, for those line items, the hours and expenses to be relieved.

Finally, the system should provide for *turnaround document capability*. In this regard, the unbilled work in process listing, by client, becomes the turnaround document. Manual notations regarding billing are made on the document, which then becomes the source document for billing data entry. The unbilled work in process listing might look like the illustration in Table 5.7.

Accounting Reports

On an accrual basis, the results of billing activities would be an addition to accounts receivable, a reduction to unbilled work in process and the difference charged or credited to a profit and loss account, and billing adjustments. The related accounting reports would consist of:

- Manual and computer-prepared billing invoices.
- Invoice journal, including invoice and billing adjustments (the difference between the invoice amount and the amount by which unbilled work in process was reduced).

Engagement Management Reports

For the billing partner (or other personnel with that responsibility), the power of computerized time accounting and billing functions becomes evident. Beginning with the planning function, use the computer to help forecast and plan regarding your group of clients as illustrated in Table 5.8. As Table 5.8 illustrates, the computer does all the clerical work, which permits you to focus on improvements. The computer retrieves the prior year key information and statistics for each client. On the first iteration, enter the assumptions without regard to corrective action (hours, average billing rate, and the amount you expect to be able to bill the client). The computer then calculates the results for you. Are the results acceptable? If not, consider:

1. Are there any tasks performed that are not absolutely necessary?
2. Could some tasks be delegated downward?
3. Could any tasks be done more efficiently?
4. Could any tasks be performed by client personnel?
5. To what extent would the client be receptive to an increase in fees?
6. Are there additional services that could be performed?

TABLE 5.8
Revenue Forecast by Client

PARTNER A – FORECAST FOR 19x3

| | 19x2 Actual | | | | | | | | Assumptions Increase/(Decrease) | | | | 19x3 Forecast | | | | | | | | |
| | Standard | | | | | Collections | | | | | | | Standard | | | | | Collections | | |
Client	Hours	Rate	Time	Exp	Total	Amount	Rate	%	Hours	Rate	Exp	Collections	Hours	Rate	Time	Exp	Total	Amount	Rate	%
Continuing clients:	0	0.00	0	0	0	0	0.00	0.00	0	0.00	0	0	0	0.00	0	0	0	0	0.00	0.00
	0	0.00	0	0	0	0	0.00	0.00	0	0.00	0	0	0	0.00	0	0	0	0	0.00	0.00
	0	0.00	0	0	0	0	0.00	0.00	0	0.00	0	0	0	0.00	0	0	0	0	0.00	0.00
	0	0.00	0	0	0	0	0.00	0.00	0	0.00	0	0	0	0.00	0	0	0	0	0.00	0.00
	0	0.00	0	0	0	0	0.00	0.00	0	0.00	0	0	0	0.00	0	0	0	0	0.00	0.00
	0	0.00	0	0	0	0	0.00	0.00	0	0.00	0	0	0	0.00	0	0	0	0	0.00	0.00
	0	0.00	0	0	0	0	0.00	0.00	0	0.00	0	0	0	0.00	0	0	0	0	0.00	0.00
	0	0.00	0	0	0	0	0.00	0.00	0	0.00	0	0	0	0.00	0	0	0	0	0.00	0.00
	0	0.00	0	0	0	0	0.00	0.00	0	0.00	0	0	0	0.00	0	0	0	0	0.00	0.00
	0	0.00	0	0	0	0	0.00	0.00	0	0.00	0	0	0	0.00	0	0	0	0	0.00	0.00
	0	0.00	0	0	0	0	0.00	0.00	0	0.00	0	0	0	0.00	0	0	0	0	0.00	0.00
	0	0.00	0	0	0	0	0.00	0.00	0	0.00	0	0	0	0.00	0	0	0	0	0.00	0.00
	0	0.00	0	0	0	0	0.00	0.00	0	0.00	0	0	0	0.00	0	0	0	0	0.00	0.00
	0	0.00	0	0	0	0	0.00	0.00	0	0.00	0	0	0	0.00	0	0	0	0	0.00	0.00
	0	0.00	0	0	0	0	0.00	0.00	0	0.00	0	0	0	0.00	0	0	0	0	0.00	0.00
	0	0.00	0	0	0	0	0.00	0.00	0	0.00	0	0	0	0.00	0	0	0	0	0.00	0.00
	0	0.00	0	0	0	0	0.00	0.00	0	0.00	0	0	0	0.00	0	0	0	0	0.00	0.00
	0	0.00	0	0	0	0	0.00	0.00	0	0.00	0	0	0	0.00	0	0	0	0	0.00	0.00
	0	0.00	0	0	0	0	0.00	0.00	0	0.00	0	0	0	0.00	0	0	0	0	0.00	0.00
	0	0.00	0	0	0	0	0.00	0.00	0	0.00	0	0	0	0.00	0	0	0	0	0.00	0.00
TOTALS	0	0.00	0	0	0	0	0.00	0.00	0		0	0	0	0.00	0	0	0	0	0.00	0.00
New and deleted clients:	0	0.00	0	0	0	0	0.00	0.00	0	0.00	0	0	0	0.00	0	0	0	0	0.00	0.00
	0	0.00	0	0	0	0	0.00	0.00	0	0.00	0	0	0	0.00	0	0	0	0	0.00	0.00
	0	0.00	0	0	0	0	0.00	0.00	0	0.00	0	0	0	0.00	0	0	0	0	0.00	0.00
	0	0.00	0	0	0	0	0.00	0.00	0	0.00	0	0	0	0.00	0	0	0	0	0.00	0.00
	0	0.00	0	0	0	0	0.00	0.00	0	0.00	0	0	0	0.00	0	0	0	0	0.00	0.00
	0	0.00	0	0	0	0	0.00	0.00	0	0.00	0	0	0	0.00	0	0	0	0	0.00	0.00
	0	0.00	0	0	0	0	0.00	0.00	0	0.00	0	0	0	0.00	0	0	0	0	0.00	0.00
TOTALS	0	0.00	0	0	0	0	0.00	0.00	0		0	0	0	0.00	0	0	0	0	0.00	0.00
GRAND TOTALS	0	0.00	0	0	0	0	0.00	0.00	0		0	0	0	0.00	0	0	0	0	0.00	0.00

Use the computer to model "what if" calculations for you. In this regard, revise the assumptions to see what the impact is and determine what steps you might take. When you are satisfied that you have exhausted the possibilities, commit your plan to writing and finalize the forecast.

Let the computer help you to monitor progress on a monthly basis. Print whatever information is useful to you for that purpose. An example is illustrated in Table 5.9.

TABLE 5.9
Realization by Client

		PARTNER A											Increase/ <decrease>	
		Prior year billings						Current year billings						
Client	Hours	Standard charges	Expenses	Net charges	Percent of standard	Per hour	Hours	Standard charges	Expenses	Net charges	Percent of standard	Per hour	Percent of standard	Per hour
Continuing clients:														
	___	___	___	___	___	___	___	___	___	___	___	___	___	___
	___	___	___	___	___	___	___	___	___	___	___	___	___	___
	___	___	___	___	___	___	___	___	___	___	___	___	___	___
	___	___	___	___	___	___	___	___	___	___	___	___	___	___
	___	___	___	___	___	___	___	___	___	___	___	___	___	___
	___	___	___	___	___	___	___	___	___	___	___	___	___	___
	___	___	___	___	___	___	___	___	___	___	___	___	___	___
	___	___	___	___	___	___	___	___	___	___	___	___	___	___
	___	___	___	___	___	___	___	___	___	___	___	___	___	___
	___	___	___	___	___	___	___	___	___	___	___	___	___	___
	___	___	___	___	___	___	___	___	___	___	___	___	___	___
	___	___	___	___	___	___	___	___	___	___	___	___	___	___
	___	___	___	___	___	___	___	___	___	___	___	___	___	___
Totals	___	___	___	___	___	___	___	___	___	___	___	___	___	___
New/deleted clients:														
	___	___	___	___	___	___	___	___	___	___	___	___	___	___
	___	___	___	___	___	___	___	___	___	___	___	___	___	___
	___	___	___	___	___	___	___	___	___	___	___	___	___	___
	___	___	___	___	___	___	___	___	___	___	___	___	___	___
	___	___	___	___	___	___	___	___	___	___	___	___	___	___
Totals	___	___	___	___	___	___	___	___	___	___	___	___	___	___
Grand Totals	═══	═══	═══	═══	═══	═══	═══	═══	═══	═══	═══	═══	═══	═══

In addition to monitoring overall realization (which is based on relief of unbilled work in process), you will also want to monitor buildups in unbilled work in process and accounts receivable. Reports that facilitate this process are:

- Aged unbilled work in process (summary totals by client).
- Aged accounts receivable (summary totals by client).

Having monitored actual results all year, it's time to begin planning next year. Let the computer do one more thing for you. Print the prior year forecast compared to actual results. Then review the variances. In what areas were forecasted results not obtained? What more could have been done? What problems could have been foreseen? Incorporate the results of this analysis into your forecast for next year.

Practice Management Reports

Managing your practice requires you to make some very difficult decisions such as:

1. What billing rates should you establish for next year?
2. What minimum fee levels should be established for services such as tax returns, monthly write-up work, and so on?
3. What personnel changes need to be made (promotions, terminations, and new hires)?
4. Which areas of the practice need improvement?
5. Should new clients be added and, if so, what type (tax, audit, industry, etc.)?
6. Where do you want to be in five years? How will you get there?

While the decisions that have to be made are certainly difficult, the task of gathering information to make these decisions need not be. In fact, using the computer can result in more and better information. Let's look at some examples.

Your computerized billing system tracks a great deal of information for you. Since you provided for analysis of billing adjustments and fee arrangements, you can obtain comparative summary statistics such as:

- Dollar amounts and percentages, by category, regarding all billing adjustments:
  a. First year start-up
  b. Staff inefficiencies
  c. Prearranged fees

d. Minimum fees

e. Client resistance to additional billings

This type of information is useful to pinpoint problem areas (staff inefficiencies) and obtain an overall understanding regarding planned versus unplanned billing adjustments.

- Dollar amounts (standard, budget, billed, and adjustments), by category, for billing adjustments applicable only to per diem clients. This information will help you determine to what extent (a) these clients are fee resistant and (b) billing rate increases may be accepted and passed through to clients.

- Number of clients and related dollar amounts, by service code and in total, regarding clients charged a minimum fee (e.g., tax return). This information will be useful in determining the impact of increases in minimum fees.

After you make the policy decision regarding billing rate increases, the revenue forecasts depicted in Table 5.8 can be prepared. The computer can then produce a consolidating forecast by billing partner as illustrated in Table 5.10.

The consolidating revenue forecast can then be challenged as to:

- Overall practice objectives.

- Forecasted hours compared to overall personnel complement.

The consolidated revenue forecast is but one of the tools available to you for preparing the overall practice revenue forecast. Another computerized tool is the personnel revenue forecast illustrated in Table 5.11. Larger firms could substitute staff levels and number of personnel at each staff level for the "name" column. The computer provides the prior year data by employee (utilization percentage represents total chargeable hours worked as a percentage of 2080 hours). At this point you can begin applying "what if" assumptions to the current year forecast figures such as:

- Number of employees

- Utilization percentage (more or less overtime, more or less non-chargeable activities, etc.)

- Realization percentage

The "what if" analysis will help you (1) to calculate a revenue forecast with results that are acceptable to you and (2) to focus on what needs to be done to achieve that forecast. When you obtain results that are acceptable and consistent with your overall practice goals, document the actions to be taken and finalize the revenue forecast.

With your forecast in place, you can now monitor results. In this regard, computerized reports that may be useful to you include:

TABLE 5.10
Consolidating Revenue Forecast by Billing Partner

REALIZATION
ALL PARTNERS

Billing partner:	Prior year billings						REALIZATION ALL PARTNERS	Current year billings						Increase/ <decrease>	
	Hours	Standard charges	Expenses	Net charges	Percent of standard	Per hour	Hours	Standard charges	Expenses	Net charges	Percent of standard	Per hour	Percent of standard	Per hour
Continuing clients:														
Partner A														
B														
C														
D														
E														
F														
G														
Totals														
New/deleted clients:														
Partner A														
B														
C														
D														
E														
F														
G														
Totals														
Grand totals														

TABLE 5.11
Revenue Forecast by Employee

Name	Prior year actual				Current year forecast			
	Billing rate	Utilization percentage	Chargeable Hours	Chargeable Dollars	Billing rate	Utilization percentage	Chargeable Hours	Chargeable Dollars
	000	000.0	0000	000,000	000	000.0	0000	000,000
	000	000.0	0000	000,000	000	000.0	0000	000,000
	000	000.0	0000	000,000	000	000.0	0000	000,000
	000	000.0	0000	000,000	000	000.0	0000	000,000
	000	000.0	0000	000,000	000	000.0	0000	000,000
	000	000.0	0000	000,000	000	000.0	0000	000,000
	000	000.0	0000	000,000	000	000.0	0000	000,000
	000	000.0	0000	000,000	000	000.0	0000	000,000
	000	000.0	0000	000,000	000	000.0	0000	000,000
	000	000.0	0000	000,000	000	000.0	0000	000,000
	000	000.0	0000	000,000	000	000.0	0000	000,000
	000	000.0	0000	000,000	000	000.0	0000	000,000
	000	000.0	0000	000,000	000	000.0	0000	000,000
	000	000.0	0000	000,000	000	000.0	0000	000,000
	000	000.0	0000	000,000	000	000.0	0000	000,000
	000	000.0	0000	000,000	000	000.0	0000	000,000
	000	000.0	0000	000,000	000	000.0	0000	000,000
	000	000.0	0000	000,000	000	000.0	0000	000,000
	000	000.0	0000	000,000	000	000.0	0000	000,000
	000	000.0	0000	000,000	000	000.0	0000	000,000
	000	000.0	0000	000,000	000	000.0	0000	000,000
	000	000.0	0000	000,000	000	000.0	0000	000,000
	000	000.0	0000	000,000	000	000.0	0000	000,000
	000	000.0	0000	000,000	000	000.0	0000	000,000
	000	000.0	0000	000,000	000	000.0	0000	000,000
	000	000.0	0000	000,000	000	000.0	0000	000,000
	000	000.0	0000	000,000	000	000.0	0000	000,000
	000	000.0	0000	000,000	000	000.0	0000	000,000
	000	000.0	0000	000,000	000	000.0	0000	000,000
	000	000.0	0000	000,000	000	000.0	0000	000,000
	000	000.0	0000	000,000	000	000.0	0000	000,000
	000	000.0	0000	000,000	000	000.0	0000	000,000
	000	000.0	0000	000,000	000	000.0	0000	000,000
Totals								

- Comparative realization reports (similar to Table 5.9)
  a. By client (unless this is an overwhelming volume of information)
  b. By billing partner
  c. By service code
  d. By client type
     (1) New, lost, and continuing clients
     (2) Fee arrangements (per diem and so on)

- Billing adjustments
    a. Current period, descending dollar sequence
    b. By category totals compared to prior year
- Comparative unbilled work in process and accounts receivable agings
    a. By billing partner
    b. Others as appropriate (service code, discipline, etc.)
- Comparative statistics such as:
    a. Days revenue in unbilled work in process and accounts receivable
    b. Changes in key rates, such as billed rate per hour
- Exception reports
    a. Clients with billings in excess of x
    b. Clients with balances in excess of x

As the previous sample reports demonstrate, the computer can be a powerful tool to help you run your practice.

6 using the computer in manufacturing operations

Controlling cost is a key ingredient for a successful manufacturing operation. In this regard, the process of controlling costs begins long before any costs are actually incurred. Questions to be answered include the following. Which products are to be produced and in what quantities? When should they be produced? What materials have to be on hand and in what quantities? Then, when costs are incurred, the following questions arise. Are actual costs exceeding budgeted costs? If so, in what areas? What are the causes? What corrective action needs to be taken?

If your present manufacturing accounting and information systems aren't meeting your needs, automating some or all of the following modules may be an effective solution.

- Bill of materials
- Inventory control
- Material requirements planning
- Master production scheduling

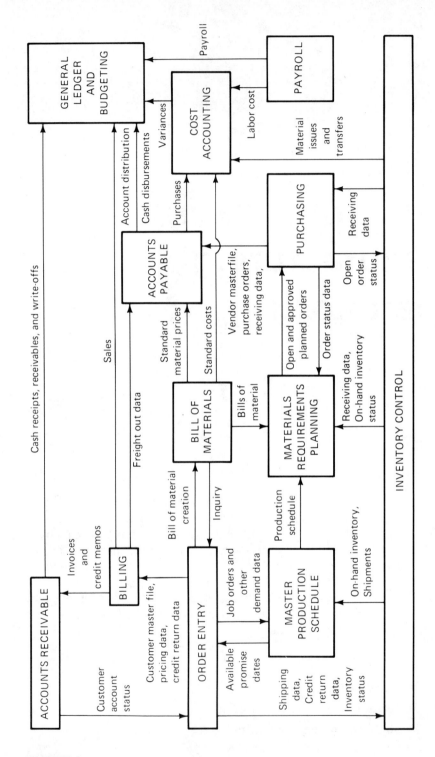

FIGURE 6.1
Sample interrelationships.

- Cost accounting
- Warranty

Although specific relationships depend upon software design capabilities and how they are implemented, Figure 6.1 illustrates major interrelationships between the accounting and manufacturing systems. Figure 6.1 is followed by a discussion of each of the preceding modules, including their purpose, key features, and reporting requirements.

BILL OF MATERIALS

The bill of materials system is the foundation for an integrated manufacturing system. In addition to providing engineering information for product design, the bill of materials system facilitates the determination (1) as to the manufacturing processes to be accomplished and (2) of material and labor requirements.

Features

1. Establish, change, or delete the relationships between material items.
2. Provide product structure inquiry information regarding both the parts list and where-used list.
3. Provide for mass change or mass replace through a single transaction. Extensions to this function would be such related functions as:
   - Same as except
   - Component replace
   - Mass add
   - Mass replace
   - Bill of material delete
   - Mass delete
4. Interface from the bill of materials system to the standard costing system and/or the material requirements planning systems.
5. Provide for "departmental" types of inputs. In this regard, departments should be limited to accessing only those departments for which they are authorized.
6. Editing all transactions to verify the propriety of deletions, changes, additions, and matching of any element already in existence.

7. Provide for component transactions, which would consist of (at a minimum) the following types of information:

Material identification	Component relationship information
Quality and/or unit of measure	Type of component
Item type codes	Parent/component relationships

8. Support of options such as the following:
   - Changes in the bill of materials to the engineering group regarding current demands.
   - "Blow-through" capability (providing pseudo items and structures for those items that must be referenced but are not physically manufactured or stocked).
   - Modular bills of materials that provide for various ways in which the product may be built.
   - Use of low-level code that indicates the level of a particular component corresponding to the lowest manufacturing level at which the component is ever used.
   - Provide for material substitutions when a part or raw material is not available.
   - Specify and process prototype and/or test products to allow for incomplete bill of materials structures.

9. Perform a cost buildup that processes and accumulates costs for all items based on a low-level coding scheme.

10. Editing all input and data file information to assure the integrity of the bill of material database, including:
    - Discrete value checking
    - Data dependency
    - Procedural editing (an item cannot be released unless certain mandatory data have been defined)

11. Provide hard-copy printouts for all changes.

12. Maintain a transaction history file based on any changes made to the bill of materials subsystem.

13. Provide database editing, including:
    - Checking all low-level code relationships.
    - Prohibiting the deletion of a part master that is part of an active bill of materials.
    - Retaining and restoring the bill of materials files whenever necessary.

- Validating that each item of a part master has a component or bill of materials relationship.
- Checking that each part in the bill of materials has a part master.

14. Maintain data on the bill of materials structure file, which would contain, at a minimum, the following:

Parent part	Component part	Quantity per assembly
Type	Operation	Engineering change ID
Lead time	Engineering change numbers	Description of engineering change

15. Notify the material requirements planning system of changes to facilitate replanning in that system. Changes are:

Order policy changes	Structural changes in
Lead time changes	the bill of materials

Reports

1. Single-level bill of material list with only first-level components.

2. Multilevel bill of material (explosion) listing that retrieves records for an entire product from the top to bottom and indicates the component relationship to the entire bill of materials.

3. Single-level where-used list that directly selects the assembly part number of a requested part.

4. Multilevel where-used (implosion) list that starts with a requested component part and retrieves its direct where-used assembly in each higher assembly until the end item (independent item) is reached.

5. Engineering change report that indicates and tracks any engineering changes scheduled for future implementation.

6. Engineering parts master list that is used as the master parts list, to be used by engineering as a turnaround document for performing bill of materials maintenance.

7. A summarized where-used list that provides information regarding the effect of a contemplated cost or component change for an item.

8. Listing of processed parts that have been added, deleted, or updated in the sequence in which they are processed.

INVENTORY CONTROL

The purpose of the inventory control module is to provide information to control production and inventory levels. Benefits to be derived include:

- Minimizing inventory investment while maintaining sufficient inventory levels to support manufacturing and marketing goals.
- Improving elapsed time from customer order placement to shipment.

Features

1. Accept standard inventory maintenance transactions for material receipts, issues, scraps/returns, and material adjustment quantities.
2. From a production work order environment, the system should transfer component information to the inventory system with regard to component allocation and material order release quantities.
3. Process material identification transactions with regard to adds, changes, and deletes to maintain all the major elements of the inventory master information.
4. Process cycle count information regarding count/recount stock and adjustments to inventory balances.
5. Validate inventory transactions regarding part number, field description, and quantity in the inventory masterfile.
6. Process order cancellation transactions by applying a negative allocation for the affected material.
7. Process stock transfers for all changes in stock locations or between plants or warehouses.
8. Provide for the following lot-sizing techniques:
   - Dynamic EOQ (economic order quantity)
   - Part period balancing
   - Lot-for-lot (discrete) logic
   - Least unit cost
   - Fixed quantity
   - Period order quantity
9. Detect whether a particular material part is slow moving or obsolete.
10. Process manual allocations.
11. Maintenance and generation of pegged requirements for detailed component demands, each of which references the next higher-level part or assembly generated by any demands.
12. Group demands into fixed length time periods (buckets) and, additionally, restrict the number of time periods that can be maintained.

13. Calculate manufacturing lead times based on order quantity.

14. Analyze the status of an item and, if certain selection criteria are met, notify material control to physically count the item.

15. Perform analyses of all parts according to predetermined classes of period usage value with classes defined in terms of a percentage of the total usage value.

16. Maintain engineering change effectivity dates for planning material availability in the future.

17. Maintain historical transactions that allow the sourcing of inventory discrepancies such as:

    - Date and quantities of last receipts.
    - Source of unscheduled issues.
    - Date of last physical inventory count to be traced.

18. Provide for two methods of controlling component material issues to orders:

    - Manual issues
    - Automatic issues

19. Interface with purchase order and sales order systems.

20. Reschedule allocation record due dates and quantities if and when the parent supply order is rescheduled or has had its quantity changed.

21. Process and provide for multiple inventory locations with balances of on hand for each.

22. Calculate or specify order points based on:

    - Manually preset order point
    - Computer-derived order point

23. Calculate safety stock where safety stock equals a constant multiplied by the mean absolute deviation (MAD) adjusted for lead time.

24. Maintain x items or part masters with the following information:

Part number	Part name	Unit of measure
ABC code	Make or buy code	Activity code
Unit cost	Order policy	Order quantity
Safety stock data	On hand quantity	Stockroom location
On order quantity	Allocated quantity	Cycle code
Date of last update	Item type	Lead time
	Order multiple	Lot size
Reorder point	Shrinkage factor	Year to date usage
Inventory account number	Annual usage	Inventory turns

25. Maintain year to date data on both receipts and issues of inventory items.

26. Maintain transaction history files and responsibility codes for input transactions that affect inventory adjustment levels.

27. Determine whether replanning of a particular item must be performed due to material status updates external to material requirements planning.

Reports

1. Inventory listing.

2. Parts list that provides for tracing structure downward through levels of a product structure or major assembly, showing component stock locations and quantity used in an assembly. The parts list is used to provide design engineering with up-to-date product structure information to:

   - Develop a parts catalog.
   - Assist manufacturing engineering with the preparation of routing documents.
   - Assist sales in preparation of customer orders.

3. Stock status inquiries that display inventory balance for selected items.

4. Stock status and/or value by location displaying inventory balance information and value of inventory for each item.

5. Cycle count report including all items selected for counting.

6. ABC classification analysis that documents inventory by usage value to determine order policies, demand control codes, and cycle count frequency.

7. Shortage reports that indicate orders that cannot be met on the scheduled date for which component material is requested.

8. Purchase requisition reports produced to notify purchasing that a firm purchase order needs to be placed based on planned lead time from the inventory master.

9. Stock status transaction register that results from transactions processed against an inventory balance and displays the update effect of the transaction.

10. Display of current on hand quantities by part number.

MATERIAL REQUIREMENTS PLANNING

Drawing on information contained in the other modules, the material requirements planning (MRP) system provides a materials plan based on current and planned manufacturing activities. In this regard, MRP should perform the following functions:

- Determine gross requirements (total materials needed for current and planned production).
- Calculate net requirements (total materials needed less inventory on hand).
- Reschedule and resequence orders.
- Create planned orders.

The benefits to be derived from an effective MRP system consist of:

- Improving the quality of decision making by identifying production problems on a timely exception basis.
- Minimizing inventory levels.
- Shortening lead times to deliver.

Features

1. User-specified variable planning time frames for individual parts or assemblies.
2. Specify which reports and displays will be generated for a particular MRP run.
3. Accept input from the master scheduling or order control system regarding:

Part number	Order type	Order quantity
Order due date	Order release action	Demand type
Required quantity	Required date	Customer order/
Commodity class		contract

4. Simulate a net change effect through the input of a transaction that specifies MRP simulation, thus permitting evaluation of the effect of inventory policy changes, master schedule changes, or any lead time changes.
5. Recognize the need for planning based on any of the following factors:
    - Changes in the master schedule.

- Engineering changes that affect usage quantity, effectivity dates, sources of an item, scrap, or yield factors.
- Inventory change transactions.
- Changes in any inventory policy that may affect safety stock or order size quantities.
- Changes in lead time.

6. Provide for net change processing that allows MRP to be performed as frequently as the user specifies.

7. Provide for regeneration of a completely new material requirements plan from the end master schedule on a cyclical basis; changes to inventory status or a materials plan since the last period are reflected in the order action recommendations, which become the output of the regenerative processing cycle.

8. Perform gross requirements determination for parts other than end items using one of two sources:
- Independent demand, which is a derivative of the master schedule and/or forecasting.
- Dependent demand, which results from order releases derived from the next higher level of an independent item.

9. Calculate time-phased net requirements.

10. Apply safety stock against net requirements.

11. Create planned orders that cover all calculated net requirements.

12. Group demands into a fixed length time period (buckets) that associates each demand with a corresponding required date based upon a "planning horizon."

13. Support firm planned orders (FPOs) to add control over planned orders by avoiding undesirable shifts in production schedules. In this regard, MRP should not permit the capability to alter either the due date, release date, or quantity of an FPO.

14. Generate replenishment orders that satisfy all net requirements once they are determined. The order quantity may be generated to satisfy either a customer order, requirements over a single time period, combined requirements over several periods, or an annualized economic order quantity.

15. Plan the date on which a planned order release must be put into effect. The release date is the required date less the purchasing or manufacturing lead time for manufactured parts and assemblies that must be exploded through all levels.

16. Provide for allocation records for components to remain open until the supply order is closed at the next higher level for that item.

17. Employ a variable planning horizon capability for individual parts or families of parts.

18. Provide for pegged requirements that generate and maintain detail component demands that reference the next higher-level part or assembly that generated this demand.

19. Provide for level-by-level explosions. The explosion process should only occur if there are changes to the materials plan that require it. The changes that would cause an explosion to update component demand data and produce planned orders are:

   - Planned order rescheduling
   - Planned order quantity changes
   - Planned order cancellations
   - Planned order placements

20. Interface to the bill of materials system to explode supply items and generate new demands for each planned order created by MRP. This explosion process should retrieve each bill of material component selected for further processing if the demand date falls between effectivity date periods and required order dates.

21. Provide for order close out, which, when final receipt for an order is processed, removes all unfilled allocations and appropriate allocation quantities in any inventory master records. When an order is canceled, the same type of processing should occur.

22. Update the following data elements, which are contained in both the master scheduling, order control, and bill of materials systems:

On hand quantities	Stock location	Customer/contract
On order quantity	Last receipt date	number
Current month scrap	Year to date usage	Order type
Order number	Order quantity	Parent assemblies
Customer/order contract	Planned order	Planned order
Order release date	quantity	due date
Completed quantity	Demand type	Mean absolute
Annual usage		deviation

23. Maintain all pegged requirements with a summary of the schedule quantity and the customer and/or order contract to which the requirement is attached.

24. Provide for consolidating and reporting projected on hand dollars by total order commitment for specified due dates.

25. Allocation records should include quantity delivered fields in addition

to quantity required fields. Allocation records must remain open until a supply or customer order is closed at the next higher level.

Reports

1. Planning action notification that action is required to maintain optimal replenishment order plans; information capability includes:
   - User-specified parameters.
   - Pegging each demand and supply reference.
   - Projection of inventory requirements for each future date.
   - Display of each product's detailed demands.
2. Master production schedule report that lists all items with MRP demands. The report indicates the MRP period along with outstanding customer order demand and dependent demand. Projected inventory should be calculated for each period.
3. Critical orders and/or net change report indicating:

Material identification	Description	Order number and type
Order status	Start date and	Balance carried forward
Due quantity	due date	Net change
Planning commentary/ action		

4. Make or buy part requirements notification.
5. Order action notices that designate, by location and/or planner, the various part numbers, the type of order, order number, and required action based upon a specified time frame.
6. Planned orders report, prepared after each run, indicating all planned part numbers, due dates, scheduled release date, order quantity, and any critical release commentary.
7. Materials planning report specifying the order and requirements detail by part and type of order, order number, release date, due date, corresponding shop date, order quantity, last activity date, and any rescheduling information.

MASTER PRODUCTION SCHEDULING

The objective of the master scheduling system is to provide necessary data from which a realistic master production schedule can be developed. Using sales forecast demand together with customer orders, current stock status, and available capacity, the master scheduling system indicates which products are to be produced, the quantities of each, and the dates by which they are to be completed. After review and judgmental revisions are made, the planned build schedule is passed to the MRP system for generation of work orders.

Features

1. Accept the following forecast data from either an automated or a manually prepared forecast:

Part number	Demand type	Customer order number
Customer order date	Schedule date	Scheduled quantity
Period date	Period quantity	Representative
Order status		product group

2. Interface with a customer order system. Information from the customer order system is received by the master scheduling system to reduce the overall forecasted demand for the product.

3. Interface with the output of the master schedule into the material requirements planning system

4. Process master schedule additions, changes, and deletions against specific customer orders.

5. Master scheduling system handling of input into the shop calendar (calendar dates, day of week, shop day, period length, normal working days, and shutdown periods).

6. Maintain a file of key resources or capacity centers with their indicated constraints and provide for update capability as follows:

   - Resource identification or work center number
   - Resource description
   - Unit of measure
   - Unit cost
   - Efficiency percentage

7. Calculate an "available to promise" amount for each applicable master-level item by time period for "make to order" master-level items.

8. Allocate customer orders against a specified forecast over a pre-determined number of periods.

9. Calculate "rough cut" resource requirements profiles for the entire master schedule by extending each master production schedule quantity by the representative resource profile and sum for the entire master production schedule.

10. Check, on a cumulative basis, available capacity versus load (available capacity is computed by multiplying the daily capacity by the number of periods between the current demand due date and a planned start date).

11. Utilize a planning bill of material concept that develops bills of material from a forecasting/customer order point of view rather than an engineering specification.

12. Track actual production versus the master production plan, requiring input and storage of actual production by time period be available.

13. Calculate net requirements for master-level items by adding safety stock and allocations and subtracting on hand inventory, released orders, and firm planned orders from gross requirements.

14. Handle production lot sizes.

15. Accumulate and subtotal demands for each item by time period representing gross requirements for master-level items.

16. Maintain a resource load profile database containing information regarding the load imposed on specific plant resources by master-level items.

17. Maintain a master schedule database for x master schedule entries consisting of:

- Customer order/demand reference number
- Part number
- Demand type
- Customer order due date
- Schedule date
- Scheduled quantity
- Period date
- Period quantity

18. Run master scheduling in a simulated mode, allowing creation of a master schedule without permanent update.

19. Data common to resource profile summaries by product include:

Number of workers	Normal hours per week	Overtime hours
Efficiency factors	Hourly rates	per week

Reports

1. Resource profile report indicating long-term manpower, machine, capacity requirements, overloads, and underloads.

2. Transaction listings of all adds, deletes, and changes to the master schedule.

3. Projected inventory values for each period-end.

4. Forecast error report comparing actual to forecasted demand both at an aggregate and individual item level.

5. Master schedule revision work sheet to be used as a production planning tool for modifying the master schedule for subsequent input to MRP.

6. Master schedule report including:

Plant manufacturing location	Part number	Part name
	Type	Source of demand
Schedule due date	Scheduled quantity	Period due date
Volume dollar summaries		

7. Shop calendar report whenever a new shop calendar is created.

8. Master schedule profile report indicating actual committed and probable committed capacity based on open orders and order history.

COST ACCOUNTING

The purpose of the cost accounting module is to integrate the results of manufacturing and other activities into the general ledger reporting system. While the manufacturing modules facilitate establishing and monitoring quantities, the cost accounting module attaches dollar amounts to these quantities.

The importance of accurate and timely financial information cannot be overemphasized. One situation will illustrate this point. The company is a manufacturer of electronic devices. In addition to its line of standard products, the company also manufactures to custom specifications. Although extremely profitable historically, the company began to experience unfavorable operating results. Accordingly, management initiated steps to improve its manufacturing information systems.

New automated systems were implemented including tracking material usage and labor efficiency by cost center. Unfortunately, the accounting side of the business was ignored and none of the manufacturing systems were integrated into the general ledger. The absence of timely and accurate financial information led to two disastrous decisions. First, believing that labor production problems had been solved, management made a decision to grant an hourly wage increase to production personnel. Second, believing that product costs had returned to their previous cost levels, management made the decision not to increase selling prices. Accurate information came in the form of the annual audit; however, by then it was too late! The assumptions made earlier in the year proved to be erroneous. The costs associated with the decisions turned out to be many times the cost of installing an integrated cost accounting system, which would have provided both timely and accurate information.

If you are not presently receiving both timely and accurate information, automation should be considered.

Features

1. Inquire as to detail cost information for all open work orders.
2. Budgeting and variance analysis capabilities.
3. "Implosion" ability (accumulate incremental cost for material, labor, and overhead) up through the product structure to arrive at a cumulative cost for each subassembly, assembly, and end product.
4. Factor in miscellaneous costs (supplies, paint, etc.) based upon a user-defined percentage.
5. Calculate variances on work orders partially completed.
6. Accommodate x work centers and x departments.

Reports

1. Inventory cost status report with multiple sort capability.
2. Storeroom issues to work in process by part number and work order (standard cost and quantities).
3. Shipments by part number (standard cost and quantities).
4. Cost of sales reports by product type and category.
5. Cost of goods manufactured summary.
6. Cost of goods manufactured and transferred from work in process to finished goods by part number and work order (dollars and quantities).
7. Job cost summary report for open work orders (quantity, statistics, material, labor, and factory overhead).
8. Job cost and unit cost summary report for work orders closed during the month.
9. Produce reports of slow moving and obsolete goods, including related costs.
10. Produce variance reports such as product type and/or product category material and labor variances.

WARRANTY

Many manufacturing companies incur significant cost to repair defects for products under warranty. The objectives of an adequate warranty system are to:

- Identify (and quantify in dollar terms) unfavorable trends that may be developing.
- Summarize nature of repairs.
- Determine whether the warranty period has expired.
- Monitor repair department performance.
- Calculate warranty reserves.

Features

1. Screen display of products still under warranty showing serial number, customer, ship date, and invoice number.
2. Ability to enter serial number when goods are shipped.
3. Automatic deleting of products from the goods under warranty file when the warranty expires.
4. Screen display of the status of open customer service reports.
5. Extensive editing of masterfile data.
6. Ability to automatically interface with:
   - Order entry system to determine whether the customer should be billed or whether the item is under warranty.
   - Shipping/sales files regarding validity of warranty.

Reports

1. Invoices with the serial numbers displayed.
2. Customer service reports regarding timeliness of repair and goods on hand to be repaired.
3. Service returns summary:
   - Reason/problem and appropriate dates
   - Product type and category
   - Defective parts
   - Disposition

- Responsible department
- Warranty information

4. Open engineering change requests.
5. Service cost and charges.

7 using the computer in distribution operations

The challenges facing companies in the distribution business are numerous. Frequently, the competition is fierce and customers are extremely price sensitive. Add to that the sheer volume of paper to be processed together with issues of timely deliver and inventory management. Manual systems frequently cannot keep up with the processing load and provide management with the information needed to manage the business. In that event, consider automating some or all of the following modules:

- Order entry (including credit authorization)
- Sales analysis
- Inventory management
- Route scheduling

ORDER ENTRY

An automated order entry system should minimize the amount of clerical effort to process orders, check the credit status of customers, and provide comprehensive management reports. The benefits to be derived may include:

- Reduction of clerical personnel.
- Elimination of clerical errors.
- Smaller lead times from order to shipment.
- Accurate and timely determination of credit limit information (sum of accounts receivable plus on order).
- Faster response to customer inquiries.
- Ability to make better and/or more timely decisions.

Features

1. Enter complete order information including customer number, salesman number, ship to address, special freight considerations, inventory item data, government contract number, whether the item is for resale, whether the item is renegotiable, and so on.

2. Check, as applicable, whether valid tax exemption certificates are on file.

3. Calculate unit price during order entry by using a quantity discount table and a product list price.

4. Verify a customer's credit status during order entry on a line item basis.

5. Enter changes on-line to the customer masterfile, including information regarding the addition of new customers, deletion of former customers, and changes to existing customers.

6. Reject user attempts to delete customers with balances of any type.

7. On-line editing for all data elements for each customer line item and customer information.

8. Apply credits to customer balances.

9. Process standard contract orders.

10. Validate shipping information including:

Ship date	Shipment type	Carrier
Carrier return date	Shipping number	Truck identification
Price	Customer product number	

11. Enter line item data including:

Item number	Unit of measure	Item description
Override terms	Quantity	Freight class
Price	Customer product ID	

12. Handle up to x items per sales order and be able to handle multiple shipments per order.

13. Invoice each shipment separately.

14. Capacity to handle up to x different quantity price breaks.

15. Schedule orders and project an order completion date. If appropriate, the order entry system should interface with the purchasing system.

16. Process standing and blanket orders.

17. Support x customers in total and x number of active customers.

18. Support x number of orders at any one time.

19. Allow for cyclical billing via a user-designated code.

20. Facilitate multiple billings to a given customer within a billing cycle.

21. Apply automatic interest or late charges to customer billings and account balances.

22. Interface directly with other modules, including inventory control, accounts receivable, general ledger, and sales analysis.

23. Provide open-item accounts receivable reports.

24. Perform automated housekeeping functions at period end, such as zeroing of month to date totals, accumulating balance forward amounts, and calculating interest and other charges.

25. Support a 13-period fiscal year.

26. Process new customers and corresponding orders during the current cycle.

27. Calculate interest charges from payment due date.

28. Apply sales tax, freight terms, and miscellaneous charges.

29. Calculate most advantageous shipping date based upon transit time to customer location.

30. Accommodate discount terms for cash and end of month payments.

31. Produce dunning letters.

32. Prepare invoices.

33. Inquiry capability for customer data by searching customer number or customer name.

34. Maintain an open item invoice file containing, at a minimum, the following:

Invoice number	Customer number	Invoice amount
Invoice date	Invoice type	Reference data
Contract data	Freight arrangements	

35. Maintain data in the customer master file including, as a minimum, the following information:

Customer number	Credit limit	Account type
Customer address	Month to date sales	Month to date
Current balance	Terms	payments
Customer contact	Billing code	Customer name
Year to date sales	Year to date payments	Salesman code
Discount percentage	Bill to address	Aged balances
Most recent date	Credit amount granted	Ship to address
credit limit	at most recent date	
checked	credit limit checked	

36. Maintain an open order file containing, at a minimum, the following items:

Order number	Shipment status	Amount
Customer number	Order type	Order date
Order responsibility	Reference data	Invoice cross
		reference

37. Perform complete editing and validation of data before system updating, including interface updates (general ledger, inventory, accounts receivable).

Reports

1. Daily orders by customer and inventory item.
2. Order confirmations and back-order notices with the capability of entering user-defined messages.
3. Back-order reports by customer and item.
4. Order backlog report with the following information:

Customer number	Customer name	Transaction date
Ship to location	Total units	Order amount

5. Masterfile change report with before and after information.
6. Masterfile contents with control totals for number of customers and hash totals.
7. Customer lists based upon user-specified criteria (alphabetical for all customers, customer number, selected lists, etc.).
8. Outstanding bills and orders (by date, number, customer, etc.).
9. Hard copy and inquiry regarding status of customer orders.
10. Credit memos.

11. Invoice registers for invoices prepared during the current processing cycle.

12. Order register for orders processed.

SALES ANALYSIS

The purpose of the sales analysis system is to provide timely summaries of historical data, to facilitate market analyses and forecasting, and to produce commission statements.

Features

1. Maintain sales data by:

Catalog number	Quantity
Charge to customer/account	Salesman
Territory	Commodity code
Sales price	

2. Provide transaction entry and editing in an on-line interactive mode.

3. Reject only those entries containing errors.

4. Maintain a suspense account for entries with validation errors.

5. Identify all errors for a given transaction for which an error condition has been detected.

6. Support x customers in total with x customers active at any time.

7. Support x salesmen in total with x salesmen active at any time.

8. Support x inventory items in total with x items active at any time.

9. Automatic end of period housekeeping, such as zeroing monthly figures and accumulating year to date amounts.

10. Support 13-period fiscal year.

11. Perform trend analysis on sales summaries.

12. Accommodate primary and secondary salesmen.

13. Accommodate "house accounts" when salesman is not applicable.

14. Accommodate present manual account number sequences.

15. Calculate both current period and year to date information, as well as comparable prior period data.

16. Accommodate the prior period adjustments and update the prior period data.

17. Provide comparison of actual data to budgeted data and provide variance analyses.

18. Produce trend reports based on prior period, current period, and budget data, and use such reports as turnaround documents.

19. Facilitate flexible or variable budgeting using rates, standards, or projected figures.

20. Maintain, as a minimum, the following product masterfile information:

Product identification	Product category
Product description	Product unit of measure
Weight	Current cost per unit
Preceding cost per unit	

21. Maintain, as a minimum, the following sales masterfile information:

Customer number	Salesman number
Product identification	Product category
Prior year sales, amount	Current year sales, amount
Prior year sales, units	Current year sales, units
Prior year sales, weights	Current year sales, weights
Commission data	Margin

22. Maintain, as a minimum, the following customer masterfile information:

Customer name	Customer number
Bill to address	Ship to address
Salesman	Balance data

23. Maintain salesman masterfile information.

24. Perform all edit tasks prior to any file updates.

Reports

1. Product masterfile listing, including analyses and/or forecasts for various categories.

2. Sales masterfile listing.

3. Product category sales analysis and forecast.

4. Salesman sales analyses (by salesman, customer, and territory).

5. Customer sales analyses (by customer type, territory, salesman, alphabetical).

6. Item sales analysis report (by category).

7. Detailed sales report.
8. Daily sales recap (by territory, salesman, customer, item) with comparison analysis.
9. Product analysis by salesman.
10. Salesman commission statements.
11. Market analysis by industry type, geographic territory, product line, type of customer, and sales history totals.

INVENTORY MANAGEMENT

The objectives of the automated inventory management system consist of:

- Avoiding stock-outs while at the same time minimizing inventory levels.
- Maintaining information on inventory items, including quantities on hand and on order.
- Preparing picking tickets.

Features

1. Provide transaction entry and editing in an on-line interactive mode.
2. Reject only those entries containing errors.
3. Maintain a suspense account for entries with validation errors.
4. Identify all errors for a given transaction for which an error condition has been detected.
5. Permit transaction entry for a subsequent period prior to closing the current period.
6. Accommodate on-line maintenance to the inventory management system.
7. Process "issues" and returns transactions including:

Quantity	Part number
General ledger account number	Issuing responsibility

8. Process adjustments to inventory quantity on hand and unit price.
9. Process transfers between inventory locations (catalog number, quantity, transfer from, transfer to, document number and/or material request number authorizing the transfer).
10. Automatic interface from order entry system, including part number, quantity, charge to customer, account number, and sales price.

11. Process receipts of inventory, including item number, quantity, account number, vendor, and purchase order number.

12. Support in-transit inventories.

13. Accommodate user-defined inventory locations such as company, division, warehouse, stock location, and material type.

14. Calculate prices by item number based on user-defined pricing methods.

15. System-generated reordering capability based on reorder levels.

16. Automatic interface to the user-defined general ledger accounts.

17. Maintain detailed transaction files to facilitate detailed listings of inventory transactions, including activity from other systems.

18. Reassign and compute "ABC" codes based on annualized and season usage, cost, margin, and sales.

19. Compute and maintain actual cost history for inventory items based on all transactions processed by the system.

20. Process quantity adjustments based on physical counts.

21. Calculate order points and economic order quantities (EOQs).

22. Automatic interface with accounts receivable, order entry, and credit authorization systems.

23. System-generated purchase orders based on user-defined criteria (inventory quantity on hand plus on order is less than min/max or reorder point, positive MRP net requirements, etc.).

24. Prepare and process cancellation notices for on-order quantities.

25. Permit discretionary "overbuy" of inventory items.

26. Automatic generation of pick lists.

27. Accommodate up to x digits for stock numbers.

28. Accommodate inactive and active part numbers and change status.

29. Accommodate two lead times (from supplier to dock and dock to stock).

30. Automatic conversion from one unit of measure to another.

31. Track inventory shrinkage.

32. Automatic rejection and notification for transactions that would cause a negative inventory quantity.

33. Process partial-case shipments.

34. Provide physical inventory aids, including input screens, forms, and the like.

35. Track committed but not shipped items.

36. Automatic rejection and notification for deletion of masterfile items regarding nonzero balances.

37. Automatic housekeeping for end of period processing, including zeroing current period balances and accumulating year to date figures.

38. Limit checks and notification for transactions above limits and inventory quantity limits.

39. Automatic update of prior period balances for prior period adjustments.

40. Accommodate bulk price updates.

41. Maintain an inventory masterfile with, as a minimum, the following information:

Warehouse	Inventory location	ABC code
Actual cost information	Order rules	Freight code
Standard cost information	Vendor cross-reference number	Order point
		Lead time
Safety stock	Lot size	Class
Item number	Description code	Item weight
Vendor number	Alternate vendor number	Tax class
Out of stock code		Price code
Purchase unit of measure	Stock unit of measure	Description
Price break information for up to x breaks	Suggested retail price	

44. Maintain a customer masterfile with, as a minimum, the following information:

Number	Name	Address
Ship to address for up to x locations	Phone number	Credit limit
	Year account opened	Credit rating
Credit rating date	Salesman number	Servicing branch code
Date of last sale	Tax information for multiple jurisdictions	

45. Maintain a vendor masterfile with, as a minimum, the following information:

Vendor number	Vendor name	Vendor address
Telephone number	Vendor minimum quantities	

46. Maintain an inventory warehouse masterfile with, as a minimum, the following information:

Item number	Warehouse number	Bin location
Reorder point	Safety stock level	Suggested order
Date of last purchase	Lead time	quantity
order	Last cost	Average unit cost
Total quantity on order	Quantity on hand	Quantity on back
Today's outs	Period to date outs	order
Receipts for period	Year to date direct	Year to date stock
This month direct sales	sales	sales
This month stock sales	Last month stock	On hand at last
Buyer code	sales	receipt
Quantity of last	Cash discount code	Quantity of last
receipt	Lead times	purchase order

Reports

1. Daily transaction listing for all inventory activity.

2. Physical inventory work sheet for cycle counts.

3. Reorder recommendation report specifying reorder point, EOQ, quantity on hand and on order, average usage, and lead times.

4. Back-order report listing all items for which requests for issue have been suspended, including item number, storage location, and required quantity.

5. Inactive inventory report summarizing items for which there has not been any activity for a user-defined (variable) period, including issues, sales, or transfers.

6. Physical inventory differences report with quantities and dollars for book figures, physical counts, and the difference.

7. ABC analysis, including current ABC from the calculated ABC, ABC quantity, ABC dollars, cumulative dollars, and percentage of total value.

8. Cycle inventory report with quantities, standard cost, and extended dollar amounts for both book and cycle count, together with actual differences compared to user-defined tolerance limits.

9. Inventory masterfile listing, including inventory number, account name, dollar amounts for beginning balance, receipts, issues, adjustments, net change, and ending balance.

10. Inventory stock status report with part number, inventory account, quantity on hand, dollar amount of quantity on hand, requirement quantity, on order quantity, allocated quantity, secondary quantity, description, and unit of measure.

11. Inventory revaluation report comparing new standard costs to old standard costs for each account and the change both in dollars and percentage.

12. Weekly or monthly transaction register listing transactions and stock movements.

13. Inventory report listing the number of months of quantities on hand for all parts within each inventory account.

14. On-line inquiry and display for individual transactions including status and level information.

15. Picking list for filling orders.

16. Inventory cross-reference listing based on user-defined criteria.

17. Warehouse transfer report of stock movement between warehouses.

18. Inventory return report.

ROUTE SCHEDULING

For some distribution companies, the use of common carriers solves delivery issues. For others, a fleet of company-operated trucks presents further challenges. The primary objective of the route scheduling system is to enable the fleet to be used in the most efficient manner.

Features

1. Load salesman orders.

2. Process breakage information (truck and warehouse).

3. Process customer information, including data relative to chain-store operations.

4. Extensive edit and validation testing.

5. Rejection only of transactions containing errors.

6. Automatic interface with the inventory control system.

7. Automatic interface with the accounts receivable system.

8. Perform route reconciliation for both presell and driver-sell methods.

9. Produce invoice registers.

10. Accommodate a 13-period fiscal year.

11. Calculate salesman commissions for both presell and driver-sell methods.

12. Accommodate up to x chain-store locations.

13. Accommodate up to x days of history.

14. Permit entering transactions for other than the customer's assigned salesman.

15. Accommodate up to x days of future orders.

16. Accommodate sales promotions.

17. Accommodate up to x customer types.

18. Maintain up to x state requirements regarding prohibited transactions.

19. Accommodate up to x customers with x customers active at any time.

20. Process multiple warehouses and multiple companies both with unique inventories.

21. Accommodate x number of active orders at any time.

22. Process prior period adjustments.

23. Allow posting to other subsystems (inventory control and accounts receivable).

24. Transaction editing and notification for:

Insufficient inventory	Nonexistent customer
Poor credit risks	Nonexistent salesman

25. Perform all editing prior to file updates.

26. Maintaining breakage information and statistics.

27. Maintain a route scheduling masterfile with, as a minimum, the following information:

Customer number	Customer name	Route number
Salesman number	Normal ordering requirements	Product/commodity type

28. Maintain a route scheduling transaction file with, as a minimum, the following information:

Customer number	Location	Amount
Delivery frequency	Ordering	Source code
Date	information	Schedule parameters

29. Maintain a load statistics file with, as a minimum, the following information:

Truck number/ID	Truck type	Availability
Size	Commodity capability	Usage history
Driver	Loading characteristics	Expected receipts

Reports

1. Preprinted invoices (for use in presell activities).
2. Truck load sheets.
3. Route scheduling work sheet indicating vehicle assignments, territory, distance, customers, driver, load, inventory, return.
4. Preprinted order forms (for use in driver-sell activities).
5. Sales analysis report.
6. Marketing and statistical reports.
7. Customer order list (for use in presell activities).
8. Ticket headers and/or gummed labels (for driver-sell activities).
9. Route reconciliation report (to help eliminate shrinkage).
10. Where applicable, a gratis report.
11. Where applicable, a case promotion report.
12. Inventory requirements report (by supplier, product).
13. Daily sales report (by route, salesman).
14. Sales (by route, by product, by day).
15. Sales to chains (weekly and/or monthly, by chain- store location).
16. Sales to other distributors (by invoice).
17. Truck breakage report.
18. Warehouse breakage report.
19. Receipts and other adjustments to inventory.
20. Return control turnaround documents.

8 computerizing finance functions

As an accountant responsible for finance functions, you devote a significant amount of your time to analyzing the future, the present, and the past. First, there is the budget for next year with all its seemingly endless versions. Then there is the continuous monitoring of current results compared to last year and budget. In the meantime, the bank wants another forecast. Management wants an analysis of expenses and the impact of reducing certain costs. Finally, there are all those special projects that you don't seem to have the time for. Will it ever end? Of course not, but it can be easier. Let the computer help you with finance functions such as:

- Budgeting
- Projections
- Economic analyses

COMPUTERIZING BUDGETING FUNCTIONS

Whether your organizational structure is simple or complex, computerizing budgeting functions can save you time. In this regard, let's consider the three phases of budgeting:

- Preparation
- Approval
- Monitoring

Budget Preparation

Irrespective of the level of detail that you gather, the budgeting process itself essentially consists of the steps illustrated in Figure 8.1. Each of these steps leading up to the budget meeting can be computerized. Let's explore what can be done.

Gather Information. The details supporting major financial statement captions and the like generally require the preparation of numerous schedules and other work papers with mathematical buildups. In this regard, there are essentially three tasks that can be computerized:

1. **Pro forma work-paper preparation:** Setting up manually prepared schedules to gather information is not only a time-consuming task, it also tends to be error prone. Line items and other important details may be forgotten. Computerizing the work papers provides assurance that, once the work papers are adequately set up, they can be printed when needed with all the relevant details. Other benefits of computerizing the work papers include (1) automatic retrieval of prior period data and (2) consistency of preparation (formats, techniques, etc.).

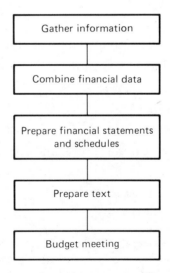

FIGURE 8.1
Budget preparation steps.

2. **Mathematical calculations:** After the details have been gathered, let the computer perform all the mathematical calculations (extensions, footings, etc.). In addition to saving you time, the computer can eliminate those embarrassing math errors that inevitably find their way into the manual budgeting process.

3. **Modeling "what-if" scenarios:** Whether you use a top-down approach (estimate revenues and costs to determine profit) or a bottom-up approach (set profit goal and work upward to determine revenues and costs), or both, assumptions have to be made and the related effects calculated. In this regard, use the computer to help you with this process. Examples of what-if scenarios that can be modeled include:

- Revenues
  a. Volume changes
  b. Price changes
  c. New products or services
- Cost of revenues
  a. Volume changes
  b. Price changes
  c. Mix of products or services
- Personnel costs
  a. Headcounts
  b. Pay rates
- Selling expenses
  a. Advertising relationships
  b. Travel and entertainment (e.g., number of trips)
  c. Commission rates
- Cash flow
  a. Borrowing levels and interest rates regarding interest expense
  b. Investment levels and related interest income
- Consumption (fuel, supplies, etc.)
  a. Volume changes
  b. Price changes

Combine Financial Data. At this point, all the work-paper schedules are complete and necessary mathematical calculations have been made (extensions, footings, etc.). The next step is to combine the data ("roll-ups") into your category totals. Let the computer do this for you also. Examples include:

- Cost buildups
- Cost-center totals
- Product line totals
- Natural account totals
- Division totals
- Capital expenditure totals
- Period totals (month, quarter, etc.)

Prepare Financial Statements and Schedules. Your final step as to financial data is preparing the summary financial statements and schedules (cash flow and the like). Inasmuch as all the necessary data are already in the computer, let the computer perform this step for you also. In addition to eliminating the preparation time (layout, math, etc.), you will eliminate time-consuming typing and proofreading (including your time to do so).

Prepare Text. Financial budgets are frequently supplemented by narratives such as written plans, analyses of alternatives, economic evaluations, and explanatory material. Consider computerizing this function also. Benefits include:

- Ease of making corrections
- Ability to preview the document prior to printing (e.g., to improve cosmetics)

Budget Approval

It is only in the rarest of occasions that the initial budget draft is approved as submitted. Revising a manually prepared budget can be an extremely time-consuming process. Changing one minor assumption at a detail level requires recalculating the effects all the way through the final summary level. When numerous assumptions are changed (which is usually the case), not only are the revisions time consuming to implement, the risk of making errors is high. In this regard, it is easy to overlook dependent relationships (e.g., changing an overhead pool affects inventory and cost of sales). If you have computerized the budget preparation process, making changes during budget approval is simple. Key in the revisions and out pops the entire revised budget package.

Monitoring the Budget

After the budget is approved, it's time to monitor actual results compared to budgeted results. In this regard, let's examine the steps in this phase:

- Compare budget to actual
- Analyze variances
- Revise the budget

Compare Budget to Actual.   Done manually, comparing budget to actual requires that you schedule both the budgeted figures and the actual figures for each of the budgeted periods (current month, quarter to date, year to date). Then you make all the variance calculations (dollar amounts, percentages) for each of the budgeted periods. By integrating the budgeting system with the general ledger system, you can totally eliminate the manual effort. Let the computer (1) retrieve both the budgeted and actual figures and (2) calculate all the variances. Your report might have headings such as those in Table 8.1.

TABLE 8.1
Budget Comparison

	ACTUAL		BUDGET		VARIANCE	
Caption	Amount	Percent	Amount	Percent	Amount	Percent

Analyze Variances.   Understanding what has caused variances to date is critical to facilitating corrective action. Unfortunately, on a manual basis, analyzing variances can be an extremely time-consuming process. Once again, the computer can do a great deal of the work for you. Examples include:

- Expense analyses (e.g., print the details of actual expenses charged to selected accounts to determine which items weren't budgeted).
- Revenue analyses (e.g., which products/services are under/over budget and by how much as to both dollars and units).
- Cost of revenues analyses (e.g., which products/services are over/under budget and by how much as to both dollars and units).

Revise the Budget.   Whether you refer to the output as a revised budget, an outlook, or an updated forecast, the components are the same—actual to date and estimate of results for the balance of the period. Computerizing this process can certainly save you time by eliminating the clerical effort involved in retrieving data and making calculations. More importantly, the computer can enable you to improve the quality of the revised budget. Ideally, the budget revision process would consist of going through the entire formal budgeting process with respect to the remaining portion of the year. If your budgeting process is not computerized, the time and effort might be overwhelming. However, if the budget preparation process is computerized, the steps could be as simple as:

- Revise the assumptions for the remaining months of the year.
- Rerun the budget preparation model.

The computer could then produce reports with headings such as those in Table 8.2.

TABLE 8.2
Revised Budget and Outlook

	OUTLOOK										
	Actual results 1/1 to 6/30		Revised budget 7/1 to 12/31		Total			Original budget		Variance	
Caption	Amount	%	Amount	%	Amount	%		Amount	%	Amount	%

COMPUTERIZING PROJECTION FUNCTIONS

Projection functions deal with the financial impact of applying assumptions to historical data. The data may be complete financial statements, specific accounts, levels of spending, and so on. In the preceding section we looked at the power of the computer to help us with "what-if" scenarios in the short term for purposes of the budget cycle. You can take advantage of the computer's power to help you with other short-term situations, such as "how can we do things better." In this regard, vary the assumptions until the results appear feasible and are desirable. Then you can prepare an action plan to achieve the results. For short-term projections, the examples

TABLE 8.3
Ten-Year Projected Pretax Profit Model

	Base year	Percent increase	PROJECTION									
			1	2	3	4	5	6	7	8	9	10
Revenues	2,000,000	7%	2,140,000	2,289,800	2,450,086	2,621,592	2,805,103	3,001,461	3,211,563	3,436,372	3,676,918	3,934,303
Cost of revenues	1,400,000	5%	1,470,000	1,543,500	1,620,675	1,701,709	1,786,794	1,876,134	1,969,941	2,068,438	2,171,860	2,280,452
Gross profit	600,000		670,000	746,300	829,411	919,883	1,018,309	1,125,327	1,241,622	1,367,935	1,505,059	1,653,850
Costs and expenses:												
Selling	200,000	6%	212,000	224,720	238,203	252,495	267,645	283,704	300,726	318,770	337,896	358,170
Administrative	200,000	1%	202,000	204,020	206,060	208,121	210,202	212,304	214,427	216,571	218,737	220,924
Total expenses	400,000		414,000	428,740	444,263	460,616	477,847	496,008	515,153	535,341	556,633	579,094
Pretax profit	200,000		256,000	317,560	385,148	459,267	540,462	629,319	726,469	832,594	948,426	1,074,756

in the preceding section apply here equally. In addition, you can use the computer to help you with long-range projections.

The role of the computer in long-range projections is identical to that in short-term projections. That is, given a historical situation, you determine the assumptions and let the computer do the math and print the results. What is different is the types of activities that you might use it for. For example, management (or the bank) wants a 10-year pretax profit and loss projection (as illustrated in Table 8.3) based on the following percentage increases: revenues, 7%; cost of revenues, 5%; selling expenses, 6%; and administrative expenses, 1%. Using pencil and paper, this little project could take you an hour or two to accomplish. If it has to be typed, add the secretarial time plus some more of your time to review the typed projection. Using the computer, you could accomplish this task in a few minutes and eliminate the typing time as well. Now suppose you are asked to change the revenue increase to 8% and the cost of revenue increase to 6%. For manual projections, you can either erase the affected line items and recalculate or start over and prepare the projection anew. In either case, there goes another hour or so. On a computerized basis, the data would have been saved and simply retrieved. Now the time to enter the revised assumptions and recalculate the effects would be less than *10 seconds*.

In addition to projecting financial statements, you can use the computer to calculate historical relationships and model "what-if" scenarios for other long-range projections as well. Examples include:

- Market share
- Profit contribution (product, category, etc.)
- Inflationary effects
- Manpower requirements
- Capacity planning
- New locations (offices, territories, etc.)
- Cost relationships
- Capital expenditure planning
- Maintenance programs
- Productivity
- Training (costs, statistics, etc.)

COMPUTERIZING ECONOMIC ANALYSES

As accountants, we are frequently faced with economic alternatives. How does situation A compare to situation B? Which of these alternatives is the most attractive? Is there a positive payback to this project? These are the types of questions that we have to deal with. Common to all of them is the time value of money. If the situations that you encounter are relatively simple, you don't need the power of a computer. For example, if all you need to do is calculate how much a fixed amount will grow into at a fixed rate for periods of equal length, you can probably do that just as quickly on a calculator. However, if the situations you deal with are more complex, consider using the computer to help you with the calculations. Our topics consist of:

- Fixed-assumption calculations
- Variable-assumption calculations
- Opportunities

Fixed-Assumption Calculations

In fixed-assumption calculations, all but one of the factors is known and your objective is to calculate the unknown factor. For example, given the term, interest rate, and principal amount of a loan, you need only solve for the payments. Or, given the positive and negative cash flows together with the time periods, you need only calculate the interest rate.

Variable-Assumption Calculations

In variable-assumption calculations, the assumptions are fixed for a given calculation but are then varied until the desired results are achieved or all the predefined calculations are made. Examples include (1) iterative calculations that require trial-and-error calculations until the closest approximation is achieved and (2) calculations made for a range of values.

Opportunities

- Asset management
- Financing alternatives
  a. Debt/equity
  b. Short-term/long-term
- Lease/purchase
- Loan amortization tables
- Make/buy
- Payback period
- Portfolio investment analysis

- Rate of return analysis (e.g., acquisitions)

Before moving on to the next chapter, here are two more thoughts regarding computerizing economic analyses. First, if they are not complex but you make them repeatedly, consider the amount of time it presently takes both to format and calculate, as well as the overall turnaround time. Second, if they are very complex but you make them infrequently, consider time sharing as a viable alternative.

9 computerizing personnel functions

The computer can be an effective tool to help you to manage assets such as cash, receivables, and inventory. It can also be an effective tool to help you to manage your most important asset, your personnel. Even if your firm is fairly small, some of the opportunities in this chapter will be of interest to you. While some of the topics are directed primarily to public accounting firms and accountants in service-oriented organizations, some topics are equally applicable to all organizations. With that in mind, our computerization topics are:

- Compensation
- Continuing professional education
- Personnel evaluation information
- Recruiting
- Requirements planning
- Scheduling
- Skills inventory

COMPENSATION

Ask anyone (who is not independently wealthy) to name their three most important employment topics and, more often than not, one of them will be compensation. Looking at the subject from your standpoint, compensation is critical because:

- Compensation directly affects your profitability.
- Compensation directly affects productivity.

Computerization compensation opportunities include compensation history and compensation planning:

Compensation History. It is easy to maintain manual records of an individual's compensation history. However, maintaining even the most rudimentary statistics requires time, which, given your everyday pressures, may not be available. Consider using the computer to automatically calculate:

- Compensation increase (percent and amount) for the past five years.
- Compensation increase (percent and amount) relative to other personnel similarly situated for the past five years.

Compensation Planning. Compensation increases affect future profitability. Let the computer help you determine the impact. In this regard, you can use the computer's ability to help you with "what-if" calculations. Use the computer to determine the amount and percent of increases and their effects on your future bottom line.

CONTINUING PROFESSIONAL EDUCATION

If your personnel must attend educational courses to meet minimum licensing or other requirements, consider computerizing educational activities. In this regard, the computer can be used to monitor compliance with requirements, maintain an information base of courses attended, including course evaluations, and plan training in areas in which additional skills are needed.

PERSONNEL EVALUATION INFORMATION

The results of performance evaluations can also be computerized. The data could then be sorted to (1) identify poor performers who need counseling regarding improvement and (2) assist in determining compensation adjustments.

RECRUITING

The recruiting process lends itself to computerization. Potential applications include:

- Interview scheduling
- Interview results
- Form letters
- Campus statistics

REQUIREMENTS PLANNING

If your overall goals include growth, a key consideration is the number of personnel required to accomplish that growth. Using the computer's "what-if" capabilities, you can make assumptions regarding employee turnover (planned and unplanned), total man-hours to be worked (regular, overtime, etc.), and work to be performed. The computer can then calculate the number of personnel (full time and part time) required for each set of assumptions. The results could then be used to determine short- and long-term policies (overtime, new hires, etc.) to accomplish overall goals.

SCHEDULING

As a service organization, you have only one thing to sell—time! In an increasingly competitive environment, your ability to earn a fair profit is directly dependent on your ability to (1) minimize the amount of time required to perform the service and (2) maximize the time devoted to performing services. An automated scheduling system can help you achieve the following:

- Minimizing the amount (to the extent under your control) of time required to perform the service is a function of the personnel skills assigned to the engagement. Matching engagement skills with personnel skills includes:

  a. As to new engagements, assigning personnel experienced with the client's industry.

b. For recurring engagements, assigning personnel who have previously worked on the engagement.

- Maximizing the amount of time devoted to performing services is a function of scheduling personnel fully and productively.

Given the preceding objectives, key features and reporting capabilities might be as follows:

Features

1. Maintain personnel data including:

Name	Staff level	Special skills
Hire date	Employee address	(industry, etc.)
Employee number	Division (audit, tax, etc.)	

2. Maintain engagement data including:

Staff assignment priority by staff level	Name	Engagement number
Prior year hours, dates, and service code by staff level	Address	Engagement executives
	Year-end	

3. Maintain moving 18-month master assignment calendar.

4. On-line data entry and editing.

5. On-line inquiry based on user-specified criteria.

6. On-line assignment calendar file update.

7. Computer-generated assignment capability based on user-specified parameters, including industry experience, client service experience, location, availability.

8. User ability to override computer-generated assignments.

9. User capability of specifying length of work week for each calendar work week.

10. Ability to perform "what-if" scenarios (e.g., all assignments for a specified staff level based on client service experience, all seniors work 44 hours during a specified period of time, etc.).

11. User ability to restore engagement assignment calendar to prior update status.

12. Maintain record counts and hash totals (employee and engagement numbers) for personnel and engagement masterfiles.

Reports

1. Before and after changes for personnel and engagement masterfiles with control totals for record counts and hash totals.

2. Masterfile listing of personnel and engagement masterfiles with control totals for record counts and hash totals.

3. Multicopy assignment notification by client with client data, personnel, staff level, dates assigned, and so on.

4. Engagement assignment calendar for user-specified period.

5. Availability listing, by staff level (with subtotals), by week and summary totals by staff level.

6. Unscheduled assignments by staff level within client by month.

7. Projected chargeable hours reports, by month, with details by staff level and summary totals for each staff level based on (1) entered assignments and (2) prior year actual for continuing clients.

8. Industry experience report by staff level.

9. Overscheduled (based on user-defined work-week hours) personnel report.

10. What-if scenarios.

SKILLS INVENTORY

All but the smallest of organizations may be able to benefit from a computerized skills inventory. In this regard, potential uses consist of:

- Matching personnel needs with engagement requirements: Assigning personnel who have experience meaningful to a specific engagement is important to a long-term client relationship. In this regard, use the computer to keep track of all experience (industry, manufacturing, retail, etc.) and type of service performed (audit, review, write-up, data processing, etc.). Then determine which personnel should be assigned to the engagement.

- Identifying important experience and skills for proposal efforts: Whether the proposal effort is informal (meeting with potential clients/customers) or formal (presentations of capabilities, services, etc.), your success is directly dependent on the perceived talents of the personnel you involve. Your up-to-date skills inventory will help you to identify the appropriate personnel to be involved in the proposal effort.

- Identifying areas for which additional skills should be obtained: Your computerized skills inventory provides you with information, by employee, of your historical experience and capabilities. In this regard, also use it to determine what experience you don't have. Consider your organizational goals in terms of where you want to be.

The opportunities in this chapter have been presented primarily on a "stand-alone" basis. Most of these modules have information that is common to them all. In this regard, efficiencies can be gained by implementing one or more of them on an integrated basis, thus eliminating entering redundant data and reducing data-storage requirements.

10 using the computer for marketing functions

As an accountant in public practice or private industry, you're concerned with your firm's future prospects for profitability. In this chapter, we will focus on profitability from the standpoint of increasing revenues. In this regard, the computer can be used to help you with your marketing effort to add new business. Our topics consist of:

- Planning marketing activities
- Monitoring marketing activities
- Computerizing the marketing database

PLANNING MARKETING ACTIVITIES

In Chapter 8, we explored planning as it relates to the budgeting process. In this section, we will explore planning from a marketing standpoint. Regardless of the time frame (short term or long term) or level of detail, marketing planning consists of the following steps:

- Diagnosis
- Prognosis
- Objectives
- Strategy
- Tactics

Diagnosis

Your first step is to determine your present market position and the related reasons for it. In this regard, you are concerned with historical data. You can use the computer to retrieve, for several periods, revenue and profitability data such as service/product and profitability mix, customer mix, and market share. Once the data have been retrieved, use the computer to analyze trends. Which services/products have increased/ decreased and by how much (dollars and percentages)? How much of the increase/decrease is attributable to volume versus price? Use the computer to fit trend lines based on the historical data.

Once the data have been gathered and trends analyzed, determine the causes. Use a survey approach to help you accomplish this task. The questionnaire should be designed to gather data as to changes in buying attitudes (existing services/products, desired services/products, prices, etc.). Use the computer to draw a random sample from both your existing customers as well as the entire marketplace. The survey results can then be sorted and analyzed by the computer. Use the analysis to assist you in determining the underlying reasons for observed trends.

Prognosis

Your next step is to determine where you are headed based on your historical results. Admittedly, some assumptions about the future will have to be made. However, you'll be better off having gone through the thought process than if you simply forge ahead blindly. Begin by using the computer to project the historical trend lines into the future. How do you measure up as to key performance ratios and statistics (revenues, mix, profitability, etc.)? If industry data are available to you, use the computer to project that also. How do your trend lines compare to those of the entire industry? Then use the data gathered in your survey regarding desired services, buying patterns, products, prices, and so on. Use the computer to revise the trend lines based on historical data to give effect to key survey statistics.

Objectives

If you are not totally satisfied with the prognosis, a change in marketing objectives is warranted. You will need to accomplish two tasks:

- Select market areas for action
- Establish revenue targets

Select Market Areas for Action.   Since you have decided to revise your marketing approach, you will need to define the markets for which action will be taken. How your organization views itself is critical in this process. For example, if a public accounting firm views itself as a provider of services to the real estate industry, its fate is linked directly to that industry and its marketing opportunities are limited. Likewise, if a manufacturing entity views itself as a producer of office desks (as contrasted with office furniture), its fate is linked to that product. Your task then is to select markets in which opportunities appear to exist (which may include markets for which new skills/products will be necessary).

Establish Revenue Targets.   After you have focused on the markets to be served, use the computer to model "what-if" scenarios (revenue, profitability, etc.) based on alternative programs. The results can then be used to establish the revenue targets.

Strategy

Your next step is to develop the overall strategy necessary to accomplish the revenue targets. At this stage you are concerned with policies, not procedures. This is a difficult step because it involves:

- Assessing numerous alternatives
- Risk taking

Assessing Numerous Alternatives.   Setting the overall strategy requires careful assessment of numerous alternatives regarding competition and customers. Examples and related questions include:

- **Quality.** Should we focus on producing the best and plan to appeal to those who are not price conscious? Alternatively, should we produce an average-quality product/service and plan to appeal to a larger, price-conscious segment?
- **Advertising.** Should we advertise? If so, what image do we want to convey? Should we advertise more than or less than our competitors?

Risk Taking.   Although numerous strategies exist, each with its own variety of risks, for our purpose we will view risk taking in terms of approaches to what competitors are doing. In this regard, there are two general approaches to risk taking:

- **Imitate successful competitors.** This approach attempts to minimize risk by using proven strategy. For example, successful competitors might use a high-price, high-quality strategy. However, there is nothing to guarantee that the marketplace will reward another firm using the same approach.

- **Deviate from what competitors are doing.** This approach involves a high level of risk because it is unproven. However, it potentially may provide greater reward because of unfulfilled market needs. For example, a firm might use a low-price, average-quality strategy to appeal to a different segment of the market.

Tactics

Whereas strategy deals with policies as to how objectives will be met, tactics deal with the procedures or specifics to be used. For example, a public accounting firm might decide to expand services to privately owned businesses (an objective). It decides to focus on an average-quality service, charge a low price, and rely heavily on advertising to develop its market (the strategy). The service will be priced between X and Y dollars and will be supported by an advertising budget of Z dollars, split evenly between media advertising, mass mailing of brochures, and seminars (the tactical decisions). In this regard, the computer can be of assistance with both tactical planning and execution.

- **Tactical planning:** Deciding on the specific tactics to be used requires consideration of the alternatives (selling prices, number of units, etc.). Use the computer to model "what-if" scenarios.

- **Tactical execution:** After the tactical decisions are made, they must be executed. In this regard, the computer can be used to maintain the database for execution. We'll explore the details in the last section of this chapter.

MONITORING MARKETING ACTIVITIES

Monitoring budgeted revenues and expense is discussed in Chapter 8. Accordingly, in this section we will focus on the statistical aspects of monitoring marketing activities and related computerization opportunities. Our topics consist of:

- Monitoring advertising programs
- Monitoring specific-purpose marketing programs
- Monitoring sales contact effort
- Monitoring overall results

Monitoring Advertising Programs

The primary purpose of advertising (newspaper, television, radio, magazines, and mass mailings) is to increase consumer awareness. In this regard, the anticipation is that, if the consumer becomes aware of your product/service, the consumer (1) will be immediately motivated to make a purchase or (2) will consider your product/service if, at a later date, a decision to make a purchase is made. Pick up any basic text on marketing and you will likely be told that there is not a direct relationship between general-purpose advertising and revenues. We will leave it to the statisticians and marketing theorists to argue that point. Whether or not there is a direct relationship is unimportant for our purposes. What is important is that there are data that, when measured, can provide meaningful input regarding advertising programs. Use the computer to collect and summarize information such as nature of advertising, extent of coverage compared to plan, leads obtained, and the like.

Monitoring Specific-Purpose Marketing Programs

Whereas general advertising is directed to large segments of the population, specific-purpose marketing programs are directed to smaller segments (e.g., known or potential buyers). Seminars on special topics are an example of this type of program. You can use the computer to:

- Select the invitees from your overall marketing database based on predefined characteristics (e.g., industry type) and prepare mailing labels.
- Maintain the acceptance list and prepare name tags.
- Summarize program results:
  a. Expected versus actual attendees.
  b. Follow-up inquiries, sales, and so on.

Monitoring Sales Contact Efforts

For businesses for which direct personal contact is an important source of obtaining new business, you can use the computer to:

- Identify desirable contacts based on predetermined characteristics (target companies).
- Assign contacts based on personnel skills (e.g., specialized industries).
- Monitor contact efforts:
  a. Quantity: number of contacts achieved versus plan.
  b. Quality: new business obtained.

Monitoring Overall Results

The specific information that you use to monitor overall results will depend on your specific objectives, strategies, and tactics. Examples of information that can be tracked and reported by the computer include:

- Market share: actual share compared to prior period and plan
- New business
  a. Actual compared to prior period and plan
  b. Source
- Consumer awareness: increase compared to prior period and plan

COMPUTERIZING THE MARKETING DATABASE

The objectives, strategies, and tactics you have defined determine the scope and content of your computerized marketing database. Accordingly, in this section we will explore potential information sources and define features (system capabilities) and sample reports. For illustration purposes, we will use information relative to a public accounting firm. If you are an accountant in industry, substitute "customer" for "client" and "product" for "service," as applicable.

Information Sources

The purpose of your marketing database is (1) to maintain and report information regarding potential clients and (2) to assist in marketing efforts (mailings, seminar invitations, contacts, etc.). Your first step then is to create the database itself. Companies such as Standard and Poors and Dun & Bradstreet maintain extensive information regarding the business community at large. One approach would be to obtain all this information and use the computer to weed out entities that are inconsistent (industry, size, etc.) with your marketing plan. Other sources of information include:

- Trade association membership listings
- Chamber of Commerce membership listings
- Research organizations
- Annual reports of public companies
- Telephone directories
- Newspaper reports
- Acquaintances
- Referral sources (attorneys, bankers, etc.)

When you have assembled the information base, you are ready to use your computerized marketing database. Let's explore its features and reports.

Features

1. On-line data entry and extensive editing (completeness, numeric data in numeric fields, etc.).
2. Maintain masterfile data including:
   - Entity type (client, nonclient, attorney, banker, investment banker, trade association, alumnus)
   - Entity form (individual, corporation, partnership, trust)
   - Entity name
   - Entity address
   - Entity telephone number
   - Key executives
     a. Name
     b. Division (finance, administration, operations, marketing, etc.)
     c. Title
     d. Publications mailing list (e.g., tax notes)
   - Entity industry
   - Entity primary service/product
   - Most recent annual revenue
     a. Amount
     b. Period
   - Ownership
     a. Type (private, public, nonprofit)
     b. Nonmanagement owners

    (1) Name

    (2) Ownership percentage

- Contact information

  a. Priority type (target, secondary)

  b. Entity personnel

  c. Our personnel

  d. Dates

      (1) Most recent planned contact

      (2) Most recent actual contact

      (3) Next planned contact

  e. Up to x characters of user-entered narrative

- Professionals serving this entity

  a. Accountants

      (1) Firm name

      (2) Type (national, regional, local)

  b. Attorneys

      (1) Firm name

      (2) Account executive

  c. Bankers

      (1) Bank name

      (2) Branch

      (3) Account executive

  d. Investment banker

      (1) Firm name

      (2) Account executive

- List source

3. Maintain up to x records

4. Maintain control totals (record count and hash totals)

5. Multilevel search/sort capability (e.g., all nonclients in the electronics industry with revenues ranging between X and Y dollars that are privately owned, all nonclients for which the attorneys are XYZ law firm, etc.)

6. Print standard forms based on user-defined multilevel criteria:

- Mailing labels

- Standard letters
- Name tags

Reports

1. Before and after image report for file maintenance, with control totals (record count, hash totals).
2. Missing field reports:
   - Entity name and missing fields by contact personnel.
   - Total records and missing fields by contact personnel.
3. Standard forms.
4. Current period and year to date information regarding transfers from nonclient to client status.
5. Masterfile contents:
   - Alphabetical by entity name.
   - Alphabetical by entity name within contact personnel.
6. Multilevel search reports based on user-defined criteria:
   - All fields printed.
   - User-specified fields printed.
7. Masterfile statistics report based on user-defined criteria.

11 using graphics to communicate better

In Chapter 1 we saw that there are three primary devices (printers, plotters, and CRTs) that are capable of displaying graphic representations. We also noted that graphics are created by either drawing lines or densely packing dots to resemble solid images. So much for the technology! In this chapter we will focus on the elements of graphics for use by accountants and specific examples of how we can use graphics to communicate better.

UNDERSTANDING FINANCIAL GRAPHICS

The effective use of graphics requires more than simply throwing together some images on a white piece of paper. Accordingly, let's explore the details of graphics for financial purposes. Our topics consist of:

- Why you should consider using graphics

- Understanding the basic elements of financial graphics
- Guidelines for the use of financial graphics

Why You Should Consider Using Graphics

As accountants, we have been trained to deal with lots of numbers. Our work papers contain many detail figures that support totals, which in turn are forwarded to other schedules, which in turn support totals, and so on. Whether the details consist of account analyses, multiperiod comparisons, or cash accumulations is unimportant. What is important is that we are so used to working with an incredible amount of detail that we often lose sight of the fact that others aren't. Furthermore, having looked at all the detail, we frequently forget that others may not have done that and, accordingly, are not familiar with the key items. When it comes to communicating the information to others, our tendency is to communicate details. After all, don't the details speak for themselves? While the literal answer to this question is "yes," a literal approach begs the question of "Why?" Why didn't we earn the same profit as last year? Why is our gross profit margin declining? Why is it taking more hours to perform the same amount of work? As accountants trained in handling many details, we may be guilty of not passing on the benefit of our familiarity with all the details. That benefit is our understanding of what the figures mean. In this regard, graphics can be an important tool. In addition to presenting the supporting details in columnar style, use graphics to illustrate what the figures mean.

Understanding the Basic Elements of Financial Graphics

Before you can effectively use financial graphics, it is important that you understand the elements. In this regard, consider the graphics shapes themselves and the other important data relationships these shapes can represent.

Shapes.   From the financial perspective, graphics shapes of interest to you are illustrated in Figure 11.1. Lines and rectangles have one thing in common—their length. In this regard, their length can be used to illustrate quantities. The longer the length, the greater the quantity. Circles provide yet another perspective. Using dividers, you can create pie slices to illustrate relative size.

Amounts.   While the shapes in Figure 11.1 convey a mental image of relative size, the reader has no way of measuring magnitudes. Accordingly,

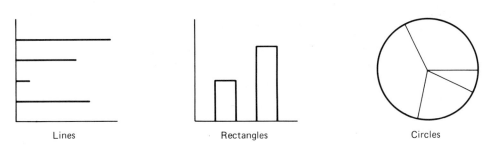

FIGURE 11.1
Graphics shapes for financial uses.

amounts need to be inserted. For lines and rectangles, the amounts should be inserted along the axis used to illustrate their length. For pie shapes, the amounts can be inserted inside the circle.

Titles.   Titles are a critical element of effective business graphics. The graphics shapes in Figure 11.1 are meaningless because the reader has no idea as to what data the shapes purport to illustrate. Also, it is important to choose the titles carefully. For example, consider the following comparisons:

- "Income" *vs.* "revenue by product"
- "Amount" *vs.* "expenditure category"

The titles that you use are critical to your use of graphics. Choose them carefully.

Guidelines for Use

How Much Graphics to Use.   Graphics can be an effective tool for communication. On the other hand, if they are used too liberally, their impact will be diluted. Use them to supplement other materials and use them sparingly.

What Should Be Illustrated.   Given that you can illustrate absolute values (totals, increases, etc.), percentages, dollars, units, and so on, you'll have to make choices. In this regard, consider what you believe the reader needs to know. For example, if sales are increasing but cost of sales is increasing even faster, illustrate the rates of increase.

Which Shape to Use.   Which shape you should use is a function of what you want to illustrate. As a general rule:

- **Rectangles:** Use multiple rectangles when you want to compare two or more like items (e.g., current and prior year revenues) over time.

- **Lines:** Use lines when you want to illustrate a trend.
- **Circles:** Use pie shapes when you want to illustrate the relative size of components for a single period (e.g., revenues by line of business).

USING FINANCIAL GRAPHICS

In the previous section we looked at the components of financial graphics and generic uses. Let's now look at a specific example and then explore other opportunities.

The type of financial data shown in Figure 11.2 was presented at a meeting with a board of directors of a closely held company. A package of financial statements was distributed to the group; the first page contained information in the format illustrated in Figure 11.2. It was followed by traditional financial statements (figures presented in columnar format). The group was talked through the data, and a senior member of the group confessed that this was the first time he truly understood the financial data presented. He also stated that he was used to, and prefers, a graphic summary of the information to be presented. As he put it, the reader's attention is drawn first to the graphic data where the mind's eye can quickly focus on relative changes and trends. Then the reader can selectively choose which numeric data to study further. The reader is not forced to sift through all the numeric data to interpret which figures are most important.

Whether you are in public accounting or private industry, the potential uses of and audiences for graphics are essentially the same. They are limited only by your imagination. Examples of potential uses follow:

1. Financial statements
   - Company wide
   - Divisions
2. Revenues
   - Major customers
   - Market share
   - Product lines
   - Price increases
3. Cost of revenues
   - Elements
   - Product lines

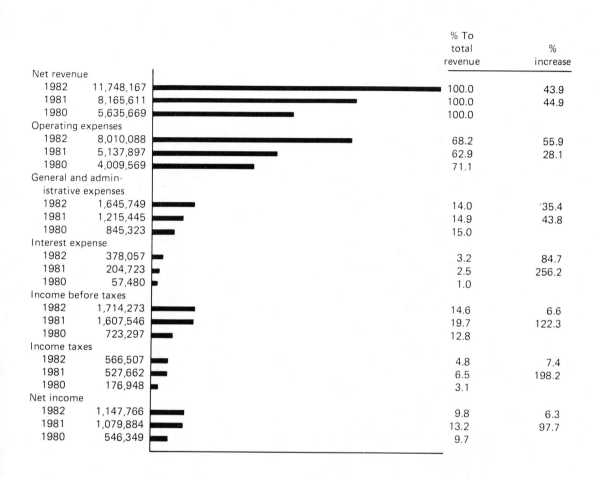

ABC COMPANY
SELECTED INCOME STATEMENT DATA
FOR THE THREE YEARS ENDED DECEMBER 31, 1982

			% To total revenue	% increase
Net revenue				
1982	11,748,167		100.0	43.9
1981	8,165,611		100.0	44.9
1980	5,635,669		100.0	
Operating expenses				
1982	8,010,088		68.2	55.9
1981	5,137,897		62.9	28.1
1980	4,009,569		71.1	
General and administrative expenses				
1982	1,645,749		14.0	35.4
1981	1,215,445		14.9	43.8
1980	845,323		15.0	
Interest expense				
1982	378,057		3.2	84.7
1981	204,723		2.5	256.2
1980	57,480		1.0	
Income before taxes				
1982	1,714,273		14.6	6.6
1981	1,607,546		19.7	122.3
1980	723,297		12.8	
Income taxes				
1982	566,507		4.8	7.4
1981	527,662		6.5	198.2
1980	176,948		3.1	
Net income				
1982	1,147,766		9.8	6.3
1981	1,079,884		13.2	97.7
1980	546,349		9.7	

(1) Each 1 represents ******$70,348.

(2) The data shown above has been derived from, and should be read in conjunction with, the basic financial statements which were examined by Ernst & Whinney and are presented only for supplementary analysis purposes for the exclusive use of management. Reference should be made to the Audit Report of Ernst & Whinney which accompanies the Basic Financial Statements.

FIGURE 11.2
Graphic income statement.

- Break-even analysis

4. Expenses
   - Commissions
   - Advertising
   - Consumption
   - Maintenance
   - Inflation
5. Forecasts
   - Income
   - Cash flow
6. Budgeting
   - Compared to prior year
   - Compared to actual
7. Variance analysis
8. Capital expenditures
9. Personnel statistics
   - Productivity
   - Wages
   - Utilization
10. Backlog
   - Absolute amounts
   - Rate of increase
   - Trends

Potential audiences include:

1. Management meetings
   - Departmental meetings
   - Meetings with senior management
   - Meetings with the board of directors
2. Meetings with outsiders
   - Bankers and other professionals
   - Potential customers/clients
   - Vendors

At this point, you might be skeptical about the cost of obtaining computerized graphics capabilities. You will be pleased to learn that, given the ever-increasing technological advancements, the price of computerized graphics is easily within your reach. The technology has advanced so rapidly that computerized graphics are available in inexpensive desktop computers, as well as in larger computers. In fact, if you already have a computer, your existing peripheral devices may be capable of creating graphics, in which case you need only acquire the application software.

12 computerizing your office of the future

Imagine that it's the end of your workday. You are about ready to leave the office and head for home. You glance at the "screen" on the side of your desk (it is attached to a movable keyboard and connected to the office computer). Before leaving, you press the button labeled "Through for the day" and the screen displays "calendar." You enter "tomorrow" and the screen displays your appointments for tomorrow. You have a meeting scheduled for 10 A.M. for which you still need to review the details before finalizing your conclusions. You enter "Pending" and the screen displays all pending matters. You select "FILE A" and the screen displays several options. You select the option "Home" and, before you leave your office, the file is on its way to your home. After dinner, you review the file on your home "workstation," make revisions, and send the revised file back to the office where the final work product is printed for the meeting.

The next day, when you arrive at the office, you enter "Today." Up pops the display of the activities for today. The screen displays three lists:

- Your calendar for the day
- Tasks for completion prior to scheduled activities for today

- Tasks that:
    a. Need to be completed for tomorrow's scheduled activities.
    b. Are optional for today but should be completed if time permits.

You attend to those tasks that need to be accomplished. Prior to the 10 A.M. meeting, you review the output that was printed after you transmitted the details from home last night. Pleased with the results, you attend your meeting. The graphics charts and supplementary data are an overwhelming success. With a smile on your face, you return to your office. The screen is flashing the message, "Urgent teleconference needed regarding LMN matter." You select "Teleconference" and your workstation initiates a teleconference. On the screen is a client and one of your co-workers. After much discussion, you reach a satisfactory solution.

After your teleconference, your screen displays:

- Secretary
    a. New
    b. In process
    c. Completed
- Other options

You select the option "Completed" and on the screen is your completed letter to "BCD Company." After scanning the letter, you add your changes and transmit the letter to your secretary. She notes that you have made final corrections and transmits the document to its destination.

The scenario described illustrates the office of the 1980s. The technology to accomplish many of the tasks described is already available on a cost-effective basis for many organizations. With that in mind, our topics are information flow and recurring documents for office automation.

INFORMATION FLOW

Figure 12.1 illustrates, from your perspective, the flow of information in your automated office. We see that there are five categories of information flow. In this section, we'll review each of these and the benefits to be derived from office automation.

Information Flow Among You and Co-workers

Consider the flow of information in a manual environment. Let's use document preparation (letters, reports, financial statements, etc.) to

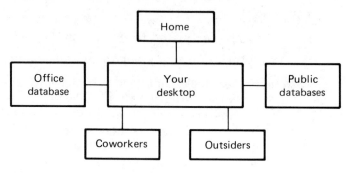

FIGURE 12.1
Automated information flow.

illustrate the flow. A document is drafted and given to a secretary to type. After it is typed, two types of changes are made. First, there are changes to correct typographical errors. Second, there are the inevitable editing changes (add a paragraph, reword a sentence, etc.). Accordingly, the affected pages (perhaps the entire document) must be retyped and the entire process repeated.

As to document preparation, there are two aspects of office automation to consider. The first aspect is the typing process itself. The use of a word-processing system can result in a dramatic reduction of clerical effort to process changes. In this regard, typographical errors can be quickly corrected, sentences can be easily modified, paragraphs can be added, deleted or moved, all without the need to retype the document itself. In addition to reducing clerical time, word-processing systems provide a level of quality (proportional spacing, left and right justification, etc.) that cannot be achieved by many electric typewriters. The second aspect of office automation in this category deals with how the information flows back and forth between you, the typist (your secretary, typing pool, etc.), and co-workers. In this regard, consider office networking as illustrated in

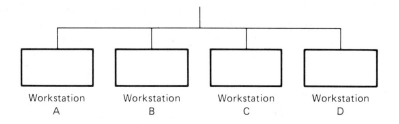

FIGURE 12.2
Workstations in an office network.

Figure 12.2. The nature of the hardware (terminals, microcomputers, etc.) located at each workstation is unimportant. What is important is that the workstations are tied together through a network and, thus, are capable of transmitting information back and forth among the workstations. Now we can really put office automation to work.

Consider the following scenario. You are at workstation A, your secretary is at workstation B, and two other co-workers are at workstations C and D. Your secretary has just finished key entering your document. The word-processing system automatically checks each word to see that it is listed as a correctly spelled and valid word in the computerized dictionary. If it is not, the word is highlighted on the screen. After your secretary makes the necessary corrections, the revised document is transmitted to you. You notice that a key point wasn't made in the last paragraph. Accordingly, you add two sentences to make the point. The document is now finished. If it is a document to be sent outside the office, you transmit it to the printer. If it is an internal memorandum, you transmit it to your co-workers at workstations C and D (you also schedule a meeting to discuss the memo contents).

Although this is but one scenario, it illustrates the dramatic potential for cost savings, more efficient use of time, and improved productivity. Consider this scenario as contrasted with the manual environment:

Description	Results
Processing changes	Elimination of need to retype entire pages or documents
Proofreading for spelling and typographical errors	Eliminated
Printing of draft copies	Eliminated
Time to physically transport documents around the office	Eliminated
Total elapsed time	Significantly reduced

Before we move on to the next category, consider yet one more potential benefit of office automation. In this regard, consider the techniques presently used in your office to create the first draft of documents. For example, if drafts of documents (letters, reports, financial statements, etc.) are created by using pencil and paper, then you are spending money for unnecessary secretarial support. Why? Compare the approach in Figure 12.3, which shows that the use of pencil drafts creates an unnecessary step. It doesn't take any more time to create the draft on a screen than it does to create the draft on paper. Therein lies your challenge! Eliminate the practice of pencil drafts and you eliminate the secretarial time to type the related draft.

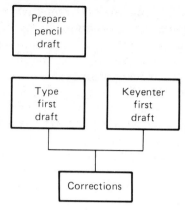

FIGURE 12.3
Approach to first drafts.

Information Flow between You and the Office Database

The fully integrated automated office presents you with a unique opportunity to eliminate the time required to create redundant data. Let's use the budgeting process to illustrate. The task is to prepare a budget for the next 12 months compared to actual for the prior 12 months. Your workstation resources include a budgeting model, but that model is not integrated with the general ledger. Accordingly, you must create your own file of historical data. That is, you have to manually enter the actual data for the prior 12 months. Contrast that approach with the integrated automated office in which you simply retrieve the actual data from the general ledger. Data redundancy is the key factor to focus on. In this regard, there are probably numerous opportunities for you to utilize an integrated automated office. You can identify these opportunities by simply opening up your file cabinets and desk drawers. What information is in there that is redundant [mailing lists, telephone numbers, work plans, calendars (events, appointments), customer and client lists, operating statistics, etc.]? Maintaining data at an office level and making it available on a need-to-know basis may significantly increase efficiency and productivity.

Information Flow between Home and Office

Life would be a lot simpler and easier if our workday could be confined to a "nine-to-five" routine. Unfortunately, that's not the case. Deadlines, special projects, and the like require us to work during the evenings. If you prefer to take work home, consider installing a workstation in your home. In this regard, when you are finished for the evening, you can send the work product back to the office for further processing (updating files, printing documents, etc.) and/or distribution. Furthermore, if you have forgotten to bring home a file or realize later than you need an additional file, simply retrieve it from the office using your home workstation.

Information Flow between You and Public Databases

A public database is simply a time-sharing service for information retrieval. The benefits of such services include:

- The ability to retrieve information more quickly and/or timely.
- The ability to retrieve information that might not otherwise be available to you.

An example of a public database is the Dow Jones service from which you can retrieve stock market data (prices, activity, trends, etc.) and daily news events. However, that's just the start. Given the ever-increasing installed base of computers, you can expect to see a wide variety of public databases. Examples of services include:

- Demographic studies
- Economic trends
- Market research and forecasts
- Product availability, pricing, and purchasing
- Salary surveys

Given the breadth and scope of services, all functional divisions within the organization can benefit by tapping into better and more timely information.

Information Flow between You and Outsiders

Automating the delivery of correspondence with outsiders also presents some opportunities. The primary benefits include cost reduction and expediting delivery. If you utilize messenger services (automobile or air) to deliver documents, consider electronic mail as a potential cost-effective alternative. In this regard, you can use the computer to store the information until evening when line charges are at their lowest. At the designated time, the computer can initiate delivery of your electronic mail. If the recipient does not have the necessary hardware to receive your communications, consider electronic courier services as another alternative.

Electronic mail can also be used to expedite delivery. If your normal distribution method is the U.S. mail, consider electronic mail to expedite delivery.

RECURRING DOCUMENTS

In the preceding section we looked at opportunities as they relate to information flow. In this section we'll explore opportunities by reference to the nature of the documents themselves. The tool for capitalizing on these opportunities is the focal point of the automated office—the word-processing system. Our goal is to eliminate preparing documents from "scratch." Accordingly, our topics are:

- Using word processing to prepare recurring documents
- Specific examples

Using Word Processing to Prepare Recurring Documents

In the previous section we saw that word-processing systems can be used to efficiently make changes (add, delete, or modify) to documents. That concept (making changes) is the key to maximizing the use of word processing. Consider the nature of documents themselves:

1. Most or all of the subject matter is identical, but the recipients are different.

2. The subject matter varies only slightly over time, but the recipient is the same.

3. The subject matter is dissimilar, but the recipient receives correspondence frequently.

4. The subject matter is dissimilar, and the recipient is not frequently corresponded with.

The first three categories represent your opportunities. Let's see how word processing can be used regarding each of these.

1. Maintain a word-processing library of standard documents and subject matters. If the subject matter is identical, use the standard document and change the recipient's name. If some of the subject matter is different, delete inapplicable material and use the subject matter library to add applicable material. If proper nouns (e.g., recipient's

name) are to be referred to in the "customized" document, insert "dummy" proper nouns in the standard document; then use the "search for/change to" feature to locate and change all these references.

2. If the subject matter varies only slightly over time but the recipient is the same, retain the prior version in your word-processing library. When it is time to issue the document again, call it up on the screen and modify only the material that requires change.

3. If the subject matter is dissimilar but the recipient recurs, maintain a mailing list and use the mailing label feature.

Examples of Recurring Documents for Which Word Processing Can Be Used

The following examples are provided for illustrative purposes only. Notwithstanding the fact that we are both accountants, too many other factors (public accounting versus private industry, work style, organizational structure, size of organization, etc.) are at work. Accordingly, use the examples to stimulate your thinking as it relates to your organization's needs. The additional time and effort will be well worthwhile. With that in mind, examples follow:

- Engagement letters
- Financial statement figures (add the current period and delete the earliest prior period)
- Footnotes to financial statements
  a. Update for current changes
  b. Standard language
- Form letters (prospective or current customers/clients, dunning notices, etc.)
- Mailing lists
- Mailing labels
- Management letters
- Memoranda (results of standard procedures, inquiries, etc.)
- Narrative plans (budgets, strategies, targets, etc.)
- Procedures (policies, audit programs, etc.)
- Projections/forecasts
- Proposals (projects, clients, etc.)
- Request for proposals

- Research (search for similar examples)
- Standard accountant's reports (compilation, review, audit)

In this chapter we have explored opportunities to automate your office from the standpoint of a single, integrated system. In Part III, we will explore purchase decisions (cost effectiveness and so on). If you conclude that total integration isn't cost effective or politically acceptable for your organization, consider using a desktop micro as an alternative to capitalize on many of the opportunities in this chapter. Accordingly, let's move on to the final chapter on application opportunities, "Using desktop micros."

13 using desktop micros

The ever-decreasing cost of desktop micros coupled with continually increasing capabilities result in some astounding opportunities for us to use them in our everyday business lives. As the name implies, you can take advantage of these opportunities right on a desktop. Given the computing power of today's microprocessors, desktop micros are being used in the following ways:

- Smaller businesses are using them to meet all the business's accounting needs (accounts receivable, accounts payable, general ledger, etc.).
- Public accountants are using them in the office and in the field.
- Accountants in private industry are using them on the top of their desks.

Some tasks are so unique and time consuming (personnel scheduling, special reports, etc.) that they warrant the purchase of a desktop micro in and of themselves. In this regard, consider purchasing specific-purpose software (packages, custom programming, etc.). Other tasks are more generalized but recur frequently. The ability of general-purpose software to accomplish these tasks is the subject of this chapter (purchasing desktop micros is discussed in Chapter 16). Accordingly, our topics consist of:

- Evolution of user friendly general-purpose software.
- General-purpose application software packages and application opportunities.

EVOLUTION OF USER FRIENDLY GENERAL-PURPOSE SOFTWARE

It doesn't make a lot of sense for us to write a computer program everytime we need to perform a specific task. Recognizing this, computer manufacturers and software houses have developed packaged software for use on desktop micros. The extent to which these packages are easy to use characterizes the degree of their user "friendliness." In this regard, four generations of packaged software have evolved.

First-Generation Software

The computer cannot perform any work for you without knowing what it is that you want to do (e.g., enter data, print a report). First-generation software uses commands to tell the computer what you want to do. The idea is that you enter one or more characters ("commands") which the package then translates into computer instructions that enable the computer to perform the desired task. That certainly is much easier than (1) learning a programming language and (2) writing a program (including testing and debugging the program) to perform the work. However, consider the effort involved to begin using the package:

1. Read the user's manual to understand what the package can do.
2. Memorize the commands, including the sequence in which the characters must be entered.

You attempt to use the package and, inevitably, you enter a wrong command. Now what? You may have to start all over again. However, if you can recover from the error, you will need to know what to do next. If you don't know what to do next, back to the user manual. Try to find the section that addresses error-correction procedures. Can't find it? Start over again!

If that isn't bad enough, consider the initial problem of memorizing the commands themselves. The best case is that the commands themselves resemble the English language (consider the fact that an EDP person developed the package). Even if the commands resemble the English language, consider the amount of time to memorize the commands themselves. Are you willing to devote all that time to memorizing commands? Isn't there a better way?

Second-Generation Software

Although still command "driven," second-generation software for desktop micros introduced the concept of the HELP function. By entering the word HELP or its equivalent, the screen displays instructions to enable the user to continue without having to start all over again. Two approaches are used:

1. The screen displays all the help functions and the user must decide which help function is applicable. While this approach is handier than retrieving a user manual, the user may be confused by all the verbiage.

2. The computer keeps track of the most recently entered command. If the help function is requested, the screen displays the commands (and their functions) that are applicable to that command.

Third-Generation Software

Entering commands on a keyboard is similar to walking around in the dark. You can't see where you are going so you have to feel your way around. Unless you grasp hold of a familiar object, you are likely to stumble around, sometimes aimlesssly. Recognizing this, third-generation vendors turned on the lights to let the user see what is happening. In this regard, two approaches evolved:

1. **Menus:** The menu approach makes extensive use of the screen to help the user. A list of options is displayed in menu format. The user reads the menu and selects the option applicable to the desired task. If additional options are applicable, another menu is displayed, and so on, until the task is accomplished. If the package is well designed and the options are clearly worded, the user can't stumble in the dark.

2. **Continual visual display of interim results:** Imagine that you are sitting at your desk either writing a letter or preparing a financial statement. At any point in time, you can look at the paper to (a) review what has been done and (b) determine what needs to be done next. That aspect of continual visual display has been incorporated into this approach. Accordingly, the user is continually able to see what has been done and determine what needs to be done next.

It is this third generation of software that led to a significant increase in the use of desktop micros. While these packages certainly are "friendlier" than their predecessors (and are quite useful), they do not approach the ideal goal of a totally user friendly system. For example, the commands peculiar to the specific package must be learned. In addition, some degree of familiarity with how the hardware works may be necessary to perform tasks such as printing reports. Finally, information may not easily be exchanged between application programs. For example, suppose you had developed a 10-year projection. What you might want to do next is present that projection in graphics form. If you can do it all, it requires (1) storing the mathematical data in a different format (and time to learn how to do that), (2) exchanging diskettes to start up the graphics program, and (3) using commands to recall the data and to create the graphic representation.

Fourth-Generation Software

Introduced in early 1983, fourth-generation software made a quantum leap in terms of user friendliness. While the technology itself wasn't totally new, it certainly was new to desktop micros. Fourth-generation software combines continual screen display with images and an electronic "mouse." This eliminates the user's need to devote a significant amount of time to productively use the system's capabilities. Let's see how it works.

The majority of the screen is a representation of your desktop. On the top of your desk is the document(s) you are currently working with (report, financial statement, etc.). Whatever changes you make to the document are instantaneously displayed.

All around the perimeter of the screen is a small area reserved for images. The images are tiny pictures of the tools you actually work with at your desk. For example, if you were through with a document, you might want to (1) put it back in a folder on your desk, (2) throw it in the trash can, or (3) file it away in a filing cabinet. Accordingly, the screen would display images of (1) a folder, (2) a trash can, and (3) a filing cabinet. These images eliminate the need for you to learn how the program works and how to store data when you are through with it.

Another extremely important feature is the ability to transfer data between application functions. For example, suppose you just finished preparing a table of figures. Perhaps you want to incorporate that table into a narrative report. Fourth-generation software permits you to transfer that information directly into the word-processing application. In other words, all the applications are (1) data compatible and (2) immediately available.

Like a real mouse, the electronic mouse has a long tail which is connected to the computer, is small enough to fit in the palm of your hand, and can nimbly scurry around your desktop. Viewed from the top, the electronic mouse looks similar to the device used for remote slide projectors [rectangular in shape with a clicking button(s)]. However, when you turn the mouse over, you see a small stainless-steel ball that rotates when you move it around your desktop. What the mouse does is translate that movement around your desk, both in terms of speed and direction, into electronic impulses that are sent through its tail into the computer.

The primary purpose of the mouse is to enable you to select options (and eliminate the need for you to memorize commands). When you move the mouse around your desktop, you also move the pointer (cursor) on the screen. Since the screen displays tiny images along the outer perimeter, you can move the mouse to point to the desired image, click the mouse button, and, instantaneously, the function is performed. An example follows: When you sit down at your desk (start the system up), the screen displays, among other things, tiny images of the tools (programs) available to you and the documents you have created and stored. You use the mouse to point to and select which documents you want to retrieve or which function you want to perform. Let's suppose you want to update the prior year's budget. You select the "19×1 budget folder."

You click the mouse to open the file (just as you would on your desk) and spread the documents across your desktop. You change the date to "19×2". Next, you revise the assumptions and recalculate the results. Next, you point the mouse to the "19×1" bar chart of the budget, move the "19×2" data into it, click the mouse to move the other documents out of the way (as you might do on your desk), and now you see the results of the bar chart.

When you are finished manipulating the data, you point the mouse to the image of the printer, click the mouse, and your reports and graphs are printed. Since you are through with the file now, you point the mouse to the image of the file cabinet, click the mouse, and your file is then stored away.

The Author's View
of Fifth-Generation Software

Fourth-generation software will suffice for the 1980s. Increased competition will drive the prices down and further enhancements will be made. However, major changes (now in the laboratories) won't be released because the market probably won't be saturated until the end of the decade. The author's speculation on fifth-generation software is just that, speculation! However, considering the things that are happening in research and development laboratories and our technology capabilities, the following scenario doesn't seem unrealistic.

When you arrive at your office you turn on the lights and glance at the screen on your desktop. Recognizing that you are 20 minutes earlier than you have been based on the running average for the last 90 days, the computer remarks, "I am sorry that your coffee isn't ready. I didn't expect you to be here this early. However, I'll start it now while you sit down. In the meantime I'll turn the screen on for you. The graphs you sent last night are ready for you and I'm prepared to initiate your conference call. Are you ready?" You glance at the graphs and respond "No, I want to make one more change. I want you to change the sales figure to 10,000,000." As soon as the words leave your mouth, the change is made and the conference call begins. After the conference call is finished, you say, "Check Joe's calendar for Friday at 10:00 A.M. If he is available, I want to meet with the XYZ Company."

As illustrated, fifth-generation software will probably bring up voice-driven systems. How long it will take to make it commercially available is anyone's guess. However, it is clear that life would be a lot simpler if we could eliminate the mouse and talk to the computer directly. The computer could take dictation, change figures for us, forecast results, remind us of what we have to do, and so on.

So much for our look into the future. Let's get back to concentrating on the present. The software already available presents opportunities you can capitalize on. Let's take a look.

GENERAL-PURPOSE APPLICATION SOFTWARE PACKAGES AND APPLICATION OPPORTUNITIES

Although there are many general-purpose software packages available, the most frequently used (because of the frequently recurring nature of the related tasks) software packages are:

- Electronic spreadsheet
- Word processing
- Graphics
- Data management

Electronic Spreadsheet

Described as the "electronic spreadsheet," this package was the major reason that desktop micros began to be used extensively. The purpose of the electronic spreadsheet is to (1) eliminate the need for you to perform mathematical calculations (foot, crossfoot, extend figures, etc.) and (2) perform "what-if" calculations by changing assumptions. Our topics consist of:

- Electronic spreadsheet concepts
- Electronic spreadsheet applications
- Electronic spreadsheet features

Electronic Spreadsheet Concepts. The electronic spreadsheet can be pictured as a columnar work sheet with many rows and columns as follows:

COLUMN

ROW	1	2	3	.... Y
1				
2				
3				
•				
•				
•				
•				
•				
•				
•				
X				

Each intersection of a row and column is referred to as a *cell*. Each cell is capable of storing numeric constants, formulas, or words/characters. The formulas are the means by which you perform mathematical and "what-if" calculations. Let's illustrate the concept:

	COLUMN		
ROW	A	B	C
1		19×1	19×2
2	Sales	100	1.10 * B2
3	Cost of sales	60	1.09 * B3
4	Gross profit	+B2−B3	+C2−C3

In this example, column A contains the captions (e.g., cell A2, sales). Column B contains the actual data for year "19×1." However, note that cell B4 has a formula in it. Instead of entering the result of subtracting cost of sales from sales, you can enter the formula "+B2−B3". This formula instructs the computer to subtract the value contained in cell B3 (60) from the value contained in cell B2 (100). Now suppose that you want to forecast figures for "19×2." The data in column C illustrate how that might be done. Suppose you forecast a 10% increase in sales and a 9% increase in cost of sales. The formulas in cells C2 and C3 instruct the computer to multiply the constants 1.10 (10% increase) and 1.09 (9% increase) by the values contained in cells B2 and B3, respectively. Cell C4 contains the formula to calculate gross profit for "19×2." This example illustrates how you can let the computer perform mathematical calculations for you. Now, as to "what-if" calculations, suppose you want to change the sales assumption to a 15% increase over "19×1." Simply change the constant in cell C2 from 1.10 to 1.15 and the computer recalculates all the results.

The remaining principal concept deals with duplication of formulas. Commonly referred to as *replication*, this concept enables you to copy all or a portion of the formulas in a given row or column. In the preceding example, suppose you also want to forecast figures for "19×3." One way to do that would be to manually enter the applicable formulas in column D. Instead of manually entering the formulas, you would simply instruct the computer to replicate the formulas in column C and place them in column D after it revises the cell references (the formula for sales would be 1.10 * C3). To illustrate further the potential benefits, let's expand our example.

Let's assume that you are doing a sales forecast for the next five years (1983 to 1987) using the following captions:

	ACTUAL		FORECAST								
	1982		1983		1984		1985		1986		1987	
	$	%	$	%	$	%	$	%	$	%	$	%
Sales												
Cost of sales												
Gross profit												
Selling expenses												
General expenses												
Pretax income												
Income taxes												
Net income												

If you were using pencil and paper, you would (1) enter the actual figures and percentages for 1982, (2) determine the assumptions, and (3) calculate the dollar amounts and percentages for 1983 to 1987 using these assumptions. What happens if you want to vary the assumptions? You have to erase the results and recalculate all the figures, a time-consuming process. Suppose you want to change the assumptions once more. Erase and change it again. Whoops, the paper just tore from erasing it too much.

Results—frustration and inefficient use of time. Is there a better way? You bet! Use the electronic spreadsheet. Enter the dollar amounts for 1982. Then enter formulas for the related 1982 percentages and 1983 dollar amounts. Replicate the formulas and let the computer do the rest. Want to change an assumption? Simply change a formula and let the computer recalculate. When you are finished, store the model and use it again the next time you want to forecast.

Electronic Spreadsheet Applications.   The potential use of electronic spreadsheets is limited only by your imagination. To get you started, consider the following potential uses in public accounting and private industry.

- Client preparation packages
- Footing trial balances
- Calculating general ledger variances (amounts and percentages; store the prior period amounts on the computer)
- Pro forma schedules with prior period balances
- Carry-forward schedules
- Depreciation calculations
- Prepaid expense calculations
- Accrued expense calculations
- Inventory extensions and footings
- Accounts receivable footings and agings
- Accounts payable footings and agings
- Overhead calculations
- Earnings per share calculations
- Debt convenant compliance
- Cash to accrual conversions
- Tax loss carry-back calculations
- Time management:
    a. Forecasts:
        (1) By individual employee, by month and in total
        (2) All employees, by month and in total
    b. Actual compared to forecast
- Practice management:
    a. Revenue forecasts:

  (1) By client

  (2) All clients

 b. Actual compared to forecast

- Budgeting:

 a. Pro forma work papers

 b. Revenues

  (1) Volume changes

  (2) Price changes

  (3) New products or services

 c. Cost of revenues

  (1) Volume changes

  (2) Price changes

  (3) Mix of products or services

 d. Selling expenses

  (1) Travel and entertainment (e.g., number of trips)

  (2) Commission rates

 e. Cash flow

  (1) Borrowing levels and interest rates regarding interest expense

  (2) Investment levels and related interest income

 f. Consumption (fuel, supplies, etc.)

  (1) Volume changes

  (2) Price changes

 g. Cost buildups

 h. Cost-center totals

 i. Product line totals

 j. Natural account totals

 k. Division totals

 l. Capital expenditure totals

 m. Period totals (month, quarter, etc.)

 n. Market share

 o. Profit contribution (product, category, etc.)

 p. Inflationary effects

 q. Capacity planning

    r. New locations (offices, territories, etc.)

    s. Cost relationships

    t. Capital expenditure planning

    u. Maintenance programs

    v. Productivity

    w. Training (costs, statistics, etc.)

- Economic analysis:

    a. Asset management

    b. Financing alternatives

        (1) Debt/equity

        (2) Short-term/long-term

    c. Lease/purchase

    d. Loan amortization tables

    e. Make/buy

    f. Payback period

    g. Portfolio investment analysis

    h. Rate of return analysis (e.g., acquisitions)

- Personnel:

    a. Compensation planning

    b. Manpower requirements

Electronic Spreadsheet Features. There are numerous electronic spreadsheets with varying capabilities and features in today's marketplace. Your first consideration is hardware oriented. That is, can the package run on the hardware you presently have or intend to purchase. The second consideration is the features and capabilities of the package itself. Key items consist of:

- User-available memory (total memory less memory required by the package).
- Up to x columns and y rows.
- Ability to sort alpha and/or numeric data.
- On-screen "help" function.
- Data compatibility with other packages and applications.
- Variable column widths.
- Recalculation order (row versus column, manual versus automatic).

- Arithmetic functions:

Absolute value	Minimum value
Average value	Modulo function
Exponent	Rounding capability
Integer portion of a value	Square root function
Logarithms	Sum of the values
Maximum value	

- Trigonometric functions (arccosine, arcsine, arctangent, cosine, sine, tangent).

- Control functions:

Error	Not applicable
False	Cell protection from data entry
True	

- Logic functions:

And	Greater than, less than, or equal to
If	Greater than or less than and not equal to
Not	Less than or greater than
Or	

- Financial functions:

Rate of return	Future value
Number of periods required	Internal rate of return
Payment amounts	Net present value
Present value	

- Tab function.

- Blank function (to clear a cell).

- Date functions.

- Column and row functions:

Replicate multiple columns or rows	Delete multiple columns or rows
Add multiple columns or rows	Move multiple columns or rows

- Display functions (alpha or numeric amounts as applicable).
  a. Alpha functions (individual or all cells):

Default characteristics	Repeating characters
Left, right, or center justify	Editing

  b. Numeric functions (individual or all cells):

    (1) Display formulas or results.

(2) Hide (make contents of a cell invisible).

(3) Format (individual or all cells):

Default characteristics	Commas
Integer	Decimal points
Left, right, or center justify	Number of digits displayed
Dollar amounts (dollar and cents)	Dollar sign
Editing	Plus or minus signs
Brackets for negative amounts	Percentage format (divide by 100)

- Procedures command (combine a series of keystrokes).
- Window function (split the screen horizontally or vertically, synchronized or unsynchronized scrolling).
- Title function (maintain horizontal or vertical titles on the screen).
- Printing functions:
  a. Print all or a portion of the screen.
  b. Printer commands (characters per inch, underlining, etc.).
- File functions:
  a. Search for file.
  b. Duplicate file detection.
  c. Save all or a portion of the work sheet.

Word-Processing Packages

Word-processing packages for desktop micros permit you to (1) edit draft documents easily and quickly (move, add, or delete paragraphs, sentences, and words) and (2) retrieve standard or recurring types of documents and quickly modify them as necessary. First let's look at some sample applications and then explore word-processing features.

Word-Processing Applications. For nonrecurring types of documents (letters, memos, etc.), word processing can significantly reduce the total and elapsed time to produce the final document. One common time-consuming task is the process of making changes. In this regard, word processing can eliminate the need to retype whole paragraphs or pages due to adding, deleting, or modifying the draft. Furthermore, word processing can be used to proofread for spelling and typographical errors.

Consider also the tremendous potential regarding recurring types of documents. You can use word processing to store them, retrieve them the next time they are needed, make minor changes, and produce the final document. Examples include:

- Engagement letters
- Financial statement figures (add the current period and delete the earliest prior period)
- Footnotes to financial statements:
  a. Update for current changes
  b. Standard language
- Form letters (prospective or current customers/clients, dunning notices, etc.)
- Mailing lists
- Mailing labels
- Management letters
- Memoranda (results of standard procedures, inquiries, etc.)
- Narrative plans (budgets, strategies, targets, etc.)
- Procedures (policies, audit programs, etc.)
- Projections/forecasts
- Proposals (projects, clients, etc.)
- Request for proposals
- Research (search for similar examples)
- Standard accountant's reports (compilation, review, audit)

Word-Processing Features. There are numerous word-processing packages with varying capabilities and features in today's marketplace. Your consideration is the features and capabilities of the package itself. Key items consist of:

- User available memory (total memory less memory required by the package)
- Up to x columns of character display
- Up to x lines maximum document size
- Data compatibility with other packages/applications
- On screen "help" function
- Templates for surrounding the keyboard (the templates indicate the functions performed by the various keys) or individual labels which can be placed directly on the key caps

- Preview function to display the document exactly as it will be printed
- File storage capabilities:
  a. Display names of documents on file
  b. Save all or a portion of the document in memory
  c. Incorporate document(s) on file into document in memory
- Document editing features:
  a. Copy, move, and delete selected portions of text
  b. Insert text
  c. Spelling check
  d. Search and replace:
     (1) Automatic
     (2) Selective
  e. Strike over
- Scrolling:
  a. Move to beginning or end of text
  b. Move to beginning of selected page
  c. Move up or down:
     (1) x lines of text (number of lines displayed on the screen)
     (2) Full page
  d. Line by line
  e. Split screens
- Formatting:
  a. Left, right, left and right, and center justify
  b. Tabs
  c. Page headings and footings (repetitive text inserts)
  d. Multiple margin and indent settings
  e. Page numbering
  f. Skip x lines
  g. New page
  h. Conditional new page (to avoid tables and the like from being broken across pages)
- Variables (replace x with y, if, then, else)
- Printing:
  a. Specify page width (characters) and length (lines)

b. Specify text width (characters) and length (lines)

c. Specify character width (characters per inch)

d. Print whole document, selected pages, or selected portions of text

e. Print multiple copies

f. Line spacing (single, double, or triple)

g. Underlining

h. Subscript and superscript

i. Print bold characters

j. Proportional spacing

k. Specify character height (e.g., oversize headings)

l. Spooling

Graphics Packages

While electronic spreadsheets enable you to use the computer to make mathematical calculations and model "what-if" scenarios, graphics packages enable you to display numeric data (perhaps the results of spreadsheet calculations) in the form of bar charts, pie shapes, and so on. Sample opportunities and features follow.

Graphics Opportunities.   A graphics capability provides you with a unique tool to illustrate rates of increase, trends, and so on. You can use graphics both for internal meetings as well as for meetings with outsiders to highlight key information. Sample opportunities follow:

- Financial statements:

    Company wide   Divisions

- Revenues:

    Major customers   Product lines
    Market share   Price increases

- Cost of revenues:

    Elements   Break-even analysis
    Product lines

- Forecasts:

    Income   Cash flow

- Budgeting:

    Compared to prior year   Compared to actual

- Expenses:

  Commissions   Maintenance
  Advertising   Inflation
  Consumption

- Variance analysis
- Capital expenditures
- Personnel statistics:

  Productivity   Wages   Utilization

- Backlog

Graphics Packages Features. There are numerous graphics packages with varying capabilities and features in today's marketplace. Your consideration is the features and capabilities of the package itself. Key items consist of:

- User-available memory (total memory less memory required by the package).
- Data compatibility with other packages/applications.
- On screen "help" function.
- Graph types (bar, line, mixed bar/line, scatter, and pie shape).
- Graph functions:

  Curve fitting   Frequency distribution   Trend generation
                                                           (forecast)

- Editing features:

  Insert and delete data points   Titles and labels
  Change graph type   Data point revision
  Scale revision

- Formatting features:

  Multiple graph sizes   Floating titles
  High-resolution screen   Numeric formatting (integer,
    display   decimal, and dollar)
  Manual or automatic labeling   Footnotes
    of axes

- Printing

  Resolution at least equal to   Underline
    screen resolution   Specify character height (e.g.,
  Single or multiple copies   oversize headings)
  Print bold letters

Data Management Packages

Data management packages (often referred to as "database management systems") enable you to manipulate and/or retrieve large volumes of related data. Sample opportunities and features follow.

Data Management Opportunities.   Any fairly large collection of data represents an opportunity for you to utilize a desktop micro. Examples include:

- Contact/target lists
- Customer/client lists
- Mailing lists
- Membership lists
- Personnel lists:
  a. Skills
  b. Applicants
- Referral sources
- Subscriber lists
- Survey results
- Telephone directories
- Vendor lists

Data Management Package Features.   There are numerous data management packages with varying capabilities and features in today's marketplace. Your consideration is the features and capabilities of the package itself. Key items consist of:

- User available memory (total memory less memory required by the package)
- Data compatibility with other packages/applications
- On screen "help" function
- Volume capabilities:
  a. Up to x records
  b. Up to x fields per record
- Editing features:
  a. Add, modify, and delete data and ability to modify initial record definition
  b. Extensive data entry editing (completeness, out of range, alpha, numeric, etc.)

    c. Before and after image reports of masterfile changes

- Search capabilities:
  a. All fields
  b. User-defined, multilevel search arguments
      (1) Up to w search arguments
      (2) All Boolean comparisons (greater than, greater than or equal to, etc.)
      (3) For example, all companies (1) whose sales volume exceeds x dollars, (2) that are located in y city, (3) are privately held, and (4) are in the z industry

- Inquiry and print capability

- Report features:
  a. Graphics
  b. Formatting:
      (1) Left, right, or center justify
      (2) User-defined reports
      (3) Tabs
      (4) Page headings
      (5) Column titles:
         —Automatic and manual
         —Descriptions
         —Character width (10, 12, 16.8 characters per inch)
         —Underlining
         —Bold print

- Page characteristics:
  a. Specific page width (characters) and length (lines)
  b. Specify text width (characters) and length (lines)
  c. Print multiple copies
  d. Specify line spacing (single, double, or triple spacing)
  e. Page numbering
  f. Preview function to display the document exactly as it will be printed

- Data fields:
  a. Specify character widths (10, 12, and 16.8 characters per inch) which are different than column headings

b. Specify fields to be printed

c. Automatic totaling of numeric fields

d. Arithmetic functions

e. Statistical functions (average, total number, range, etc.)

In Part II, we have explored a vast number of application opportunities. At this point we need to turn our attention to determining which of these opportunities make sense for us and how to go about purchasing hardware and software.

PART III

selecting computer hardware and software

At this point you no doubt have some great ideas on how you could capitalize on the opportunities presented in previous chapters. You may also have developed some innovative ideas of your own for utilizing the computer to help you in your business. If you haven't yet thought through all the considerations of implementation, I strongly urge you to do so. The pitfalls are many and the horror stories are all too common. What you need to do next is a function of your present computer usage. In this regard, let's take a look at how Part III is organized.

Chapter 14 deals with defining requirements and vendor considerations. It should be read by everyone.

Chapter 15 is dedicated to:

1. First-time users who need to purchase a larger micro or mini. While much of the material is equally applicable to mainframes, implementation of the techniques should not be attempted without the assistance of experienced EDP personnel.

2. Users who already have a "larger" micro or minicomputer and can use its capabilities to add enhancements or new applications.

Chapter 16 is dedicated to:

1. First-time users who can implement all needs on a desktop computer.

2. Users who already have a "larger" micro or mini; implementation of new applications will be done on a desktop computer.

To assist you further in determining whether Chapter 15 or 16 would be most relevant to you, use the following generalized guidelines regarding expenditures (software and hardware):

- Desktop   Up to $10,000   Chapter 16

- Larger micros and minis   More than $10,000   Chapter 15

These ranges are for guideline purposes only; however, they should facilitate focusing on your specific needs. In addition to purchasing software and hardware, you should consider other computerization alternatives such as time sharing and service centers. The material in Chapter 14 can be used for this purpose.

14 steps to take before selecting a vendor

DEFINING COMPUTER REQUIREMENTS

A recent survey disclosed an alarming percentage of dissatisfied computer users. An analysis of the survey results indicated that many of the problems encountered could have been avoided. Information needs often were defined in vague terms or, in some cases, were not defined at all. All too frequently, the users themselves simply had not committed enough time and resources during the planning process. There are five steps that you should take prior to deciding to computerize:

1. Define your goals.
2. Document your present systems and volumes.
3. Identify and document your information requirements.
4. Identify and document systems for automation.
5. Identify and evaluate processing alternatives.

Define Your Goals

The first step you should take is to define your firm's goals. While a documented statement of where you want to go will not ensure that you get there, it will help you to focus on where you want to be and avoid wandering aimlessly. This process will also provide you with an opportunity to challenge your reasons for wanting to computerize. What role do you envision that the computer will play in your business? How will the computer help you in both the short and long term?

A second benefit to be derived from this process is proper sizing of computer resources. For example, if rapid expansion is one of your objectives in reaching increased market share, that clearly needs to be considered for purposes of hardware selection (main memory, disk storage, input devices, etc.). On the other hand, if your plan is to grow slowly, stating that will help you to avoid overbuying computer resources. One of my good friends is a CPA who has his own small practice. His practice has been growing fairly rapidly and he has decided to expand it even more rapidly. He recognizes that the computer may be a useful tool to help him expand. Accordingly, he has been interviewing vendors to see what they have to offer. So far he has seen four vendors and considered the following alternatives:

- In-house mini.
- In-house micro.
- Service center with on-line data entry and two day delivery of output.
- Time sharing with on-line processing (reports printed in the office).

He asked my advice as to which of these alternatives made the most sense for him considering that (1) he plans to open two more offices in the next year or so and (2) his practice may double each year for the next two years! Being the good friend that I am, I suggested that he consider a different approach. Instead of looking at what the vendors had to offer, he would be better served by taking some time to commit his expansion plans to writing. I asked him to write down on paper where he is now and where he wants to go. How many clients does he have? How many tax returns and financial statements does he prepare? How many man-hours are required to achieve the present level of revenues? Then I asked him to forecast, by year, what his volumes would look like next year, the year after that and so on for five years. How many employees would this require? What revenue volume does he want to achieve? How much clerical support would this require? Unfortunately, he and many other entrepreneurs don't take the time to think these things through! If you can relate to this, unless you are prepared to take the time to plan where you are going, you may be headed for a computer disaster. You will either have to spend up to two or more times as much as you should to ensure adequate capacity, or you may have to start all over again within a relatively short period of time (a time-consuming and costly process). The bottom line of all of this is clear. Devote sufficient time now to avoid disasters or be prepared to pay a much larger price later.

Document Your Present Systems and Volumes

The second step you should take is to define your present systems. Admittedly, it is tempting at this point to channel your energy toward thinking about the new systems. Don't! At least, not yet. Your present systems are the fundamental building blocks for the design of those new systems. Take the time to document them. What you need to do, for each application is:

A. Gather sample input (source) documents.

B. Gather sample reports and generated documents.

C. Prepare a flow chart from origination of source documents through posting of ledgers and report preparation.

D. List the following on a work sheet:

    1. Input:

        a. Names of input fields

        b. Field length

        c. Present transaction volumes (monthly average and peak month)

        d. Estimated transactions volumes in three years (monthly average and peak month)

    2. Output:

        a. Report, ledger, or document title

        b. Names of output fields

        c. Present frequency of preparation

        d. Present volumes (document counts, number of pages, etc.)

        e. Estimated volumes in three years (document counts and the like)

    3. For each task (prepare a source document or report, calculate invoice extensions and footings, etc.), calculate the amount of time devoted to the task each month and the total for all tasks.

Notice the inclusion of estimated volumes in three years. The purpose of including these estimated volumes is to:

- Minimize the possibility that you outgrow computer resources too rapidly.
- Provide for the possibility of phasing in additional resources over time.

The estimated volumes should tie in directly to the goals you defined in the preceding step. As we will shortly see, all the preceding documentation will help you to analyze where bottlenecks are occurring or may occur and determine which tasks can be computerized (and determine the related cost savings). It will also provide the basis for calculating the extent of computer resources required. A sample work sheet for a billing application of a public accounting firm might look like that in Table 14.1 (if you are in private industry, envision the source document to be a shipper).

Identify and Document Your Information Requirements

Having documented your present systems, you are ready to identify and document your information requirements. Devote a significant amount of time and energy to this step. The potential rewards are well worth the effort. The approach I would suggest you use is as follows. For each of the applications you documented in the previous step:

1. Review the relevant application opportunities presented in previous sections. They will provide useful ideas.

2. Review the goals you defined earlier in this chapter. What information do you need to help reach those goals? What information would help you to manage your business better? What historical information do you need to prepare better forecasts? Budgets? The goals you defined should "drive" your information systems, not vice versa.

3. Review the input items you documented in the previous step. What additional information about these data items would be useful to you? In our billing example, one of the input items was service code. It might be useful to you to have a report of billings, by client, within service code. Add to that the related standard time (hours times rate) and expenses and you have a realization report by service code. Focus on each of the input items to see what additional information would be useful to you.

4. Identify your information requirements. Use an outline format to do this. For each category of information you identify, prepare an outline of the data that you need. This process will help to assure that all your requirements are identified; more importantly, it will help you to focus on substance, rather than form! This is the area where you need to express your creativity. A sample outline follows:

TABLE 14.1
Billing Work Sheet

Input: XX timesheets per month averaging XX line items per month; estimated average in three years: XX line items per month.
XX timesheets for peak month with XX line items for peak month; estimated peak in three years: XX line items per month.

FIELD NAME	FIELD LENGTH
Timesheet period	XX
Employee name	XX
Employee staff classification	X
Employee billing rate	XX
Client name	XX
Service code	X
Number of hours for this client	XX
Out-of-pocket expenses for this client	XX
Total record length	XXX
Total monthly characters (record length times line items):	
Present:	
Average	XXXX
Peak	XXXX
Three years:	
Average	XXXX
Peak	XXXX

Output: Unbilled work in process ledger, XX clients in total; average active clients, XXX; peak active clients, XXX.

FIELD NAME	FIELD LENGTH
Client name	XX
Service code	X
Employee name	XX
Employee hours	XX
Timesheet period	XX
Employee billing rate	XX
Extended dollars	XX
Out-of-pocket expenses	XX
Employee subtotal	XX
Service code subtotal	XX
Client subtotal	XX
Grand total	XX

(Continued on following page)

TABLE 14.1 (Continued)

Output: Invoice, XX invoices per month (peak, XXX invoices)

FIELD NAME	FIELD LENGTH
Invoice number	XX
Client name	XX
Client address	XX
Attention of	XX
Service description	XX
Service billing	XX
Out-of-pocket expenses	XX
Invoice total	XX

Output: Billing journal, XX line items per month (peak, XX line items)

FIELD NAME	FIELD LENGTH
Date	XX
Client name	XX
Invoice number	XX
Fees	XX
Out-of-pocket expenses	XX
Invoice total	XX
Write-off	XX
Credit to work in process	XX
Total fees	XX
Total out-of-pocket expenses	XX
Total write-offs	XX
Total credit to work in process	XX
Total billings	XX

CLERICAL TIME TO PROCESS EACH MONTH

TASK	HOURS
Time accounting: post hours from timesheets to work in process, calculate extensions and footings, and prepare unbilled work in process summary by client	XX
Billing:	
Type bills and journalize	XX
Relieve work in process ledger	XX
Accounts receivable: post billings	XX
	XXX

Outline of Information Requirements—Revenue System

1. Work in process ledger
   a. Details by client
   b. Aging report
   c. Control report (reconciliation of changes)
2. Invoices
3. Billing journal
4. Billing realization report
   a. Service code order
   b. Alphabetical order by client
5. Chargeable hours by month by client
6. Chargeable time analysis by employee
7. Revenue forecast
8. Budget comparison

5. Document your information requirements. Prepare a report layout ("mock-up") of each report or document that your information system requires. Include the basic accounting output as well (invoices, journals, etc.). This step is important for a couple of reasons:

   a. Report layouts will help to assure that all data items have been considered and none omitted (try adding some after you have computerized; it may be cost prohibitive or impossible).

   b. Report layouts are useful for communicating what is intended to others (vendors, associates, etc.).

It may be tempting to consider paper size and characters per inch limitations at this point. The disadvantage of doing this is that you devote too much time to mechanics at this point. For now, assume that you have 132 character positions, including spaces and margins. The important thing is to get a working pictorial display of your information requirements. We'll examine these other considerations later. In addition to the data themselves, on each report indicate the frequency of preparation, report period, and number of pages. A sample report follows on the next page.

Identify and Document Systems for Automation

By now you should be on solid ground to identify the systems that should be automated. Your present system is documented and you understand its limitations and volumes. Your goals are defined so you know where you want to be. Your information requirements are documented and will help you to achieve your goals. Now, which systems should you automate? What criteria should you use for making that decision? Let's begin by looking at a shopping list of what I'll refer to as "good reasons" and "poor reasons."

BILLING REALIZATION REPORT—CLIENT SEQUENCE

Frequency: monthly
Current month
Year to date

Number of lines: peak month
Present XX Three years XX
Present XX Three years XX

Client	Standard					Billed				
	Hours (1)	Rate (2)	$ (3)	Exp (4)	Total (5)	Total (6)	Exp (7)	Fees (8)	Rate (9)	% (10)
									(8/2)	(6/5)
A	XX	XX.XX	XXXX	XX	XXXX	XXXX	XX	XXXX	XX.XX	XX
B	XX	XX.XX	XXXX	XX	XXXX	XXXX	XX	XXXX	XX.XX	XX
Totals	XXX	XX.XX	XXXXX	XXX	XXXXX	XXXXX	XXX	XXXX	XX.XX	XX

Good Reasons

- Reduce clerical time
- Eliminate clerical errors
- Eliminate clerical backlog
- Avoid adding clerical personnel
- Reduce paper flow and time delays

- Expedite cash flow
- Increase productivity
- Improve customer service
- Provide new or better management information
- Obtain a competitive edge

Poor Reasons

- Popular thing to do
- Competitors have computers
- Salesmen assure results
- Expect radical reduction of clerical staff
- Expect immediate cost savings

Although dramatic reduction in clerical staff and immediate cost savings have occurred, these situations are few and far between. Unfortunately, I have also seen instances of computerization simply because managers thought it was the thing to do. Finally, as you well know, salesmen don't refer you to better products and don't earn commissions without sales. Discount what they promise and you won't go wrong!

Identifying systems for automation is a fivefold process:

1. Prepare a summary schedule of your information systems.
2. Select systems for automation.
3. Specify system relationships and summarize key features.
4. Document file requirements.
5. Summarize volume requirements.

Prepare a Summary Schedule of Your Information Systems. The purpose of this schedule (which is illustrated later) is to assure that you consider all systems and acknowledge intangible benefits (new or better information).

Select Systems for Automation. During the process of documenting your present systems, you calculated the hours and related dollars associated with clerical processing. Bring each of the dollar amounts

PRELIMINARY AUTOMATION DECISION

System	Decision	Savings	Reasons for decision
Revenue:			
Time accounting	Automate	$ XXX	Eliminate time to identify and correct out-of-balance conditions
Billing	Automate	XXX	Eliminate clerical time to prepare
Accounts receivable	Automate	XXX	Eliminate all clerical time
Management reports	Automate	NA	Provide new information to improve chargeable time, increase engagement profitability, and measure progress
Payroll	Manual	NA	Volume doesn't warrant
Accounts payable	Automate	0	Clerical time approximately the same
Fixed assets	Manual	NA	Volume doesn't warrant
General ledger	Automate	XX	Eliminate clerical time to prepare financial statements
Word processing	Automate	XX	Reduce clerical time to correct errors (retyping) and type standard letters
Client bookkeeping	Automate	XXX	Eliminate service center fees and clerical time to prepare financial statements
Infome tax:			
Planning	Automate	XXX	Eliminate professional time to prepare and revise projections
Return preparation	Automate	XXX	Eliminate clerical errors and time to prepare pro formas; improve quality
Target companies	Automate	NA	Identify new opportunities and monitor progress
Total monthly savings		$XXXX	
Present value over three years		$XXXX	Present value calculated using an interest rate of XX%
Present value over five years		$XXXX	

forward to the summary schedule. Select the systems that have potential for automation based on cost considerations. For those you do not intend to automate, delete the clerical dollar amounts and also document your reasons. Total the cost savings column. Calculate the present value over three and five years. If it is your intention to cost justify automation, your expenditure for computer resources should fall within the cost savings range of three to five years. A word of caution at this point: you can't eliminate fractions of people (unless you can substitute part-time for full-time personnel). Make sure the cost savings figures make sense in this regard.

In addition to cost justification, there may be another valid reason for automating—new or better information. New or better information is an intangible benefit; while the cost of new or better information can be precisely determined, sometimes the benefits cannot. Examples of intangible benefits include:

- Increasing market share
- Identifying costs of unprofitable products or services with a view toward:
  a. Reducing costs
  b. Increasing prices
- Improving productivity
- Better utilization of resources

Before proceeding to the next step, challenge the potential utilization of a computer to assist you in producing and utilizing new and better information. At this point, you can add any additional systems that have significant intangible benefits.

Your summary schedule for the preliminary automation decision might look like the chart on the opposite page.

Specify System Relationships and Summarize Key Features. You have made a preliminary decision as to which systems to automate. The next step is to document (1) how the automated systems will interact and (2) the key features of each system. The documentation prepared at this step will play a key role in communicating requirements to vendors. Sample documentation for the preceding revenue system follows:

Time Accounting. Timesheets and cash disbursements (for out-of-pocket expenses) are the primary source for updating work in process. Standard hourly rates will be maintained by the system. The system will calculate standard time charges and update work in process for both standard time charges and out-of-pocket expenses. Work in process will be automatically relieved by billings.

Key features are the following capabilities:

- Handle user-defined service codes.
- Handle narrative comments re time charges.
- Handle advance billings (retainers, monthly billing, etc.).
- Produce file maintenance reports, including hash totals.
- Generate general ledger entries.
- Produce work-in-process listing by client to facilitate the billing process.
- Handle adjustments.

Billing.   Completed (manually notated) work-in-process listings by client are the primary source for relieving work in process, generating invoices and the monthly billing journal, and updating accounts receivable. Key features are:

- Partially relieve hours or expenses.
- Apply advance billings to specific items in work in process.
- Generate general ledger entries.
- Produce management reports.
- Relieve work in process for manual billings.
- Forecast billings, by client and service code, based on historical information using "what-if" techniques.

Accounts Receivable.   Manual and computer-generated billings together with cash receipts are the primary source for updating accounts receivable. Key features are the following capabilities:

- Handle adjustments (billings, write-offs, etc.).
- Apply cash to specific invoices.
- On-line inquiry.
- Age by invoice.
- Open item technique versus balance forward.
- Produce management reports.

While some of the preceding material may seem obvious to us (ability to do this and that), don't fall into the trap of assuming that all vendors assume likewise. Some vendors take a "stand-alone" approach to subsystems; this means that you have to input the same information more than once. For example, a billing subsystem may not automatically relieve inventory (unbilled work in process or manufacturing inventories). In this case, you would have to input the information once to relieve inventory and twice to record revenue and increases in receivables.

For each of your systems, specify the relationships and key features. The information in Part II of this book provides examples of key features for many frequently encountered systems for both public accounting and private industry, respectively. Use the examples as a reference list of things to consider.

Document File Requirements. In a manual environment, we think of source documents, ledgers, journals, and reports (generated documents, financial statements, etc.). Conceptually, these terms have a one-to-one relationship with their data-processing counterparts, as illustrated:

Manual	*EDP*
Source documents	Input
Ledgers	Masterfiles
Journals	Transaction files
Reports	Output

It is true that, in a very narrow sense, some transaction files may be the input to update a masterfile (e.g., weekly sales transactions updating accounts receivable). However, in terms of what the system is designed to do (generate invoices, maintain account balances, etc.), the relationships shown are more meaningful. Source documents represent input. Ledgers (containing balances at a point in time together with semipermanent types of information such as name and address or billing rate) are represented by masterfiles. Journals contain a chronological history of transactions. Their counterparts are transaction files. Finally, generated documents and other reports are represented by output.

In a manual environment, if we want additional information such as historical statistics, we simply abstract the relevant information. If we are going to let the computer do that for us, all the relevant information must be stored and available. Thus, the need to plan carefully for file requirements. In this regard, we need to focus both on ensuring that all required data elements are considered and that the storage capacity of the files themselves is large enough to handle the volumes.

Using the documentation developed for your present systems and your additional information requirements, for each system, do the following:

1. Masterfiles

   - **Input identification:** Determine what information must be maintained to enable the computer to relate the input transaction to its masterfile counterpart (customer name and number, part number, account number, etc.).

- **Calculations:** Determine what information must be maintained to enable the computer to:

    a. Calculate extensions (unit price, quantities, billing rates, credit limits, etc.).

    b. Calculate new balances (e.g., prior quantities and or dollar amounts).

- **Output:** Determine what information must be maintained to enable the computer to generate documents (invoices, shippers, etc.) and ledger balances.

2. Transaction files:

- **Management reports:** Determine what information must be maintained to produce the desired reports.

- **Audit trails:** Determine what information must be retained (temporarily or permanently) to produce the appropriate audit trails.

For each system, prepare a schedule of the masterfile and transaction file volumes. Using the preceding time accounting system, the schedule would look like the one in Table 14.2. Note that the fields included in the table do not include extended dollars, subtotals, and grand total. The computer calculates these when reports are produced (unbilled work in process, general ledger entries, etc.). The fields included in the masterfile and transaction file are necessary and sufficient to produce the output reports as defined.

Summarize Volume Requirements. The final step in documenting systems for automation consists of preparing lead schedules of volumes for input, files, and output.

Input. The input section of the work sheets you prepared for your present systems contains the volume information you will summarize. If there are any new data fields needed as a result of defining your information requirements, add the field name and length to your work sheets and recalculate the record length. From each of the work sheets, bring forward the record length and the monthly transaction volumes. Your summary schedule for input would be formatted like the one in Table 14.3.

The input volume summary will enable you to estimate the number of input devices (CRTs) you will need. First, consider how you are organized along functional lines and where you would want CRTs regardless of volumes. In our example, it has been assumed that CRTs will be placed in

TABLE 14.2
Time Accounting Files

Field Description	Field Length	
	Work in Process Masterfile	Transaction File
Client name	XX	XX
Client number	XX	XX
Employee name	XX	XX
Employee number	XX	XX
Timesheet period	XX	XX
Service code	XX	XX
Employee hours	XX	XX
Out-of-pocket expenses	XX	XX
Total record length	XXX	XXX
Masterfile volumes	**Present**	**Three Years**
Total record length	XXX	XXX
Peak active clients	XXX	XXX
Product	XX,XXX	XX,XXX
Peak timesheet line items	XXX	XXX
Product	X,XXX,XXX	X,XXX,XXX
Number of months open items in unbilled work in process	X	X
Maximum file size	XX,XXX,XXX	XX,XXX,XXX
Transaction file volumes	**Present**	**Three Years**
Total record length	XXX	XXX
Average line items per month	XXX	XXX
Average monthly volume	XX,XXX	XX,XXX
Annualize	12	12
Annual file size	XXX,XXX	XXX,XXX

the bookkeeping department, at secretarial stations, and in the professional staff area.

Next you will calculate the number of CRTs you will need in each location, based on the monthly number of input characters (all four columns). For purposes of this calculation, use the data-entry rate shown next. Calculate the number of CRTs needed in each location, using a safety factor of, say, 25%. For example, assuming a present peak workload of 1

TABLE 14.3
Input Volume Summary

| System | Location | Record length | Monthly no. of input characters | | | |
| | | | Present | | Three Years | |
			Average	Peak	Average	Peak
Revenue:						
Time accounting		XXX	XXX,XXX	XXX,XXX	XXX,XXX	XXX,XXX
Billing		XXX	XXX,XXX	XXX,XXX	XXX,XXX	XXX,XXX
Cash receipts		XXX	XXX,XXX	XXX,XXX	XXX,XXX	XXX,XXX
Cash disbursements		XXX	XXX,XXX	XXX,XXX	XXX,XXX	XXX,XXX
Client bookkeeping		X,XXX	XXX,XXX	XXX,XXX	XXX,XXX	XXX,XXX
General ledger		XXX	XXX,XXX	XXX,XXX	XXX,XXX	XXX,XXX
Total accounting	Bookkeeping		XXX,XXX	XXX,XXX	XXX,XXX	XXX,XXX
Word processing	Secretary	NA	Varies			
Income tax:	Staff					
Planning		XXX	XX,XXX	XXX,XXX	XX,XXX	XXX,XXX
Returns		X,XXX	XXX,XXX	XXX,XXX	XXX,XXX	XXX,XXX

million characters per month for accounting, the number of CRTs needed would be:

$$\frac{1 \text{ million per month} + 25\% \text{ safety factor}}{5000 \text{ per hour}^* \times 8 \text{ hours} \times 22 \text{ days}} = 1.42$$

Round the calculation up to the nearest whole number. In this example, two CRTs would be required. Make this calculation for all four columns and for all locations. The results of these calculations are your estimates of the number of CRTs needed presently and in three years.

Files. The individual system file schedules you prepared contain the information you will summarize. Bring forward the information shown in Table 14.4. The totals for your masterfiles are the starting point for determining the amount of on-line disk storage you will need presently and in three years. You will need additional storage for programs, temporary work files, and so on. These amounts will be supplied by the vendor. For purposes of making a preliminary estimate, add an additional 75%. You probably won't be far off. Transaction files are not normally kept on-line

---

*This is an estimate of the number of data-entry characters per hour for purposes of estimating the number of CRTs that may be required. The actual number of characters will vary substantially depending upon skill levels and the nature of the application.

TABLE 14.4
Files Volume Summary

System	File Description	Masterfiles Peak month characters		File Description	Transaction files Annual number of characters	
		Present *(in thousands)*	Three Years *(in thousands)*		Present *(in thousands)*	Three Years *(in thousands)*
Revenue:						
Time accounting	Work in process	XX,XXX	XX,XXX	Timesheets	XXX	XXX
	Billing rate	X	X			
Billing	Accounts			Billings	XXX	XXX
Cash receipts	receiv-able	X,XXX	X,XXX	Receipts	XX	XX
	Client address	XX	XX			
Client bookkeeping	Clients	XX,XXX	XXX,XXX	Client trans.	XXX	X,XXX
Accounts payable	Accounts payable	X,XXX	X,XXX	Purchases	XX	XX
				Distribution	XXX	XXX
				Disbursements	XX	XX
General ledger	Chart of accounts	XX	XX			
	GL balances	X,XXX	X,XXX	GL distribution	XXX	XXX
Word processing	Letters	XXX	XXX			
	Labels	XXX	XXX			
Income tax:						
Planning	Projections	XXX	XXX			
Returns	Returns	XX,XXX	XXX,XXX	Tax input	XXX	XXX
Target companies	Targets	X,XXX	X,XXX			
Totals		XXX,XXX	XXX,XXX		X,XXX	XX,XXX

because (1) they are not needed frequently and (2) they are voluminous and, therefore, expensive to be kept on-line. A more common approach is to use floppy diskettes or tape devices for storing transaction files. When needed, the data can be loaded in and stored in a temporary work file. After the data are manipulated, the desired reports can be printed. The transaction volumes you have calculated will enable vendors to propose solutions for your final determination.

Output. The report layouts you prepared contain the information you

TABLE 14.5
Output Volume Summary

Report title	Freq.	Printer location	Number of lines per period Present	Number of lines per period Three years
Revenue:		Accounting		
Unbilled work in process				
Chargeable time analysis	B		XX	XXX
Chargeable hours by client	A		X,XXX	X,XXX
CLient details	M		XX,XXX	XX,XXX
Aging by client	M		XXX	XXX
Control report	M		XX	XX
Billing				
Invoices	M		X,XXX	X,XXX
Journal	M		XXX	XXX
Realization reports:				
Service code:				
Current month	M		XXX	XXX
Year to date	M		X,XXX	X,XXX
Alpha by client				
Current month	M		XXX	XXX
Year to date	M		XXX	XXX
Revenue forecast	A		XXX	XXX
Budget comparison	M		XX	XX
Accounts receivable				
Client details	M		X,XXX	X,XXX
Aging	M		XXX	XXX
Cash receipts journal	M		XXX	XXX
Control report	M		X	X
Cash balance control	D		X	X
Accounts payable:		Accounting		
Purchase journal	M		XXX	XXX
Distribution journal	M		XXX	XXX
Cash requirements	W		XXX	XXX
Vendor open invoices	M		XXX	XXX
Checks	M		XXX	XXX
General ledger:		Accounting		
Chart of accounts	R		XXX	XXX
GL entries	M		XXX	XXX
Financial statements	M		XXX	XXX
Trial balance	M		XXX	XXX
Word processing	D	Secretary	X,XXX	X,XXX

(Continued on following page)

TABLE 14.5 (Continued)

Report title	Freq.	Printer location	Number of lines per period Present	Three years
Income tax:				
Projections	D	Tax department	XXX	XXX
Tax returns	D	Accounting	X,XXX	X,XXX
Client bookkeeping	M	Accounting	X,XXX	XX,XXX

Frequency legend:
D–daily, W–weekly, B–bimonthly, M–monthly, Q–quarterly, A–annual, R–request

BY PRINTER LOCATION

Frequency	Accounting Present	Three Years	Tax department Present	Three Years	Secretary Present	Three Years	Total Present	Three Years
			(In thousands of lines)					
Daily	X.X	X.X	.X	X.X	X.X	X.X	X.X	XX.X
Weekly	.X	.X						.X
Bimonthly	.X	.X						.X
Monthly	X.X	XX.X					X.X	XX.X
Quarterly								
Annual	X.X	X.X					X.X	X.X
Request	.X	.X					.X	.X
Totals	X.X	XX.X	.X	X.X	X.X	X.X	X.X	XX.X

will summarize. Bring forward the report title, frequency of preparation, and number of lines for each report as shown in Table 14.5.

In this example, notice that a preliminary decision was made regarding the placement of printers. Output must be available quickly enough to enable the user to continue the normal work flow without unreasonable delay. In the example, suppose there was only one printer and it was currently in use for volume printing of income tax returns. Suppose further that a tax projection was just input. While the tax professional could wait until the printer becomes available, that would be disruptive and inefficient. Furthermore, a client might be waiting for the results, making the delay an intolerable situation. In the example, a low-speed, inexpensive dot matrix printer for tax projections might be a cost-effective solution. The printer near the secretary's desk might be a low-speed correspondence-quality printer. Finally, the volume in the accounting department would probably require a high-speed line printer to accommodate that workload.

The same consideration exists in private industry. To minimize delays and expedite cash flow, printers might be placed in the warehouse and billing departments to expedite printing of picking tickets, shipping documents, and customer invoices.

After you have identified the locations for printers, summarize the volumes by frequency. These volumes will be used as a guide to select printers with print speeds and qualities to accommodate your workload. You can revise these preliminary requirements later based on cost considerations.

Identify and Evaluate
Processing Alternatives

Identify Processing Alternatives. Hardware costs have been decreasing and will continue to decrease in the future. These cost reductions make a single multipurpose in-house computer more attractive. However, you shouldn't casually dismiss other alternatives without further consideration. Alternatives available to you include:

- Service centers
- Time sharing
- Desktop computers to supplement computing needs

The historical service center approach has centered around using messengers to pickup hard-copy input documents. Input was keyed and processed at the service center and hard-copy output was sent by messenger to the customer. Contrast this with the time-sharing approach in which the input and output devices are located at the customer's site. Data are keyed in, transmitted over telephone lines to the central site, processed, and the results of processing returned for printing at the customer's site.

Over recent years, the distinction between the two has blurred. Many service centers today have input devices installed at the customer's site. Some also offer in-house printing capability. The primary difference between the two has narrowed to the operating methodology within the computer installation itself. Time-sharing vendors allow users to determine when they want to process. From the user's standpoint, it looks as if the computer is dedicated to his or her task. All programs and data files are on-line, and the results of processing can quickly be returned. The service center tends to be schedule oriented. Users submit data and receive results according to a specified time schedule (batch-oriented processing).

The principal advantages of using service centers or time-sharing vendors are:

1. The responsibility for managing computer resources, including performing maintenance, lies with the vendor.

2. The user's initial investment in computerization is minimized.

The principal disadvantages of using service centers or time-sharing vendors are:

1. Potentially higher average cost per transaction from the very beginning; incremental cost per transaction increases as volumes increase.

2. Less flexibility in accommodating modifications to programs.

3. Dependence on vendor's financial stability after conversion.

4. As to service centers, time delays in receiving processing results.

5. Dependence on a single vendor for continued support and enhancements.

Another alternative is available to you as well—the use of desktop computers to supplement your other computing needs. Review the material in Chapter 2 and in the chapters on application opportunities. Don't dismiss this alternative too quickly.

Evaluate Processing Alternatives. If the intangible disadvantages (items 2 to 5) of using service centers or time-sharing vendors are overwhelming from a methodology of operating standpoint, dismiss them as alternatives and focus your attention on in-house computers. If not, include them for further consideration.

Up to now, you have gathered information as to potential cost savings and intangible benefits. However, you do not have any hard information regarding how much automation is going to cost you. You already have devoted a significant amount of time and effort in defining and documenting your information requirements. However, there is still much to do (as we shall shortly see), and you still don't have any assurance that the ultimate cost/benefit analysis will result in a decision to computerize. Accordingly, at this point you should consider performing a preliminary feasibility study as follows:

1. Perform research

2. Calculate present value range for the investment

3. Perform cost/benefit analysis

Perform Research. Services such as Data Pro publish extensive information regarding vendor hardware and software prices. Use the facilities of a public library or local college or university to gather cost information based on your volume requirements. If you feel uncomfortable doing this, consider using an outside consultant to help you with this phase. In addition, talk to other accountants who are similarly situated (volumes, type of business, etc.) and who have already computerized.

Calculate Present Value Range for the Investment. Using the results of your research, calculate a cost range for your hardware and software requirements. Reduce that range by the present value of tax benefits over three years (depreciation and investment tax credit).

Perform Cost/Benefit Analysis. Compare the present value of your anticipated cost savings to the present value for the investment. If the cost savings is close to or greater than your calculated investment, proceed on. If not, consider the intangible benefits. Are the intangible benefits significant enough to outweight the cost differential? Admittedly, this is a difficult question to answer! Nonetheless, it must be dealt with. Reconsider your goals. Review the material under "Good Reasons and Poor Reasons." If you were contemplating a larger micro or minicomputer, consider whether a desktop computer might be a partial solution. Make your decision. If you decide not to proceed, document your reasons. Put away your work papers for six to twelve months. Then review your situation again. Vendor prices will drop and your cost savings may increase. The combination may make your project feasible at that time.

SELECTING A VENDOR

So you have decided to proceed. Great! Your next step is dealing with vendors. Before you do that, there are a few pitfalls that you should understand, irrespective of your potential dollar expenditure. They are:

- Letting salesmen sell.
- Selecting a vendor based solely on price.
- Considering too few vendors.
- Selecting inexperienced vendors.

Letting Salesmen Sell

A major benefit of documenting your information requirements is to put you in control of the selection process. Don't be interested in what salesmen tell you their product will do. This often leads to distracting technical discussion or gimmicks and features. What you want to know is whether their product will meet your requirements.

Selecting a Vendor Solely on Price

While price is, of course, an important element, it is but one of several criteria that are important. Others include experience, reputation, geographic location, training capability, and financial stability. We'll explore these further later.

Considering Too Few Vendors

Many dissatisfied users have fallen victim to this pitfall. Frequently, only one or two vendors were considered. That's not enough to get overall good results. Why not? You stand a very good chance of missing out on price breaks that are sometimes passed down by manufacturers. The fewer vendors you select for consideration, the fewer are your opportunities to take advantage of these price breaks. Further, you may select a vendor whose prices are not competitive. In addition, if you limit your evaluation to one or two vendors, you will increase the chances of selecting a vendor that is not reputable. Suggestions for the number of vendors to consider will be given in the chapters that follow.

Selecting Inexperienced Vendors

Inexperienced vendors are a pitfall for two reasons. First, they may not have the expertise to deliver the goods and services you will need. Do you want to risk being stuck with a partially completed, partially implemented system? Second, you will be making a multiyear commitment to computerization. It is difficult enough for well-established vendors to compete successfully in the marketplace. Continued innovation is required, which, in turn, requires financial resources and commitment toward research and development. Select an inexperienced vendor and that vendor may not be around in six months, let alone over the useful life of your systems.

Forearmed with knowledge of the pitfalls, you are ready to deal with vendors. Detailed suggestions and strategies are provided in Chapters 15 and 16. If you will be adding new software to existing hardware, utilizing service centers or time-sharing vendors, or purchasing a larger micro or minicomputer, read Chapter 15. If you will be purchasing a desktop micro, read Chapter 16.

15 purchasing larger micros and minis

Chapter 14 provided a framework for defining and documenting your information systems requirements. In this chapter, we will explore the purchasing process itself. Our main topics consist of:

- Communicating requirements to vendors.
- Selecting vendors to submit proposals.
- Evaluating vendor proposals.
- Evaluating final candidates.
- Negotiating the vendor contract.

After discussing the details of each topic, we will conclude this chapter with a comprehensive case study.

COMMUNICATING REQUIREMENTS TO VENDORS

The systems requirements documentation you prepared put you in the driver's seat. Your objective is to stay there. Your approach to dealing with vendors should be businesslike and professional. The primary vehicle for your communications is the time-tested and proven technique, the Request for Proposal (RFP). Undoubtedly you are familiar with the concept—solicit bids, evaluate them, and, finally, select the best.

Why is the RFP so important and why does it minimize your risk of failure? Let's explore the RFP components and see why each detail is important.

Understanding the RFP Components

The RFP components and their purpose consist of the following:

Major Component	Purpose
General information	Set the stage and define your rules
Proposal guidelines	Provide for uniform vendor responses
System requirements	Communicate your requirements
Vendor questionnaire	Obtain vendor proposed solutions for evaluation

Collectively, these RFP components provide for effective two-way communication. Your needs are described completely and accurately. The framework you provide for uniform vendor responses helps assure that (1) you obtain complete information about their background and capabilities and (2) they respond completely as to the details of their proposed solution. During the overall evaluation process, you will determine whether they have responded accurately. In the meantime, you will need to understand the details of the RFP.

Understanding the RFP Details

The case study at the end of this chapter illustrates each of the following RFP details. Refer to it as needed for clarification.

Section	Item	Description
I.	GENERAL INFORMATION	
	1. Intent of RFP	Communicate your requirements
	2. Vendor inquiries	Tell the vendor whom to contact
	3. RFP addenda	Reserve the right, if necessary, to modify the RFP
	4. Important dates	Facilitate vendor planning to be responsive to your timetable

5.	Acceptance of vendor proposals	Reserve the right to reject proposals and inform vendors that they must respond completely
6.	Vendor selection	Inform vendors that factors other than price are important to you
7.	Guidelines for evaluation	Inform vendors of evaluation criteria
8.	Notification	Extend professional courtesy of providing feedback to unsuccessful candidates
9.	Financial statements	Inform vendors that you are interested in their financial position
10.	Proposal costs	Inform vendors that proposal effort is not billable
11.	Confidentiality	Have vendor state whether any proposal material is confidential
12.	Contractual obligations	Make vendor aware that proposal will be integrated into final contract
13.	Contract negotiations	Reserve right to negotiate final contract
14.	Intent to bid	Provide vehicle to determine whether additional candidates will be needed and thereby avoid potential delays
15.	Withdrawal notification	Request professional courtesy of notification
16.	Demonstrations and benchmarks	Inform vendors that proposals must be for "working systems"
17.	Terminology	Define any terms unique to your business

II. PROPOSAL GUIDELINES

1.	Proposal format	Communicate form and content of required vendor response
2.	Copies	Inform vendor to whom copies should be sent and how many

3.	Multiple proposals	Provide for the possibility that vendors may have more than one solution (the second solution may be best for you but if vendors are permitted to submit only one proposed solution, you'll never see the second solution)
4.	Exceptions to RFP	Periodically, vendors have a viable cost-effective solution that has not been contemplated; permit them to offer it and explain why
5.	Supporting materials	Instruct vendors as to how to cross reference to facilitate your review
6.	Vendor terminology	Discourage vendor jargon and instruct vendors to utilize your terminology
7.	Documentation	Inform the vendor to include the cost of needed documentation in the bid
8.	Vendor contracts	Require vendor to include all applicable contracts

III. SYSTEM REQUIREMENTS

1.	Present systems	List present systems and specify computerization plans
2.	Input requirements	Attach your input volume summary schedule
3.	File requirements	Attach your file volume summary schedule and supporting detail schedules
4.	Output requirements	Attach your output volume summary schedule and report layouts

IV. VENDOR GENERAL QUESTIONNAIRE

1.	Background	Obtain general information regarding vendor background, experience, and skills

2. User groups	A proven useful source for maximizing use of features, communicating solutions to software problems. Determine whether vendor has a user group
3. Training	A critical element of successful implementation; training capabilities and costs should be a major consideration
4. Bid summary	Provide the vendors with a framework for summarizing costs
5. Implementation	Require vendor to respond to your timetable
V. VENDOR HARDWARE AND SYSTEM SOFTWARE QUESTIONNAIRE	Summarize costs, define hardware and service capabilities, warranty period, and uncover hidden charges
VI. VENDOR APPLICATIONS QUESTIONNAIRE	
1. Narrative overview	Provide vendor with overview
2. Reports	Determine whether vendor can provide
3. Key features	Determine whether vendor can provide

As you can see, there is much more to purchasing computer systems than merely asking vendors for price quotes. The detailed RFP will help you to avoid many pitfalls and get the necessary information to evaluate vendor proposals.

If you already have a computer and want to add new applications, list each of your present hardware components (manufacturer, model number, quantity, and capacity) in Section III.2. Revise your transmittal letter to indicate that you presently have a computer system.

SELECTING VENDORS
TO SUBMIT PROPOSALS

Now that you have prepared a RFP tailored to your needs, your next step is to select vendors to submit proposals. Considerations at this point consist of:

- Understanding vendor sources.
- Selecting an appropriate number of vendors for proposal solicitation
- Identifying vendor candidates.

Understanding Vendor Sources

There are essentially three categories of vendor sources:

- Hardware manufacturers, including their distributors.
- Software houses, including their distributors, which develop and market application software.
- Turnkey vendors and OEM (original equipment manufacturers) suppliers, which provide total systems (hardware and software).

These three categories in turn suggest three strategies:

- Select hardware vendors and locate software houses that develop software to run on the hardware vendors' machines.
- Select software houses and locate the hardware on which the software will run.
- Select turnkey vendors/OEM suppliers who can provide total solutions.

The first strategy emphasizes hardware and should be avoided by small- and medium-sized businesses. The second strategy requires that you locate software houses that can supply all the applications you need and which will all run on the same hardware. Unless you are prepared to hire a consultant or have significant in-house EDP expertise, this strategy should also be avoided (if you already have a computer and simply want to add applications, this strategy might be viable for you). The strategy of dealing with one vendor who can provide a total solution (hardware and software) is generally the best approach for a small- or medium-sized business.

Selecting an Appropriate Number
of Vendors for Proposal Solicitation

While your chances of locating the best solution increase with the number of proposals you receive, recognize that you will have to respond to vendor questions and devote the time to evaluate each proposal (not to mention the costs of reproducing and mailing the RFP itself). Consider the following approach. Select 10 to 12 vendors with the idea in mind that 4 to 5 of them will be eliminated fairly quickly (cost prohibitive, no experience, etc.). Perform preliminary evaluations of the remaining proposals and narrow the list to approximately three finalists for detailed evaluations.

Sources for Identifying Vendor Candidates

You have numerous sources for identifying vendor candidates. Among them include:

- Competitors of comparable size who are satisfied users.
- Well-known hardware manufacturers who can provide referrals to turnkey vendors and the like.
- Trade magazines and newspapers.
- Trade shows.
- Technical publications such as Data Pro.

When selecting vendor candidates, consider developing a list that has a representative balance from the preceding categories. Once you have developed your list, it is a good idea to contact each candidate by telephone before sending the RFP. In this fashion, you can determine whether they are interested in proposing and add additional candidates to your list as needed.

EVALUATING VENDOR PROPOSALS

The absence of objectivity is a major pitfall in selecting a vendor. As we have seen, numerous factors other than cost are important to you. How then can you measure the responses to the hundreds of detail items in your RFP? How can you compare one vendor's response to another vendor's response? The answer is to use a rating mechanism. By assigning relative values to items you consider important, you can rank each vendor's response. The rest is a mathematical exercise, and the result is an objective total ranking for each vendor. The overall approach is as follows:

- Determine a cost limit.
- Determine the relative importance of general characteristics to applications suitability (defined later).
- Determine overall rating approach:

a. Point values

b. Normalizing mechanisms

- Evaluate general characteristics:

  a. Identify categories

  b. Rank vendors by category

  c. Perform preliminary evaluation

- Evaluate application suitability:

  a. Determine relative importance

  b. Rank vendors by application

  c. Perform preliminary evaluation

- Summarize preliminary evaluations:

  a. Scale results

  b. Rank vendors

  c. Select finalists

Using this outline, let's explore the details.

Determine Cost Limit

No one would argue that cost is not a major consideration in computerization. However, there is a way that you can keep costs in mind and, at the same time, permit an orderly and objective evaluation of all important elements. How? Determine a cost limit. The cost limit is the point at which you would not consider the vendor's proposal no matter what else the vendor has to offer. Upon receipt of a proposal that exceeds this limit, you simply set it aside. The remaining proposals can then be objectively evaluated.

Determine Relative Importance of General Characteristics to Applications Suitability

General characteristics relate to the vendor's background, the general capabilities of the hardware and system software, and the vendor's overall approach to application software. Application suitability, on the other hand, relates directly to the ability to process as specified in the RFP and produce the requested output. As a rule of thumb, begin by considering each of these two areas to be of equal importance. If you will be dealing with sophisticated processing (fast response systems with remote terminals and the like), add some weight to the general characteristics. If your information needs can be met only with custom programming and are unique, add some weight to application suitability.

Determine Overall Rating Approach

You can make a rating mechanism as simple or complicated as you desire. Examples follow:

1. **Point value rating mechanisms:** a simple approach that results in point values being assigned to each category. The available points are distributed among the various rating categories.

| | | Awarded | | |
| | | Vendor | Vendor | Vendor |
Category	Maximum	A	B	C
A	10	8	9	2
B	15	11	11	13
C	10	8	8	10
Total	35	27	28	25

2. **Normalizing rating mechanisms:** a more complex approach that tends to lessen the difference between vendor rankings by category and reduce the affect of poor scores in a relatively few categories.

Category A	Maximum	Vendor A	Vendor B	Vendor C
Vendor points	10	8	9	2
Vendor grades	*	2	3	1

*Formula = no. of vendors × (vendor points/maximum points); results are then ranked and grades are assigned.

As the illustration shows, vendor C is still ranked third in category A; however, the normalizing technique lessens the gap. In fact, if you work through the math, you'll find that vendor C ties with vendor B for first place for all three categories overall. Contrast this with the previous method in which vendor C comes in third. In the materials that follow, a point value rating mechanism will be used to illustrate concepts. In this regard, we will assume a maximum point score of 220 points, comprised of 100 points for general characteristics and 120 points for applications suitability.

Evaluating General Characteristics

As we noted earlier, general characteristics relate to the vendor's background, the capabilities of the proposed hardware and system software, and the vendor's overall approach to application software. That description is a little too vague for our purposes. We need to identify the specific categories that will be evaluated. For purposes of illustration, we will use the following categories:

Category	Maximum Points	Description
Hardware and system software capabilities	20	This characteristic concerns the overall operating characteristics and processing performance of the proposed hardware configuration and software design. Consideration is given to such items as the processing speed, hardware reliability, available utilities, the variety and capabilities of the languages supported, and any special features offered beyond the basic requirements.
Application software approach	20	This characteristic relates to the overall approach to application programming. Consideration is given to the sufficiency of controls, modularity of design, and documentation.
Vendor experience and reputation	15	This characteristic relates to the stability and reputation of the vendor. Factors considered include financial ratings, years of demonstrated success, organization size, and references obtained from users.
Total cost	15	This characteristic relates to the total cost of the system in relation to proposed benefits.
Maintenance support	10	This characteristic relates to the vendor's support of the hardware and software after installation.

(Continued on following page)

(Continued)

Category	Maximum Points	Description
Ease of operation	10	This characteristic includes both hardware and software. Consideration is given to the level of knowledge required to start the system up and load and execute the applications.
Expandability	10	This characteristic relates to hardware expansion capabilities to accommodate increased processing requirements.
Training	10	This characteristic relates to the vendor's approach to implementation and the level and quality of training provided.
Backup capabilities	5	This characteristic relates to the availability and ease of use of utilities to back up system, program, and data files.
Implementation schedule	5	This characteristic relates to the timeliness and reasonableness of the vendor's proposed implementation schedule.
Environmental requirements	5	This characteristic relates to the physical and environmental requirements of the proposed hardware configuration.

The points assigned to each category are a function of the individual category's overall importance. For example, a rapidly growing business might be dependent upon expandability to accommodate planned growth. In this case, expandability would be given a higher maximum point value.

After identifying the specific categories, you will need to develop quantitative and/or qualitative criteria. These criteria then form the basis for awarding points to each vendor. Examples follow:

Category	Poor	Rating Average	Outstanding
Vendor experience and reputation	1 year experience 5 employees Weak financial position	5 years experience 20 employees Average financial position	15 years experience 50+ employees Good financial position
Total cost	$100,000	$90,000	$80,000

Category	Poor	Rating Average	Outstanding
Maintenance support	No bug correction Response time: subject to availability	Bugs corrected for 90 days Response time: within 2 days	Bugs corrected forever Response time: within 2 hours
Ease of operation	Full-time operator required Screen formats poorly designed	Limited operator intervention Simple screen formats	Minimum operator intervention Simple screens, help, and menu screens

At this point we have identified the categories and developed the criteria for awarding points to vendors. You are ready to rank the vendors within each category and perform the preliminary evaluation of general characteristics. A sample of the completed evaluation follows.

		Points						
		Vendor						
Category	Maximum	A	B	C	D	E	F	G
Hardware and system software	20	15	13	12	9	18	15	14
Application software approach	20	14	14	13	10	17	14	15
Vendor experience and reputation	15	13	12	12	9	13	11	12
Total cost	15	12	11	12	13	11	10	12
Maintenance support	10	8	7	8	7	8	9	9
Ease of operation	10	8	9	9	8	8	9	8
Expandability	10	9	8	9	6	9	8	9
Training	10	8	7	9	7	9	8	9

(Continued on following page)

| | | Points | | | | | | |
| | | Vendor | | | | | | |
Application	Maximum	A	B	C	D	E	F	G
Backup capabilities	5	4	4	3	4	4	4	4
Implementation schedule	5	3	4	4	5	4	4	4
Environmental requirements	5	4	5	4	4	4	4	3
	125	98	94	95	82	105	96	99

Evaluating Application Suitability

The methodology for evaluating application suitability is identical to that for evaluating general characteristics. List each application to be computerized and determine its relative importance. In this regard, you might assign 10 points to the most important application and 5 points to the least important application. A prioritized list might look like the following sample:

Application	Maximum points
Income tax planning and return preparation	10
Client bookkeeping	10
Time accounting, billing, and receivables	10
General ledger	7
Word processing	7
Target companies	6
Accounts payable	5

Our next task is to identify the topics that will form the basis for evaluating vendors for each application. Here, again, the topics come directly from the RFP—the vendor's ability to produce the output reports and provide the key features you have defined. Refer to the applications questionnaire in the sample RFP at the end of this chapter. Note the inclusion of the column labeled "response." The response column requires the vendor to insert a response according to predefined categories, as follows:

Code	Meaning	Description
S	Standard	Requirement provided as a standard part of the package
E	Enhancement	The requirement will be met by an enhancement to package without added charge
R	Report writer	The user can satisfy this requirement by using the capabilities of the report writer provided with the package
C	Custom	The requirement will be met by customizing the package; the additional charge is included in the fee proposal
A	Alternative	A suitable alternative is being presented and is explained
U	Unavailable	Requirement will not be provided at any cost

By requiring vendors to respond according to predefined categories, there will be little, if any, confusion as to the vendor's responsibility. In addition, you have defined the criteria for ranking the response. For example, you could assign descending point values (5 for "standard," 4 for "enhancement," 3 for "report writer," 2 for "custom," 1 for "alternative," and zero for "unavailable") for each of the responses. Then total the points for each response in the application and "scale" the total:

1. Number of response items   20
2. Maximum score at 5 points per responses   100
3. Sample vendor score   80
4. Application value   10
5. Vendor points for this application   8
   $(80/100 \times 10)$

After evaluating all vendor responses for each of the applications, tabulate the results. A sample follows.

		Points						
		Vendor						
Application	Maximum	A	B	C	D	E	F	G
Income tax planning and return preparation	10	7	8	8	6	9	8	9
Client bookkeeping	10	8	8	7	6	8	8	9

(Continued on following page)

		Points						
				Vendor				
	Maximum	*A*	*B*	*C*	*D*	*E*	*F*	*G*
Time accounting, billings, and receivables	10	7	9	8	7	8	8	8
General ledger	7	5	6	6	6	6	6	6
Word processing	7	5	5	6	5	6	6	5
Target companies	6	4	5	5	4	5	5	5
Accounts payable	5	5	4	5	4	5	5	5
	55	41	45	45	38	47	46	47

Summarize Preliminary Evaluations

Now we are in a position to summarize the results and rank the vendors. Bring forward the total raw scores for general characteristics and applications suitability. Earlier we discussed the relative importance of general characteristics relative to applications suitability. We assigned a relative importance of 1.0 to 1.2 for these two areas, respectively. We would then scale the results and rank the vendors as follows:

		Points						
				Vendor				
	Maximum	*A*	*B*	*C*	*D*	*E*	*F*	*G*
General characteristics:								
Raw score	125	98	94	95	82	105	96	99
Percent to maximum	100	78	75	76	66	84	77	79
Category value	100	100	100	100	100	100	100	100
Points earned	100	78	75	76	66	84	77	79
Category importance	1.0	1.0	1.0	1.0	1.0	1.0	1.0	1.0
Scaled points	100	78	75	76	66	84	77	79

(Continued on following page)

		Points						
					Vendor			
Category	Maximum	A	B	C	D	E	F	G
Applications suitability:								
Raw score	55	41	45	45	38	47	46	47
Percent to maximum	100	75	82	82	69	85	84	85
Category value	100	100	100	100	100	100	100	100
Points earned	100	75	82	82	69	85	84	85
Category importance	1.2	1.2	1.2	1.2	1.2	1.2	1.2	1.2
Scaled points	120	90	98	98	83	102	101	102
Total scaled points	220	168	173	174	149	186	178	177
Rank		6	5	4	7	1	2	3

The preceding framework provides us with an objective basis for selecting final candidates. As to how many to choose, I would suggest at least two. If the vendor that ranked number 3 is not far behind the vendor ranked number 2, include that vendor also. Your next step is to evaluate the final candidates.

EVALUATING FINAL CANDIDATES

The homework you have done has been well worth it. You've taken the time to read each proposal and objectively rank the candidates. You have selected two or three vendors for final consideration. The two remaining tasks are:

- Verifying vendor representations.
- Making the final decision.

Verifying Vendor Representations

The written proposals you reviewed represent promises of what the vendors say they will do. Before you commit to one of them, you should obtain some assurance that they can and will perform. In this regard, always do the following:

- Check vendor references.
- Attend demonstrations.

Check Vendor References. One of your RFP requirements was to supply several references. While you would expect that the vendor would refer you to "satisfied" users, the very existence of satisfied users provides you with some of the assurance you are seeking. Furthermore, checking user references frequently discloses both strengths and weaknesses not otherwise obvious in the written proposal. Accordingly, do the following:

- Contact the reference by telephone and explain the importance of the call.
- Provide a brief summary of the hardware and software you are considering. Ask the reference to describe their environment (industry, hardware, software, volumes).
- Solicit qualitative evaluations (excellent, average, and poor) in each of the areas of your RFP.
- Ask the reference to comment on specific strengths and weaknesses.

Attend Demonstrations. Demonstrations provide you with the opportunity to see the hardware and software in action. Accordingly, you can verify that the proposed hardware and software exist and perform as described. Key points to consider are:

- **Arrangements:** Inform the vendor as to your requirements (see below).
- **Location:** The demonstration should be at a reference (user) site. This will permit you to observe "live" processing. In this regard, be aware that demonstrations at vendor offices generally utilize "dummy" data and often utilize incomplete demo programs.
- **Hardware and software:** The equipment and software demonstrated should be the same as that you are considering buying.
- **Capabilities:** Use the proposal as a checklist for verifying capabilities. Observe sample reports and live processing, including ease of use, response time, and error-correction procedures. In addition, the volumes being processed should be similar to yours to verify capacity requirements.
- **Attendees:** In addition to your representatives, the vendor representatives should include the personnel who will be assigned to support your installation.

- **Format:** Allocate sufficient time to a lengthy question and answer period to clarify any questions.

An example of what can go wrong in this area can best be illustrated by the following unfortunate situation. A company had outgrown its existing computer capabilities. A particular turnkey vendor was selected because (1) the vendor was experienced and had a substantial number of employees, (2) the hardware was well known and ideally suited to the company's needs, and (3) the vendor's responses to the features portion of the RFP were outstanding. The company requested a demonstration, which was held at the *vendor's* office. Only the basics were demonstrated and the company did not use the RFP as a checklist. In addition to the demonstration, user references were checked. Unfortunately, the users were much smaller companies whose needs were different. One of the company's key requirements was the ability to obtain cost-center information, including profit and loss statements by cost center. The hardware was installed and the application software was delivered, but the software didn't work! The company was being used as a test site for new programs developed by the vendor. The programs used at the demonstration and by existing users were earlier versions without the capabilities specified in the company's RFP. Months went by with unfulfilled promises. All this aggravation and expense (including the ultimate attorney fees) could have been avoided had the company insisted on proper demonstration at a user's site.

Making the Final Decision

Selecting one of the final two or three candidates is primarily a subjective process. If more than one finalist survived the reference checking and demonstrations, they all should have viable solutions (if only one survived, you already have your choice). If this is the case, consider the following:

1. **Ease of use:** Which vendor's system seemed to be the easiest to use?

2. **Chemistry:** Consider the people aspect. Which group did you feel most comfortable with? Which group appeared most knowledgeable? Which group appeared most supportive?

3. **Enthusiasm and integrity:** Recognizing that the vendor's job is to sell, which group seemed the most sincere? Which group truly appeared to believe in their product?

Considering all the information obtained to date, make the final decision. After you have done this, provide constructive feedback to the vendors you didn't select (they have invested a lot of time and effort; tell them how to improve). Having chosen a vendor, there is one more vendor pitfall to consider—the vendor contract.

NEGOTIATING THE VENDOR CONTRACT

Notwithstanding your confidence in the chosen vendor, the worst thing you could do is simply "sign on the dotted line." Vendor standard contracts are generally designed to do one thing—protect the vendor. While vendors may argue that contract revisions will delay your installation, you shouldn't proceed without a contract that protects your interests as well. Points to consider include:

- **Proposal:** The RFP and proposal should be incorporated into the contract.
- **Prices:** Specify details, all-inclusiveness and provide protection against increases, including recurring maintenance charges.
- **Payment:** Provision for time-phased payment schedule based upon vendor performance (delivery, installation, and completion of acceptance testing).
- **Dates:** Specify dates for delivery and installation of hardware and software.
- **Hardware performance:** Specify operating characteristics and warranty against defects.
- **Maintenance:** Provide for hardware and software maintenance; specify vendor response time and provide for suspension of maintenance fees in event of excessive downtime (define it).
- **Software enhancements:** Specify rights to receive enhancements.
- **Installation:** Specify vendor's responsibility and related costs.
- **Ownership:** Provide licenses to use all licensed software and title transfer for purchased hardware and software; provide for transfer of ownership of software in event of vendor insolvency or bankruptcy.
- **Indemnification:** Provide for indemnification regarding patents and copyrights.
- **Acceptance:** Provide for testing of hardware and software.
- **Confidentiality:** Provide for vendor and user confidentiality.
- **Termination:** Specify user contract termination rights.
- **Software:** Specify user rights to source code, including vendor or user modifications.
- **Errors:** Specify vendor obligations for corrections.
- **Conversion and implementation:** Specify vendor obligations.
- **Training:** Specify extent of vendor supplied training and charges for additional training if needed.

- **Upgrades:** Provide for credits for trade-ins.
- **Other locations:** Specify user rights and vendor charges to use software at additional locations.

After you have read the vendor's standard contract, prepare a list of changes you want to make. You can expedite the negotiation process by drafting the revisions. Inasmuch as your revisions may be extensive, prioritize your list. This will help you in planning for compromise in the event of controversy. Finally, use your attorney to help you with the entire contract revision process.

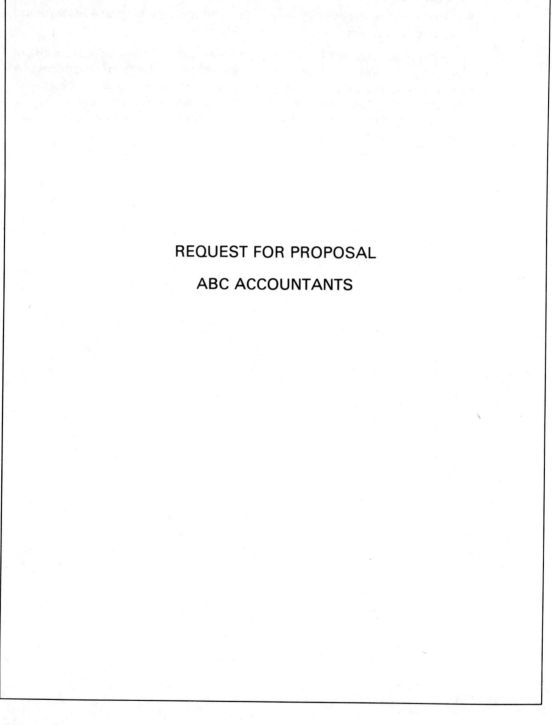

REQUEST FOR PROPOSAL

ABC ACCOUNTANTS

LETTERHEAD

June 30, 19XX

XYZ VENDOR COMPANY
1234 Vendor Street
Vendor City

Gentlemen:

ABC Accountants (ABC) is now soliciting bids for a computer system as specified in the enclosed Request for Proposal (RFP).

Multiple proposals may be submitted by each vendor. Vendors should provide schematics for each of the proposed configurations. For multiple proposals, please provide secondary responses to questions only where the answers differ from the primary responses.

While system specifications represent those features considered required, vendors are invited to take exception as described in the section entitled "Proposal Guidelines." It is important that vendors clearly justify any exceptions taken in terms of costs and benefits to ABC. This provision is intended to provide vendors with greater flexibility in responding to this RFP.

We believe that our RFP approach will simplify the bidding process while providing ABC with a consistent base of required information. Responses to the questions in the RFP, together with related cost data and supporting documentation will be used to make the final selection.

It is the objective of this RFP to solicit as many meaningful proposals as possible in order to give ABC a range of alternatives from which to choose. To facilitate this objective, we will be pleased to work with your organization in answering any questions concerning the requirements of ABC as outlined in this RFP. Vendor proposals must be submitted on or before August 15, 19XX (Proposal Due Date). Further information regarding these key dates and the appropriate vendor actions is provided under general information. All questions should be directed to my attention.

We appreciate your consideration and assistance in this matter. We are looking forward to the receipt of your proposal and to the development of a closer relationship in the near future.

Very truly yours,

ABC Accountants

_____

By John F. Accountant
Partner

Enclosures:
  Request For Proposal
  Vendor Questionnaire (2)

TABLE OF CONTENTS

Section	Description	Page
I.	General Information	iv
II.	Proposal Guidelines	vii
III.	System Requirements	ix
IV.	Vendor General Questionnaire	xvi
V.	Vendor Hardware and System Software Questionnaire	xxii
VI.	Vendor Applications Questionnaire	xxxviii
	A. Revenue	xxxviii
	B. Client bookkeeping	*
	C. Accounts payable	*
	D. General ledger	*
	E. Word processing	*
	F. Income tax	*
	G. Target companies	*

*Not illustrated in RFP but follows the identical format.

SECTION I
GENERAL INFORMATION

1. INTENT OF RFP

   The intent of this RFP is to establish the specifications for a data-processing system for ABC Accountants (ABC). The specifications contained herein are intended to provide vendors with sufficient information to enable them to prepare an acceptable response to this RFP.

2. VENDOR INQUIRIES

   All inquiries to this RFP should be submitted in writing to:

   > John F. Accountant
   > ABC Accountants
   > 1234 Accountant Street
   > Accountant City
   >
   > (213) 123-4123

   Inquiries should make reference to specific section numbers of the RFP and, where appropriate, paragraph numbers. A vendor's questions and answers to these questions will be communicated to all vendors.

3. RFP ADDENDA

   In the event that modifications, clarifications, or additions to the RFP become necessary, all vendors will be notified and receive, in writing, addenda to the RFP.

4. IMPORTANT DATES

   The following dates are significant in terms of this RFP:

RFP issue date	June 30, 19XX
Intent to bid date	July 15, 19XX
Proposal submission date	August 15, 19XX
Vendor selection date	September 15, 19XX
Desired hardware installation date	October 15, 19XX
Desired conversion date	November 15, 19XX

5. ACCEPTANCE OF VENDOR PROPOSALS

   ABC reserves the right to accept or reject any or all bids, to take exception to these RFP specifications, or to waive any formalities. Vendors may be excluded from further consideration for failure to fully comply with the specifications of this RFP.

6. VENDOR SELECTION

   ABC reserves the right to make an award based solely on the proposals or to negotiate

iv

further with one or more vendors. The vendor selected for the award will be chosen on the basis of greatest benefit to ABC, not necessarily on the basis of lowest price.

7. GUIDELINES FOR PROPOSAL EVALUATION
   Vendor proposals will be evaluated using a comprehensive set of criteria. A partial list of these criteria is presented below:

   - Does the vendor properly understand the problem?
   - Are system software checklists completed?
   - Are vendor capabilities stated in the proposal?
   - Is vendor approach stated in the proposal?
   - Are the system requirements addressed in the proposal?
   - Is vendor participation and responsibility clearly defined?
   - Is customer participation and responsibility clearly defined?
   - Availability of high-quality service and maintenance?
   - Are one-time implementation fees, start-up costs, and time estimates clearly stated?
   - Are estimated monthly recurring fees clearly defined?
   - Is requested vendor information complete?
   - Is requested proposal information complete?
   - Is requested system information complete?
   - Can the vendor meet the time constraints and proposed schedule?

8. NOTIFICATION OF VENDOR SELECTION
   All vendors who submit proposals in response to this RFP will be notified of the results of the selection process.

9. FINANCIAL STATEMENTS
   Vendors may be requested to submit financial statements prior to final selection. These may be optionally included in the proposal.

10. PROPOSAL PREPARATION COSTS
    All costs incurred in the preparation and presentation of the proposal shall be wholly absorbed by the vendor. All supporting documentation and manuals submitted with this proposal will become the property of ABC unless otherwise requested by the vendor at the time of submission of the proposal.

11. CONFIDENTIAL MATERIALS
    Any material submitted by any vendor that is to be considered as confidential in nature must be clearly marked as such.

v

12. **CONTRACTUAL OBLIGATIONS**

The selected vendor shall be considered as the prime contractor and shall assume total responsibility for installation and maintenance of all hardware and software in the vendor's proposal. Furthermore, the proposal contents of the selected bid shall be considered as contractual obligations. Failure to meet obligations may result in the cancellation of any contracts.

13. **CONTRACT NEGOTIATION**

ABC reserves the right to negotiate a contract with the selected vendor. This contract may include methods of procurement, (1) purchase, (2) lease/purchase, and/or (3) lease in any combination, and may, at the discretion of ABC, include a third-party financial institution or contract negotiation team.

14. **INTENT TO BID**

Vendors intending to submit proposals should respond in writing no later than the intent to bid date.

15. **WITHDRAWAL NOTIFICATION**

Vendors who receive this RFP and do not wish to bid should reply with a letter of "No bid" no later than the intent to bid date. Vendors who wish to withdraw from the bidding are requested to submit a letter of withdrawal.

16. **DEMONSTRATIONS AND BENCHMARKS**

ABC reserves the right to require any vendor to demonstrate and/or benchmark any hardware or software in the vendor's proposal. After the initial evaluation of vendor proposals, vendors can anticipate that demonstration will be requested.

17. **TERMINOLOGY UNIQUE TO OUR INDUSTRY**

The terms "work in process" and "unbilled work in process" represent hours worked and chargeable to a client, together with any out-of-pocket expenses, for which the client has not yet been biled. The term "inventory" represents both "unbilled work in process" and "accounts receivable."

vi

SECTION II
PROPOSAL GUIDELINES

1. PROPOSAL FORMAT
    To obtain vendor information in a form which ensures that the evaluation criteria can be systematically applied, vendors are requested to submit their proposal in the following general format:

    Letter of transmittal: Each proposal shall include a letter of transmittal that bears the signature of an authorized representative of the vendor and that also includes the names of individuals authorized to negotiate with ABC, as well as the names of vendor-appointed sales representatives.

    Vendor questionnaire: The vendor questionnaire is an integral part of the RFP. Extra copies have been included to assist vendors in preparing their proposal. The vendor should present all information in a concise manner, nearly arranged, typed, and in terms understandable to a non-EDP-oriented reader.

    Vendor attachments: Attachments include vendor standard contracts, lists of users of similar processing systems, vendor financial statements, and other materials.

2. NUMBER OF COPIES
    Vendors should prepare two (2) copies of their proposal.

3. MULTIPLE PROPOSALS
    Vendors who wish to submit multiple proposals for various models of hardware or versions of software are invited to do so. It is requested that the vendor select one proposed system as the ''primary'' system and supply complete information for this system. Secondary proposals need only include information that differs from the primary proposal. Secondary proposals should follow the same format as the primary proposal.

4. EXCEPTIONS TO THE RFP
    It is anticipated that vendors may find instances where their hardware or software does not function in a manner consistent with the specifications of this RFP. In such cases, it is permissible to take exception to the RFP. All that is required is that exceptions be clearly identified and that written explanations for the exceptions should include the scope of the exceptions, their ramifications, and a description of the advantages to be gained by ABC.

5. SUPPORTING MATERIALS
    Each specification section of the RFP includes a series of questions to be used as an aid in making a selection. All questions, unless specifically instructed to do otherwise, should be answered in terms of the system quoted for the primary proposal. The answers to each question should be documented, wherever possible, by stating title and page number of the

vii

supporting documentation. For multiple proposals, provide secondary answers to these questions only where the answers differ from the primary proposal.

6. VENDOR TERMINOLOGY
   Vendors should make every attempt to use terminology in their proposals that is consistent with that of ABC. Comparable terminology may be substituted where appropriate if the vendor provides clear and concise definitions.

7. DOCUMENTATION
   As part of each bid, the vendor shall include the cost of two sets of all available hardware and system software manuals in each category, copies of the Table of Contents of each, and individual prices for single items.

8. VENDOR CONTRACTS
   Vendors should submit, as part of their proposals, a copy of their standard contracts. If appropriate, both hardware and software contracts should be included. Standard addenda to these contracts should also be included for evaluation but need not be filled in.

viii

SECTION III
SYSTEM REQUIREMENTS

1. PRESENT SYSTEMS
    ABC's present accounting and information systems are as follows:

System	Present processing	Computerize in house
Revenue:		
Time accounting	Manual	Yes
Billing	Manual	Yes
Accounts receivable	Manual	Yes
Payroll	Manual	No
Accounts payable	Manual	Yes
Fixed assets	Manual	No
General ledger	Service bureau	Yes
Word processing	Manual	Yes
Client bookkeeping	Manual	Yes
Income tax:		
Planning	Manual	Yes
Return preparation	Manual	Yes

The remaining portions of this section set forth our present volumes as well as our volume estimates three years into the future. Our accounting and information needs have been identified and draft report layouts are also included.

ix

2. INPUT VOLUMES

INPUT VOLUME SUMMARY

System	Record Length	Present Average	Present Peak	Three Years Average	Three Years Peak
Revenue:					
Time accounting	XXX	XXX,XXX	XXX,XXX	XXX,XXX	XXX,XXX
Billing	XXX	XXX,XXX	XXX,XXX	XXX,XXX	XXX,XXX
Cash receipts	XXX	XXX,XXX	XXX,XXX	XXX,XXX	XXX,XXX
Cash disbursements	XXX	XXX,XXX	XXX,XXX	XXX,XXX	XXX,XXX
Client bookkeeping	X,XXX	XXX,XXX	XXX,XXX	XXX,XXX	XXX,XXX
General ledger	XXX	XXX,XXX	XXX,XXX	XXX,XXX	XXX,XXX
Total accounting		XXX,XXX	XXX,XXX	XXX,XXX	XXX,XXX
Word processing	na	Varies			
Income tax:					
Planning	XXX	XX,XXX	XXX,XXX	XX,XXX	XXX,XXX
Returns	X,XXX	XXX,XXX	XXX,XXX	XXX,XXX	XXX,XXX

x

3. FILE REQUIREMENTS
a. Summary

FILES VOLUME SUMMARY

System	Masterfiles: File description	Peak month characters: Present (in thousands)	Peak month characters: Three years (in thousands)	Transaction files: File description	Annual number of characters: Present (in thousands)	Annual number of characters: Three years (in thousands)
Revenue:						
Time account-ing	Work in process	XX,XXX	XX,XXX	Timesheets	XXX	XXX
	Billing rate	X	X			
Billing	Accounts			Billings	XXX	XXX
Cash receipts	receivable	X,XXX	X,XXX	Receipts	XX	XX
	Client address	XX	XX			
Client bookkeeping	Clients	XX,XXX	XXX,XXX	Client trans.	XXX	X,XXX
Accounts payable	Accounts payable	X,XXX	X,XXX	Purchases	XX	XX
				Distribution	XXX	XXX
				Disburse-ments	XX	XX
General ledger	Chart of accounts	XX	XX			
	GL balances	X,XXX	X,XXX	GL distri-bution	XXX	XXX
Word processing	Letters	XXX	XXX			
	Labels	XXX	XXX			
Income tax:						
Planning	Projections	XXX	XXX			
Returns	Returns	XX,XXX	XXX,XXX	Tax input	XXX	XXX
Target companies	Targets	X,XXX	X,XXX			
TOTALS		XXX,XXX	XXX,XXX		X,XXX	XX,XXX

xi

b. Details

TIME ACCOUNTING FILES

	Field length	
Field description	*Work in process Masterfile*	*Transaction file*
Client name	XX	XX
Client number	XX	XX
Employee name	XX	XX
Employee number	XX	XX
Employee billing rate	XX	XX
Timesheet period	XX	XX
Service code	XX	XX
Employee hours	XX	XX
Out-of-pocket expenses	XX	XX
Total record length	XXX	XXX
Masterfile volumes	*Present*	*Three years*
Total record length	XXX	XXX
Peak active clients	XXX	XXX
Product	XX,XXX	XX,XXX
Peak timesheet line items	XXX	XXX
Product	X,XXX,XXX	X,XXX,XXX
Number of months open items in unbilled work in process	X	X
Maximum file size	XX,XXX,XXX	XX,XXX,XXX
Transaction file volumes	*Present*	*Three Years*
Total record length	XXX	XXX
Average line items per month	XXX	XXX
Average monthly volume	XX,XXX	XX,XXX
Annualize	12	12
Annual file size	XXX,XXX	XXX,XXX

Note: Details of other files are not illustrated but would be included here.

xii

4. OUTPUT REQUIREMENTS
a. Volume summary

OUTPUT VOLUME SUMMARY BY SYSTEM

Frequency legend: D–Daily   W–Weekly   S–Semimonthly   M–Monthly
Q–Quarterly   A–Annual   R–Request

Report Title	Freq	Printer Location	Present	Three Years
			Number of Lines per Period	
Revenue:		Accounting		
Unbilled work in process				
Chargeable time analysis	S		XX	XXX
Chargeable hours by client	A		X,XXX	X,XXX
Client details	M		XX,XXX	XX,XXX
Aging by client	M		XXX	XXX
Control report	S		XX	XX
Billing				
Invoices	M		X,XXX	X,XXX
Journal	M		XXX	XXX
Realization reports:				
Service code:				
Current month	M		XXX	XXX
Year to date	M		X,XXX	X,XXX
Alpha by client:				
Current month	M		XXX	XXX
Year to date	M		XXX	XXX
Revenue forecast	A		XXX	XXX
Budget comparison	M		XX	XX
Accounts receivable				
Client details	M		X,XXX	X,XXX
Aging	M		XXX	XXX
Cash receipts journal	M		XXX	XXX
Control report	M		X	X
Cash balance control	D		X	X
Accounts payable:		Accounting		
Purchase journal	M		XXX	XXX
Distribution journal	M		XXX	XXX
Cash requirements	W		XXX	XXX
Vendor open invoices	M		XXX	XXX
Checks	M		XXX	XXX
General ledger:		Accounting		
Chart of accounts	R		XXX	XXX
GL entries	M		XXX	XXX
Financial statements	M		XXX	XXX
Trial balance	M		XXX	XXX

xiii

REQUEST FOR PROPOSAL   June 30, 19XX

Word processing:	D	Secretary	X,XXX	X,XXX
Income tax:				
Projections	D	Tax depart- ment	XXX	XXX
Tax returns	D	Accounting	X,XXX	X,XXX
Client bookkeeping:	M	Accounting	X,XXX	XX,XXX

OUTPUT VOLUME SUMMARY BY PRINTER LOCATION

	Printer Location							
	Accounting		*Tax department*		*Secretary*		*Total*	
	Present	*Three Years*	*Present*	*Three Years*	*Present*	*Three Years*	*Present*	*Three Years*
Frequency	*(In thousands of lines)*							
Daily	X.X	X.X	.X	X.X	X.X	X.X	X.X	XX.X
Weekly	.X	.X						.X
Bimonthly	.X	.X						.X
Monthly	X.X	XX.X					X.X	XX.X
Quarterly								
Annual	X.X	X.X					X.X	X.X
Request	.X	.X					.X	.X
TOTALS	X.X	XX.X	.X	X.X	X.X	X.X	X.X	XX.X

xiv

b. Report layouts

BILLING REALIZATION REPORT: CLIENT SEQUENCE

Frequency—monthly   Number of lines—peak month
Current month   Present: XX   Three years: XX
Year to date   Present: XX   Three years: XX

| Client | *Standard* | | | | | *Billed* | | | | |
	Hours (1)	Rate (2)	$ (3)	Exp (4)	Total (5)	Total (6)	Exp (7)	Fees (8)	Rate (9) (8/2)	% (10) (6/5)
A	XX	XX.XX	XXXX	XX	XXXX	XXXX	XX	XXXX	XX.XX	XX
B	XX	XX.XX	XXXX	XX	XXXX	XXXX	XX	XXXX	XX.XX	XX
TOTALS	XXX	XX.XX	XXXXX	XXX	XXXXX	XXXXX	XXX	XXXX	XX.XX	XX

Note: Other report layouts are not illustrated but would be included here.

xv

SECTION IV
VENDOR GENERAL QUESTIONNAIRE

1. VENDOR BACKGROUND

   a. Attach a brief narrative regarding your business history.

   b. How long have you actively participated in the data-processing industry?

   Comments

   _____ Less than 2 years _____

   _____ 2 to 5 years _____

   _____ Over 5 years _____

   c. As to our industry, provide the following information:

   Number of years you have actively participated in our industry. _____

   Percentage of your total revenues derived from our industry. _____

   Number of your employees committed to our industry. _____

   d. How many data-processing systems have you installed to date?

	This year	In total
None	_____	_____
1 to 10	_____	_____
Over 10	_____	_____

   e. Will you commit to a full implementation schedule?

	Yes	No
Site preparation	_____	_____
Equipment delivery	_____	_____
Equipment installation	_____	_____
User training	_____	_____

xvi

    f. What is your yearly gross sales volume?

        Hardware   _____

        Software   _____

        Combination   _____

          Total   _____

    g. Indicate contractual agreements that would be applicable if your proposal is ultimately accepted by us. Attach sample copies.

        _____ Hardware purchase

        _____ Hardware maintenance

        _____ Systems software purchase

        _____ Systems software license

        _____ Systems software maintenance

        _____ _____

        _____ _____

    h. List references of installed users:

Name	Title	Telephone	City
_____	_____	_____	_____
_____	_____	_____	_____
_____	_____	_____	_____
_____	_____	_____	_____

2. VENDOR USER GROUPS

If a user group does not exist, leave this section blank.

How long has the group been in existence? _____

State annual membership fee, if any. _____
If there is a national users group, complete the following:

Name of chairman _____

Address _____

City, state, zip code _____

xvii

REQUEST FOR PROPOSAL   June 30, 19XX

    Telephone number (_____) _____

    Number of currently active members _____

    How many meetings does the group hold per year? _____

  If there is an active local chapter, complete the following:
    Chairman _____

    Address _____

    City, state, zip code _____

    Telephone number (_____) _____

3. VENDOR-SUPPLIED TRAINING
    a. Describe the extent and type of free training included in your fee proposal.

        _____

        _____

        _____

        _____

        _____

    b. Describe all pertinent vendor-supplied training courses. For each course, include the
        following information:
            Cost of course
            Location
            Duration
            Frequency of offering
            Prerequisites
            General description

        _____

        _____

        _____

        _____

        _____

        _____

        _____

        _____

        _____

                            xviii

4. VENDOR BID SUMMARY
   a. System costs:

Hardware cost (see hardware section for detail) $ _____

System software cost (see system software section for detail) $ _____

Application software cost (details below) $ _____

Application subsystem	Monthly maintenance	Base price	Enhancements	Total
_____	_____	____	_____	____
_____	_____	____	_____	____
_____	_____	____	_____	____
_____	_____	____	_____	____
_____	_____	____	_____	____
_____	_____	____	_____	____
_____	_____	____	_____	____
_____	_____	____	_____	____

Total application software cost $ _____

Shipping $ _____

Site preparation (estimated: air, power, floor, etc.) $ _____

Installation costs (estimated) $ _____

Conversion costs (estimated) $ _____

User training costs $ _____

Travel costs $ _____

Documentation $ _____

Other costs, if any (describe):

_____ $ _____

_____ $ _____

Total system cost $ _____

xix

REQUEST FOR PROPOSAL   June 30, 19XX

    b. Monthly recurring costs:

	Usage	Maintenance
Hardware under leasing arrangements (describe)	$ _____	$ _____
System software	$ _____	$ _____
Application software	$ _____	$ _____
Representative monthly cost	$ _____	$ _____

    c. Maintenance and support:

	Hourly cost	Proposed cost
Hardware maintenance	_____	_____
Operating system maintenance	_____	_____
Training	_____	_____
Application maintenance	_____	_____
Programming	_____	_____
Systems analysis	_____	_____

    d. Quotation period:

Period through which proposal bid is fixed _____

Authorized negotiator _____

5. SYSTEM IMPLEMENTATION SCHEDULE

    a. Hardware installed and operational within _____ days of contract acceptance.

    b. Application system operational as follows:

Application system	Days from contract acceptance
_____	_____
_____	_____
_____	_____
_____	_____
_____	_____

xx

   c. Complete documentation available within _____ days

   d. User training to be completed within:

      System operations _____ days

      Application software _____ days

   e. Attach representative implementation plan based on vendor's experience and ABC's constraints set forth in this RFP, showing development, testing, conversion, training, and implementation milestones by application.

xxi

SECTION V
VENDOR HARDWARE AND SYSTEM SOFTWARE QUESTIONNAIRE

1. HARDWARE
    a. Hardware Equipment List
        List all equipment and system hardware components (i.e., CPU, peripherals, cables, etc.) included in the proposed hardware configuration. The first page or pages should be the components recommended for initial installation. Additional components recommended for future upgrades should be listed on separate, properly labeled pages. Continue on additional pages as needed.

System component	Model, Part	Description	Price		
			Purchase	Monthly maint.	Rental
_____	_____	_____	_____	_____	_____
_____	_____	_____	_____	_____	_____
_____	_____	_____	_____	_____	_____
_____	_____	_____	_____	_____	_____
_____	_____	_____	_____	_____	_____
_____	_____	_____	_____	_____	_____
_____	_____	_____	_____	_____	_____
_____	_____	_____	_____	_____	_____
		Totals	_____	_____	_____
		Sales tax	_____		
		Grand total	_____		

    b. Describe the expertise required for our personnel to operate the proposed initial hardware configuration. _____

    _____

    _____

    _____

xxii

c. Overall Capacity
The maximum capacity of the proposed hardware and upgrade capabilities are:

	Proposed	Next largest	Largest
Model	_____	_____	_____
Main memory	_____	_____	_____
Disk storage:	_____	_____	_____
Fixed: Number of drives	_____	_____	_____
Capacity per drive	_____	_____	_____
Removable: Number of drives	_____	_____	_____
Capacity per drive	_____	_____	_____
Printers: Number	_____	_____	_____
Speed	_____	_____	_____
Terminals, number	_____	_____	_____
Tape drives, number	_____	_____	_____

Elaborate on required software conversion activities and costs (CPU and software conversion) to accomplish upgrade.

_____

_____

_____

_____

_____

d. Central Processing Unit

Manufacturer _____ Model No. _____

Date of first delivery _____

xxiii

REQUEST FOR PROPOSAL   June 30, 19XX

Mean time between failures _____

Recommended memory _____

Maximum memory available for this model _____

Type of memory _____

Memory expansion increments _____

Word length _____

Maximum partition size _____

Cycle time _____

Maximum memory needed by operating system _____

	Yes	No
Power fail, auto restart	_____	_____
Real-time clock	_____	_____
Automatic program load	_____	_____
Battery backup	_____	_____

Describe any other features available. _____

_____

_____

_____

e. Disk and tape devices

Type of drives proposed

| | *Disk* | | | *Tape* | | |
| | *Hard disk* | | | | | |
	Fixed	*Removable*	*Floppy*	*Cartridge*	*Reel*	*Cassette*
Number of drives	____	_____	_____	_____	____	_____
Manufacturer	____	_____	_____	_____	____	_____
Model number	____	_____	_____	_____	____	_____

xxiv

REQUEST FOR PROPOSAL   June 30, 19XX

    Date of first
      delivery   ___ _____ ____ _____ __ _____

    Mean time between
      failures   ___ _____ ____ _____ __ _____

    Capacity   ___ _____ ____ _____ __ _____

    Maximum number
      available   ___ _____ ____ _____ __ _____

    Average access
      time   ___ _____ ____

    Data transfer
      rate   ___ _____ ____ _____ __ _____

    Describe other features. _____

_____

    Is backup processing accomplished by using system utilities? Yes _____ No _____

    Describe recommended approach for backup processing. _____

_____

_____

    Amount of time required to copy entire disk units to disk or tape depending upon
    backup approach recommended above. _____

_____

f. Printers

	Type (dot matrix, etc.)			
	Printer 1	*Printer 2*	*Printer 3*	*Printer 4*
Manufacturer	_____	_____	_____	_____
Model number	_____	_____	_____	_____
Date of first delivery	_____	_____	_____	_____
Mean time between failure	_____	_____	_____	_____
Number recommended	_____	_____	_____	_____

xxv

REQUEST FOR PROPOSAL   June 30, 19XX

     Maximum number available
       with central processor
       proposed   _____   _____   _____   _____

     Data transfer rate   _____   _____   _____   _____

     Rated speed worst case   _____   _____   _____   _____

     Describe character sets. _____

_____

_____

_____

     Describe other features and options. _____

_____

_____

_____

     Describe other printers available (model number, rated speed, cost). _____

_____

_____

_____

g.   Remote devices

     Manufacturer _____

     Model number _____

     Date of first delivery _____

     Mean time between failures _____

     Number recommended _____

     Maximum number available with central processor proposed _____

     Terminal type (serial, editing, intelligent) _____

     Data transfer rate _____

     Describe how terminals are set up with controllers. _____

_____

xxvi

REQUEST FOR PROPOSAL   June 30, 19XX

Maximum distance from CPU direct wired without signal regenerator. _____

_____

Maximum distance from CPU direct wired with signal regenerator. _____

_____

Briefly describe approach for user programming/control of terminals (special programming language, etc., required). _____

_____

Display characteristics: Characters/line _____

   Lines/page _____ Special symbols _____

Describe capabilities of printer attached to terminal, if available. _____

Terminal characteristics	Yes	No
Keyboard detachable	_____	_____
Cursor positioning up and down	_____	_____
Cursor positioning left and right	_____	_____
Cursor blinking	_____	_____
Character, field blinking	_____	_____
Variable brightness/intensity	_____	_____
Partial screen transmit	_____	_____
Character repeat	_____	_____
Audible alarm	_____	_____
Full screen transmit	_____	_____

Use this area to elaborate on any of your responses to questions in this section. _____

_____

_____

_____

_____

xxvii

h. Installation
    Do you provide physical planning services? Yes _____ No _____

    If yes, describe services and costs. _____

    _____

    _____

    _____

    Indicate services included as part of installation:

    Physical planning   _____

    Facility preparation   _____

    Machine checkout   _____

    System generation   _____

    Other (describe)   _____

    _____

    Environmental requirements for equipment in computer location:

    Square feet required   _____

    Temperature range   _____

    Humidity range   _____

    Power   _____

    Raised floor   _____

    Air conditioning   _____

    Separate power line   _____

    List all hardware components to be installed in the computer location and power
    required for each:

    Device   Power

    _____   _____

    _____   _____

    _____   _____

    _____   _____

xxviii

When are the machine and software considered installed and when do applicable financial charges begin? _____
For all devices proposed for installation outside the computer location, fully describe any special environmental requirements.

Device	Power	Humidity	Temperature
_____	_____	_____	_____
_____	_____	_____	_____
_____	_____	_____	_____
_____	_____	_____	_____

i. Warranties
Indicate which portions of the proposed configuration are warranted and date warranty commences:

	Check	Length of time	*Indicate date warranty commences (shipment, receipt, acceptance, etc.)*
CPU	____	_____	_____
Memory	____	_____	_____
Tape drives	____	_____	_____
Disk drives	____	_____	_____
CRT terminals	____	_____	_____
System interfaces	____	_____	_____
Printers	____	_____	_____
_____	____	_____	_____
_____	____	_____	_____

j. Maintenance
Primary service location for servicing ABC:

Name _____

Street address _____

City, state, zip code _____

xxix

REQUEST FOR PROPOSAL   June 30, 19XX

    Telephone _____

    Distance from ABC _____

Number of field engineers at the above location. _____

Number of similar systems currently serviced there. _____

Address of secondary service location. _____

Will you guarantee that hardware maintenance will be available for any equipment proposed for a five-year period? Yes _____ No _____

Guaranteed service call response time. _____

Will all spare components be inventoried at the primary service location? Describe procedures. _____

_____

_____

Location of alternate parts supply. _____

Average response time for field engineers to arrive:
    On weekdays _____ On weekends _____

Average time to correct a problem (mean time to repair). _____

_____

Describe preventive maintenance policy and procedures. _____

_____

_____

When the manufacturer (or vendor) initiates an engineering change for a component of the proposed configuration, will the system be modified free of charge? Yes _____ No _____

If no, describe associated costs. _____

_____

Describe any extra maintenance services/costs not included in the proposed maintenance contract. _____

_____

_____

xxx

Describe provisions for rebates on rental charges and maintenance costs for extended periods of downtime. _____

_____

_____

Describe provisions for penalty payments from vendor to customer for extended periods of downtime. _____

_____

_____

Does the proposed maintenance contract include extra charges for:

	Yes	No
Weekends	_____	_____
Nights	_____	_____
Travel	_____	_____
Cases when trouble isn't found	_____	_____
User errors	_____	_____
Operator errors	_____	_____
Vendor holidays	_____	_____

If yes as to any of the above, explain extra charges. _____

_____

_____

_____

_____

_____

_____

_____

_____

_____

xxxi

2. SYSTEM SOFTWARE
   a. System software summary
      Specifically list all system software included as part of the proposed configuration including the following types of software: operating systems (OS), assemblers (AS), compilers (CO), interpreters (IN), text editors (TE), word processors (WP), database management systems (DB), report generators (RG), and file utilities (FU) (sort/merge, copy, delete, etc.).

Description (name, version, and release date)	Type	Price			Number Installed
		Purchase	Monthly Maintenance	Monthly Lease	
_____	____	_____	_____	_____	_____
_____	____	_____	_____	_____	_____
_____	____	_____	_____	_____	_____
_____	____	_____	_____	_____	_____
_____	____	_____	_____	_____	_____
_____	____	_____	_____	_____	_____
_____	____	_____	_____	_____	_____
_____	____	_____	_____	_____	_____
_____	____	_____	_____	_____	_____
_____	____	_____	_____	_____	_____
_____	____	_____	_____	_____	_____
_____	____	_____	_____	_____	_____
_____	____	_____	_____	_____	_____

xxxii

b. Operating system
   Indicate those features listed below that will be provided as part of the proposed operating system software:

	Yes	No	Comments
Multiprogramming	___	___	_____
Multitasking	___	___	_____
Task scheduling	___	___	_____
Priority assignment	___	___	_____
Memory mapping	___	___	_____
Spooling	___	___	_____
Job accounting	___	___	_____
User accounting	___	___	_____
Password accounting	___	___	_____
Record level lock	___	___	_____
Library management	___	___	_____
Device diagnostics	___	___	_____
Console log	___	___	_____
Automatic file allocation	___	___	_____
Multilevel interrupt	___	___	_____
_____	___	___	_____
_____	___	___	_____
_____	___	___	_____
_____	___	___	_____
_____	___	___	_____
_____	___	___	_____

xxxiii

Is operating system memory allocation made on the basis of:

	Yes	No	Comments
Fixed partitions?	_____	_____	_____
Dynamic contiguous allocation?	_____	_____	_____
Dynamic noncontiguous allocation?	_____	_____	_____
Other _____	_____	_____	_____

How many batch or background programs may be concurrently executing? _____

How many foreground programs may be concurrently executing? _____

May a user dynamically create and delete disk files? Yes _____ No _____

c. Programming languages
Indicate languages available on the proposed configuration:

	Interpretive	Pseudo-compiled	Compiled
Assembly	_____	_____	_____
ALGOL	_____	_____	_____
APL	_____	_____	_____
BASIC	_____	_____	_____
COBOL	_____	_____	_____
FORTRAN	_____	_____	_____
PASCAL	_____	_____	_____
PL1	_____	_____	_____
RPG	_____	_____	_____
_____	_____	_____	_____

xxxiv

d. Utilities
Which of the following features is supported by the proposed system in an on-line, terminal-oriented mode?

	Yes	No	
Source code preparation, editing	_____	_____	_____
Compilation or assembly	_____	_____	_____
File cataloging	_____	_____	_____
Program execution	_____	_____	_____

If a stand-alone sort utility is available, how long will it take to sort 5000 records that are 80 characters long using a 10-character sort key? _____

_____

e. Support software
If any of the following features are available, briefly describe capabilities, limitations and system resource requirements, etc.

Report generator/writer _____

_____

Query language _____

_____

Database management _____

_____

Print spoolers _____

_____

Screen formatters _____

_____

f. Installation
Describe extent of services included as part of the installation:

Systems software testing _____

_____

Data conversion _____

_____

xxxv

Application systems testing _____

_____

Parallel running _____

_____

Operator training _____

_____

User training _____

_____

g. Warranties
   How long is the software warrantied?

   Systems software _____ days   Application software _____ days

   When do the terms of the software warranties begin (shipment, receipt, installation, acceptance, other)?

   Systems software _____   Application software _____

   What medium is used to deliver the systems software? _____

   How many complete sets of supporting technical systems software documentation will be provided free? _____

h. Maintenance

   Is a hardware maintenance contract a prerequisite for systems software maintenance?

   Yes _____ No _____

   Describe the types or levels of systems software maintenance available, specify location of service (on site or off site), and indicate contractual response times:

   _____

   _____

   What are the standard and optional services provided under the system software maintenance contract and the related costs?

   _____

   _____

   What must ABC do to receive a new version or release of a system software product to

   which it is licensed? _____

xxxvi

For how many months will the proposed system be covered by a system software maintenance contract after a new version or release is available if ABC decides not to upgrade?

_____

What is the fastest way for ABC to obtain assistance in the event of a system software-related failure or a failure whose cause is unclear?

_____

_____

Other vendor comments: _____

_____

_____

_____

_____

xxxvii

SECTION VI

VENDOR APPLICATIONS QUESTIONNAIRE

System requirements, including volumes and required reports, are included in Section III of this RFP. This section uses the following general format:

1. For each application, a narrative overview of processing is provided together with a brief description of system interrelationships.

2. Vendors are requested to respond as to whether the required reports will be provided. In this regard, the report layouts in Section III are not the only way to present the information. Vendors may deviate from the requested format provided that all the required information is presented. Vendor responses should be in accordance with the response codes shown below.

3. Vendors are requested to respond as to whether the indicated features will be provided. Vendor responses should be in accordance with the response codes shown below.

RESPONSE CODES

Code	Meaning	Description
S	Standard	Requirement provided as a standard part of the package
E	Enhancement	Requirement will be met by an enhancement to the package without additional charge
R	Report writer	User can satisfy this requirement by using the capabilities of the report writer provided with the package
C	Custom	Requirement will be met by customizing the package; the additional charge is included in the fee proposal
A	Alternative	A suitable alternative is being presented and is explained
U	Unavailable	Requirement will not be provided at any cost

REVENUE SYSTEM

1. Narrative overview
    Time accounting: Timesheets and cash disbursements (for out-of-pocket expenses) are the primary source for updating work in process. Standard hourly rates will be maintained by the system. The system will calculate standard time charges and update work in process for both standard time charges and out-of-pocket expenses. Work in process will be automatically relieved by billings.

xxxviii

Billing: Computer-generated work in process listings by client will be manually notated ("turnaround document") and are the primary source for relieving work in process, generating invoices and the monthly billing journal, and updating accounts receivable.

Accounts receivable: Manual and computer-generated billings together with cash receipts are the primary source for updating accounts receivable.

2. Reports

Report Title	Frequency	Response	Comments
Unbilled work in process:			
Chargeable time analysis	Semimonthly	_____	_____
Chargeable hours by client	Annual	_____	_____
Aging by client	Monthly	_____	_____
Control report	Monthly	_____	_____
Billing:			
Invoices	Monthly	_____	_____
Journal	Monthly	_____	_____
Realization reports:			
Service code:			
Current month	Monthly	_____	_____
Year to date	Monthly	_____	_____
Alpha by client:			
Current month	Monthly	_____	_____
Year to date	Monthly	_____	_____
Revenue forecast	Annual	_____	_____
Budget comparison	Monthly	_____	_____
Accounts receivable:			
Client details	Monthly	_____	_____
Aging by client	Monthly	_____	_____
Cash receipts journal	Monthly	_____	_____
Changes control report	Monthly	_____	_____
Cash balance control	Daily	_____	_____

xxxix

3. Features

Feature	Response	Comments
Ability to handle user-defined service codes		
Ability to handle narrative comments re time charges		
Ability to handle advance billings (retainers, monthly billings, etc.)		
Ability to produce file maintenance reports, including hash totals		
Ability to generate general ledger entries		
Ability to produce work-in-process listings by client to facilitate the billing process		
Ability to handle adjustments		
Ability to partially relieve hours or expenses		
Ability to apply advance billings to specific items in work in process		
Ability to generate general ledger entries		
Ability to relieve work in process for manual billings		
Ability to forecast billings, by client and service code, based upon historical information using "what-if" techniques		
Ability to handle adjustments (billings, write-offs, etc.)		
Ability to apply cash to specific invoices		
On-line inquiry capability		
Ability to age by invoice		
Open-item technique versus balance forward		

xl

16 purchasing desktop micros

The fundamental concepts of purchasing desktop micros are identical to those involved when purchasing larger systems. Given your information requirements, you need to identify potential solutions and select the best alternative. While the concepts are identical, a totally different approach will be necessary and appropriate. Accordingly, in this chapter we will:

- Review the characteristics of desktop micros.
- Explore the reasons for using a different approach.
- Define an approach to purchasing desktop micros.

CHARACTERISTICS OF DESKTOP MICROS USED IN BUSINESS

As we saw in Chapter 1, it is becoming increasingly difficult to distinguish between the various classes or sizes of computers. Nonetheless, it is important for our purposes that we have a clear understanding of what we mean by the term desktop micro. Accordingly, let's review the characteristics of desktop micros that distinguish them from other computers:

- Cost
- Main memory
- Distribution method
- Use

Cost

Although cost is a function of, among other things, the extent and quality of peripheral devices, in general we are talking about systems that cost less than $10,000, including software.

Main Memory

The typical desktop micro has a range of 64 to 256K of main memory (although some manufacturers may provide the ability to add more main memory). This characteristic distinguishes them from their smaller counterparts, the "home computer." Application software developed for desktop computers generally requires at least 64K of main memory and frequently more.

Distribution Method

Desktop micros are generally purchased in retail stores, which in turn are owned by the hardware manufacturer or independent dealers.

Use

Desktop micros are used in two ways. First, they are used as stand-alone solutions to meet the needs of a single user. Typical applications include forecasting, budgeting, cost analysis, and word processing. Second, for businesses with small volumes, they are used to process the entire accounting function.

EXPLORING THE REASONS FOR
USING A DIFFERENT APPROACH

In Chapter 15, the Request For Proposal (RFP) is a critical element in purchasing larger micros and minis. However, when it comes to purchasing desktop micros for business, a totally different approach is both warranted and necessary. The primary reasons for a different approach are (1) cost and (2) the vendor's role.

Cost

As with all purchase decisions, the amount of time and effort devoted to the decision should be proportionate to the amount of the puchase. If you glance through Chapter 15, you will note that the RFP is a rather lengthy document, requiring considerable preparation time. Add to that the time and effort involved to evaluate vendor responses. The result would likely be an investment of time and effort disproportionate to the amount for the purchase of the desktop micro. Furthermore, experience indicates that the purchase of a desktop micro can typically be readily justified on the basis of:

- Cost savings
- Accuracy and timeliness of information
- Better quality of information for decision-making purposes

Vendor's Role

The second reason for using a different approach is the role that the vendor plays. As to larger micros and minis, the vendor plays a very active role and plays that role for a considerable length of time. In addition to the hardware and software, you would, in essence, be purchasing the vendor's experience in planning, installation, problem solving, and ongoing ability to maintain and enhance your systems. Should modifications be necessary, it is critical that the vendor have the experience and ability to make those modifications.

As to desktop micros, the vendor's role is totally different. Since the computer will be placed on a desktop and doesn't occupy much space, there is no need for a vendor's extensive site preparation and installation planning skills. Furthermore, the use of packaged software generally obviates the need for custom programming modifications. Finally, hardware and software warranty and maintenance arrangements are predefined, in writing, by original manufacturers and software houses; the vendor from whom you purchase hardware and software does not have any role in determining these arrangements. As you can see, the role of the desktop micro vendor is much more limited. In fact, that role consists of (1) displaying and demonstrating various products and (2) facilitating maintenance services should they be necessary.

HOW TO PURCHASE
DESKTOP MICROS

In Chapter 14, we discussed how to document volumes and information requirements. These steps are equally applicable when purchasing desktop micros. Having completed these steps, you are ready to purchase your desktop micro. Steps to take consist of:

- Identify vendor candidates.
- Screen vendor candidates.
- Attend demonstrations and evaluate vendors.
- Select the best alternative.

Identifying Vendor Candidates

There are literally hundreds of microcomputer hardware and software vendors competing in the marketplace. However, most of them don't have the financial resources to compete effectively and, accordingly, won't survive for very long. It's true that you might save a few dollars by shopping for lesser known vendors. However, the risk simply isn't worth it. With that in mind, the best advice is to deal with industry leaders with proven track records. Your approach is as follows:

Identify the Industry Leaders.   Research companies such as The Yankee Group conduct periodic surveys. Their compiled results for 1982 compared to 1981, for new shipments (cost of $1000 to $10,500; *minimum* hardware consisting of keyboard, CPU, 64K RAM, two floppy disk drives, and a video monitor) were as follows:

	1982		*1981*	
Vendor	*Market share*	*Rank*	*Market share*	*Rank*
Apple	28.6%	1	28.1%	1
IBM	18.5	2	3.3	5
Tandy (Radio Shack)	17.3	3	20.2	2
Commodore	5.3	4	6.6	3
Hewlett-Packard	3.7	5	4.8	4
All others	26.6		37.0	
Totals	100.0%		100.0%	

Sources for identifying software vendors include magazine advertisements and publications by research companies such as International Data Corporation (IDC), Datapro, and Auerbach. Locate several of the dealers in your area. In this regard, the yellow pages should be helpful. If that doesn't work, contact the manufacturer's local or regional headquarters.

Screen Vendor Candidates

The purpose of your initial visit is to screen the dealers. In this regard:

- Meet the owner/manager and tour the facilities. Do you get a sense of comfort that the store is well run and they know what they are doing? Do they have on-site maintenance capability? If not, eliminate them.

- Provide the dealer with a list of your applications, together with the volume summaries prepared in Chapter 14. If they do not have software packages for all of your applications, eliminate them.

- Obtain product brochures and price lists. Use these to get an overall sense of the product line and to prepare yourself for your next visit.

- Schedule a demonstration appointment. Ask the owner/manager to identify the employee who is most technically competent to demonstrate their systems and schedule an appointment with that person.

Attend Demonstrations
and Evaluate Vendors

During your demonstration visit you need to accomplish three tasks: (1) determine whether the application software meets your needs; (2) determine associated hardware requirements; and (3) determine total system costs.

Application Software. Review the material you prepared in Chapter 12 regarding information requirements (reports and features). Use that material as a checklist during the demonstration to determine whether the application software meets your needs. Use copies of the Software Demonstration Checklist at the end of this chapter to evaluate each application. Prioritize your applications and devote the majority of your time to your most important applications.

Hardware Requirements. Two key factors influence your hardware requirements. The first factor is the minimum configuration required for your application needs. In this regard, the application packages will determine the minimum amount of main memory required. Your application volumes will determine the minimum requirements of peripheral devices. The second factor relates to your judgmental preferences regarding cost versus productivity or quality trade-offs. In this regard, the two key considerations relate to (1) hard disk versus floppies and (2) printer characteristics.

1. **Hard disk versus floppies.** Vendor application software programs are delivered on floppy diskettes. Frequently, the user has an option regarding whether the data will be maintained on floppies or hard disk. Even though your application volumes may not require hard disk, you may want to consider using a small hard disk (say 5 to 6 megabytes) for storing data to eliminate disk swapping and utilize faster access speeds. Make sure that the dealer explains these options to you.

2. **Printers.** Most manufacturers offer a wide range of models with varying capabilities. The bottom of the line typically might be an 80 character per second dot matrix printer without graphics or text features (underlining, bold printing, proportional spacing, etc.). Although your application needs may not require additional speed or other features, the cost to obtain them generally isn't significant to the total expenditure. Make sure that the dealer explains these options to you. Consider also the possibility of purchasing two printers, a dot matrix printer for documents to be distributed internally and a letter quality printer for documents to be distributed outside the firm.

Require the dealer to demonstrate the application software packages on the hardware that is being recommended. This will ensure that (1) it actually runs on that hardware (don't assume that it will) and (2) you have an opportunity to evaluate the ease of use of the entire system. Use the Hardware Demonstration Checklist at the end of this chapter to evaluate the recommended hardware.

Total System Cost. Use the Vendor Price Quotation form at the end of this chapter to collect cost information and a price quotation. In this regard, note that the form provides for two prices, one for the minimum configuration and another to address the hardware options available to you. Also note that the form provides for a discount from list price. In this regard, you should be aware that the retail list price may not be indicative of actual current selling prices (artificially high list prices, promotions, etc.). Thus, there is a need to determine the purchase price.

SELECT THE BEST ALTERNATIVE

The forms and checklists provided at the end of this chapter will help you to collect data necessary to evaluate each of the vendor's proposed solutions. Modify them as necessary if you have any special requirements. What remains then is to discuss two issues: the extent of your information requirements and the selection process itself.

Extent of Your Information Requirements

If your information requirements are extensive or particularly unique, you may find that none of the vendors can satisfy each and every requirement. In that event, consider the following options:

1. **Compromise.** Generally the best option if most of your requirements are met.

2. **Vendor custom modifications.** Generally this option will not be viable because (a) the software house is unwilling to make modifications at any cost or (b) the cost is prohibitive. However, at least consider it.

3. **Modifying the programs yourself.** This option also is generally not viable because few vendors make the source code available (either by not providing it or by copy protection schemes). However, if the vendor will make the source code available to you (generally at significant additional cost) and you have the requisite skills or can hire a software house to make the changes, you might consider this option.

4. **Custom programming.** If perhaps all but one application meet your needs, consider contracting with a software vendor to program the remaining application. Obtain a price quote and, if you proceed, follow the RFP guidance in Chapter 15. Alternatively, consider programming the application yourself if the application is not complex and you have the requisite skills (or are willing to obtain them).

5. **Changing strategies.** If deficiencies are widespread across applications and extensive, a desktop micro may not suit your needs. Consider turnkey vendors and the approach set forth in Chapter 15.

Selection Process

The checklists provide for the awarding of points in each of the various areas; however, it is not intended that the purchase decision be made simply by adding up the points and selecting the vendor with the greatest total. Rather, the primary purposes of the forms and checklists are:

1. To help assure that you consider all the important factors during the demonstrations.

2. To relieve you of the burden of having to remember all the details of how each vendor fared.

3. To cull out vendors that are deficient in areas important to you or whose quoted prices are excessive.

If you interviewed industry leaders, those that survived the evaluation process probably will all be at least satisfactory for your purposes. The final decision will be subjective in nature. Points to consider include overall ease of use and features provided over and above those you required. Make your final decision and enjoy the exciting world of the desktop micro. However, you're still not through—read Chapter 17.

SOFTWARE DEMONSTRATION CHECKLIST
FOR DESKTOP MICROS

Vendor _____ Salesperson _____ Date _____

	Points (1)
Functionality	
Ability to produce desired information	_____
Contains desired features	_____
Response time for data entry and retrieval	_____
Ease of use	
Menus	_____
Help function	_____
Easy to learn	_____
Screen formats easy to use	_____
Clarity and helpfulness of error messages	_____
Documentation	
Index completeness	_____
Examples	_____
Clarity	_____
Comprehensiveness	_____

(1) Point scale = 0 to 5; 0 = poor, 5 = excellent.
(2) Hardware on which application is demonstrated must be the same as that recommended.

User oriented   _____

Description of error messages _____

Glossary _____

HARDWARE DEMONSTRATION CHECKLIST
FOR DESKTOP MICROS

Vendor _____ Salesperson _____ Date _____

Microprocessor (Mfg/Model) _____ Eight bit _____ Sixteen bit _____

Points
(1)

Vendor
  Friendliness _____

  Knowledge of the hardware _____

  Support availability:

    Maintenance _____

    Training _____

  Proximity to you _____

CRT and Keyboard
  80 columns _____

  24 rows _____

  Character resolution _____

  Type-ahead feature _____

  Detachable keyboard _____

  Separate numeric keypad _____

  Graphics _____

  Upper- and lowercase characters _____

---

(1) Point scale = 0 to 5; 0 = poor, 5 = excellent.
(2) Hardware on which applications are demonstrated must be the same as
    that recommended.

Printer
  Speed: *Manufacturer and Model*   *Characters per second*

    Letter quality _____   _____   _____

    Dot matrix   _____   _____   _____

  Carriage width 80 _____ 132 _____   _____

  Multiple copies   _____

  Proportional spacing   _____

  Graphics   _____

  Tractor feed   _____

  Automatic paper feed   _____

Storage Volumes and Expandability

                        Recommended   *Maximum*

  Main memory   _____   _____   _____

  Floppy disk drives:
    Number   _____   _____   _____

    Storage capacity   _____   _____   _____

    Hard disk capacity _____   _____   _____

Backup
  Ease of use   _____

  Speed   _____

Documentation
  Index completeness   _____

  Comprehensiveness   _____

  Clarity   _____

VENDOR PRICE QUOTATION

1. **HARDWARE**
   List all equipment and system hardware components (i.e., CPU, peripherals, cables, etc.) required for the application software.

Description	Manufacturer	Model/Part	Capacity	Warranty period	Price for configuration	
					Optional	Minimum
_____	_____	_____	_____	_____	_____	_____
_____	_____	_____	_____	_____	_____	_____
_____	_____	_____	_____	_____	_____	_____
_____	_____	_____	_____	_____	_____	_____
_____	_____	_____	_____	_____	_____	_____
_____	_____	_____	_____	_____	_____	_____

Total hardware price _____ _____

2. **SYSTEM SOFTWARE**
   List all the system software for the configuration, including utilities, operating systems, etc.

Type	Description: name, version, and release date	Warranty period	Price
_____	_____	_____	_____
_____	_____	_____	_____
_____	_____	_____	_____

Total system software price _____

3. **APPLICATION SOFTWARE**
   List all application software.

Package name and version	Software developer	Warranty period	Price
_____	_____	_____	_____
_____	_____	_____	_____
_____	_____	_____	_____

Total application software price _____

4. **SUPPLIES AND OTHER COSTS**

Description	Quantity	Price	Price

5. **TOTAL PRICE**

	Configuration	
	Optional	Minimum
Total of 1 to 4 above		
Discount		
Subtotal		
Sales tax		
Total net price		

Optional maintenance arrangements (describe, including period and cost):

_____

_____

Date through which price quotations above are fixed: _____

_____
Company Name

By _____
Authorized signature

_____
Title

_____
Date

17 implementing new systems

Notwithstanding some vendors' claims to the contrary, there is much more required for a successful implementation than simply "plugging in the computer." Consider all your time and effort to date, let alone the monetary commitment. If you don't take steps to help assure a successful implementation, you risk losing all your investment to date. The guidance provided in this chapter assumes an environment of more than one user. If you plan to implement a desktop computer for yourself (no other users), some of the material won't be relevant to you individually. In this event, simply scan the materials and proceed to the next topic. With that in mind, the major implementation steps are:

- Preparing the implementation plan.
- Monitoring implementation issues.
- Integrating controls.
- Performing postimplementation evaluation.

PREPARING THE
IMPLEMENTATION PLAN

The most critical step in the entire implementation process is the preparation of the implementation plan itself. The preparation of a formal plan provides you the opportunity to anticipate problems and think through related solutions in a relaxed environment, rather than waiting for the problems to surface and reacting in a crisis mode. Preparing your plan consists of two steps:

- Determine the implementation approach.
- Determine the contents of the implementation plan.

Determining the Implementation Approach

If you were told that 15% to 20% of all new automobiles purchased are not operational, you would likely consider that misinformation. Certainly, there is an occasional "lemon" automobile, but 15% to 20% seems inconceivable. The reality is that the percentage is correct; however, the industry is not automotive, it's the small business computer industry! Add to that the fact that less than 10% are installed on schedule and more than 50% are not installed within one year. Compared to that, the automotive industry is a gem. While vendors are a frequent cause of small computer failures, a lot of the credit should be given to the users. Common causes of failures are:

- Management apathy.
- Unreasonably short or ambitious schedules.
- Poor communications.
- Inability to finalize design requirements.
- Viewing the computer as a simple cure for complex problems.

This brings to mind one situation that I encountered not too long ago. A small business was growing rapidly and saw the need to computerize the order-entry function. So they bought a computer system. When I toured their facilities, I noticed that the system wasn't being used. I asked why, and got the following responses:

- From the owner, "I thought we could get it up and running in a couple of weeks but the system doesn't do what we want it to! Besides, I can't be bothered with it right now."

- From the order-entry department, "That computer was the owner's idea. Furthermore, we don't know how to use it."

In determining your approach, consider the following:

- Use a team approach.
- Identify implementation issues.
- Assign responsibilities.
- Prepare a time-phased implementation plan.

Use a Team Approach.   Nothing dooms a project to failure like a system "forced" upon those who have to use it. Avoid this problem by assembling a project team. The project team should include (1) the vendor, (2) users representatives, and (3) where applicable, a data-processing representative. Select a project team leader. That person need not be a technician, experienced in EDP matters. To the contrary, it is more important that the project team leader have good communication skills and a high level of energy. There is a lot of work ahead and a key ingredient is the project team's morale (enthusiasm and apathy have one thing in common—they are both contagious). The primary role of the project team leader is to keep the morale up and the project on target.

Identify Implementation Issues.   The existence of a computer in your office will be a source of concern. Computerization results in change. While the old way may not be as good, it is familiar and comfortable. In addition, there is the common fear of the computer itself. You can partially overcome these concerns with frank open discussion of how the computer will help. Solicit the project team's concerns. This will go a long way toward opening communication lines and breaking down the fear barriers.

Assigning Responsibilities.   Application implementation is a user function, not a data-processing function. Each user should be assigned the responsibility for implementation of their respective applications. The added benefit here is that you will have broken down the project into manageable pieces.

Prepare a Time-phased Implementation Plan.   Working as a group, the project team should develop the plan overview. If the vendor has implementation responsibilities, use the vendor's plan as a starting point. Challenge it in terms of both content and timing. Revise it as necessary. This is *your* project, not the vendor's. You need to manage and control the project to accommodate the needs of your business. As a general rule, the plan overview should contain the major tasks on a time-phased basis. In this regard, Gantt charts are particularly useful since they present a graphic

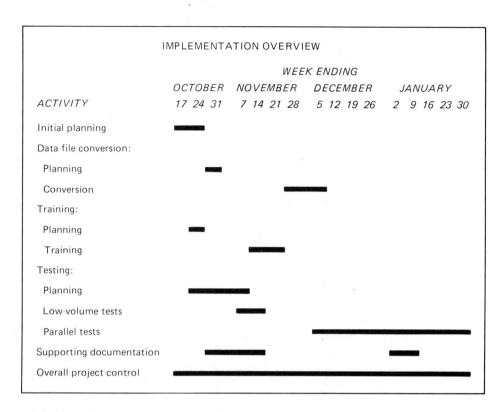

FIGURE 17.1
Phased timetable.

portrayal of the sequence of events and how they interrelate. An example is shown in Figure 17.1

After the plan overview has been prepared and agreed to by the project team, work can begin on the implementation checklists. Your objective is to list, by activity area, each of the key tasks to be accomplished. As a minimum, the checklist should include:

- Task identification
- Responsibility assignments
  - a. Vendor
  - b. Company personnel
- Level of responsibility
  - a. Perform
  - b. Review
  - c. Monitor

- Completion dates
  a. Target
  b. Actual
- Hours required for each task

The checklist might take the format shown in Figure 17.2.

IMPLEMENTATION CHECKLIST—PLANNING						
Task iden-tification	Company personnel			Vendor level	Completion date	
	Name	Level	Hours		Target	Actual
Determine project timetable	Roger S.	Perform	8	Review	10/15	10/15

FIGURE 17.2
Sample implementation checklist format.

Appendix B contains sample checklists. Modify them according to your own needs. After preparing the checklists, review the time requirements for each individual by month. If each individual can devote the time required, proceed with the plan. If not, revise responsibilities as necessary.

Determining the Implementation Plan Contents

The specific contents of an implementation plan are a function of the size of the organization, the sophistication of the hardware and software, and the nature and extent of application processing. The plan contents are determined by addressing the "what" questions. What needs to be done? What can go wrong? Asking these sorts of questions will surface issues that you can incorporate into your plan and be prepared to deal with. Considerations include testing, converting existing computerized applications, initial data-file creation, site preparation, insurance, computer operations, forms, and training.

Testing. Many vendors will tell you that the amount of testing already done is sufficient. The vendors themselves tested the programs after they were designed. Furthermore, you attended demonstrations during which additional testing was accomplished. Isn't that enough? The answer is an emphatic "NO!" for two reasons. First, the mysteries of data processing are endless. What works in one installation simply doesn't work in another installation. When you combine the specific hardware and software provided by the vendor with your unique people and transactions, you create an environment that cannot be simulated anywhere else. The second reason for further testing is to provide training. The time allotted during demonstrations was, of necessity, limited. Further testing permits you to become intimately familiar with how to use the systems before you go "live." A common approach to testing consists of two types of tests: low volume and parallel testing.

The purpose of low-volume testing is to test the programming logic and related error detection and correction procedures. In this regard, design two to three valid transactions of every type that you would expect the system to accept and process. Then design transactions containing errors of every type imaginable (invalid account numbers, numeric data in alphabetic fields, and vice versa, missing data, out-of-range amounts, illogical responses to program prompts, delete masterfile accounts that have balances, out-of-balance journal entries, etc.). Although you want to maintain a high level of professionalism, you can also make this phase an entertaining process (e.g., award prizes for creative error conditions). At this point you can also solicit suggestions for testing from the vendor. In fact, some vendors have packaged "test systems" that provide for dummy masterfile accounts and dummy transactions. Challenge these as to their sufficiency but, by all means, use them as a source. Then list all your tests on a work sheet. An example follows:

Nature of test	Expected results	Actual results
Process a shipment for a customer not on the masterfile	Transaction rejected; appropriate error message given	
Omit required fields and attempt to process purchase transaction	Transaction rejected; appropriate error message given	
Delete a customer with a balance	Deletion not performed; appropriate error message given	

Fill in the second column as to what you think will happen (mathematical results, error messages, etc.). Then perform the tests. If the actual results match your expected results, proceed to the next step. If not, discuss the problem with the vendor. If there are programming errors that cannot be corrected, you have two choices—return the software or live with the conditions and design controls around the errors. As an aside, after completion of the low-volume testing, you will derive a sense of comfort that you understand the strengths and weaknesses of the systems and that you, not the machine, are in control.

If you are implementing accounting systems, you should also plan to perform parallel ("high-volume") testing. There are two reasons for running parallel. First, there may be error conditions that you didn't anticipate during low-volume testing. High-volume testing with live data will provide reasonable assurance that all error conditions have been encountered. If you encounter serious problems, you still have the old system to fall back to. The second reason for running parallel is to permit you to go through the period-end closing procedures using your business volumes. This in turn raises the question as to the length of the parallel period. As a rule of thumb, plan to run parallel for at least one month. If all goes well, you can discontinue running parallel and convert over to the new system. If you encounter problems, continue running parallel until all the problems have been worked out. You should also plan to go through all the period-end closing cycles (monthly, quarterly, and year end). Ideally, your final parallel month would be the last month of the fiscal year. This would enable you to go through all the balance forward routines. If your timing doesn't permit this, consider making an extra backup copy of the files and use these to test the period-end closing procedures.

Converting Files from Existing Computerized Applications.　Converting existing computerized files eliminates the necessity to rekey all the historical data. In this regard, there are two considerations you need to be aware of. The first is the existence of the capability itself. The lack of standardization in the data-processing industry in terms of programming languages, operating systems, and the hardware itself creates incompatibility. A file created by one machine more often than not cannot be read by another machine. To overcome this problem, some vendors have developed conversion programs to reformat files created on other vendors' machines. If you have existing computerized applications for which data-file conversion is planned, be aware that timing is of the essence. The old files must be updated, copies forwarded to the conversion location (vendor or other third party), and converted files returned on a timely basis to be utilized on the new system. In this regard, consider performing a dry run. That is, using a low-volume file from an earlier period, arrange to have it converted. This will provide you with reasonable assurance that the conversion process works and will also give you a good indication of the turnaround time.

Initial Data-File Creation.　For existing manual applications and new applications that utilize masterfiles or historical transaction files, the initial data files for the computerized application will have to be created. If the data are voluminous, initial file creation will be a time-consuming process with the potential for fouling up your implementation timetable. Consider whether you have the manpower to accomplish this task internally. If not, plan to hire temporary personnel to alleviate the workload strain.

Site Preparation. Depending on the environmental requirements of your hardware, the extent of site preparation can range all the way from ascertaining that you have sufficient electrical outlets to full-scale facilities construction. The key points to consider are:

- Unique operating environment (isolation, air conditioning, etc.).
- Electrical requirements (power supply, transformers, cables, breakers, etc.).
- Telephone connections for modems.
- Floorspace and clearance.
- Hardware delivery timetable.

Insurance. Review the adequacy of insurance coverage, including fire, theft, and business interruption.

Computer Operations. Utilization of computer resources and timely processing and report preparation require a well-planned and disciplined operating environment. The key points to consider are scheduling and recurring operating procedures:

1. **Scheduling.** If your EDP resources are far greater than your needs, you probably don't need to worry about scheduling. However, chances are that you don't have that luxury. If that is the case, determine when information (invoices, management reports, etc.) is needed, where it is going to come from, and how long it will take to input new data, update files, and print the reports. For shared input devices, determine who will use them and when. Assign priorities and prepare a formal operating schedule (hourly, daily, weekly, monthly, and yearly).

2. **Recurring operating procedures.** The simple things we take for granted frequently come back to haunt us. Suppose the person responsible for running the system calls in sick? Or worse yet, quits! What then? How will you get the system up and running? What else needs to be done? The information needed to answer these types of questions should be fully documented and incorporated into a data-processing operating procedures manual. Begin by reviewing the vendor's operating manual. Determine which topics are not addressed in sufficient detail. Supplement these materials as necessary. Points to consider include:

- System startup procedures

  Power-up sequence   Log on procedures
  Communications startup

- Program run procedures

  Error message responses   Schedules, including
  Error logs   cutoff times

- Password procedures

  Authority   Change schedule

- Backup procedures

  On site/off site   System software
  Data files   Documentation
  Application programs

- System recovery procedures
- System shutdown procedures

  Power-down sequence   Log-off procedures
  Communications shutdown

- Preventive maintenance schedules
- Document retention
- Program modifications

  Testing   Approvals
  Documentation

- Supply reordering
- Contingency plan

  Alternate site and persons to contact   Requirements
  Equipment resources

Forms. Consider all the various forms that will be needed. Preprinted forms (letterheads, labels, checks, invoices, etc.) should be ordered well in advance so that supplies are available when needed for the new system. In addition, consider other internal forms that need to be designed and implemented (control forms).

Training. Consider who needs to be trained, as well as the level (overview, in depth) and type (operator, user, programmer) of training required. Sources include vendors, user groups, and self-study courses. Schedule the training and monitor progress.

MONITORING IMPLEMENTATION PROGRESS

Monitoring implementation progress is the responsibility of the project team leader. The project team should meet weekly regardless of the significance of the prior week's activities. There are four primary purposes for weekly meetings:

- Problem solving.
- Keeping communication lines open and maintaining high morale.
- Comparing actual results to planned results.
- Documenting matters discussed and conclusions reached.

Problem Solving

During an intense process such as data-processing implementation, problems can develop and escalate. In addition, problems encountered by one team member may have previously been encountered by another team member. A weekly meeting facilitates sharing of common problems, experiences, and potential solutions. Finally, poor decisions can thwart the entire implementation effort. Weekly meetings provide a forum for reviewing the events of the week and resolving issues that have arisen.

Keeping Communication Lines
Open and Maintaining High Morale

Acting as a cohesive unit, each team member needs to be kept informed of the group's progress, as well as new matters that may affect their areas of responsibility. Furthermore, team members may become so frustrated that they set a problem aside and refuse to deal with it. A weekly meeting will alert all team members as to problems that may affect them individually. In addition, the project leader will have timely information to react to morale problems that may be developing.

Comparing Actual Results
to Planned Results

During each weekly progress meeting, the team members should report progress made in their respective areas. The requirement to report progress will, in and of itself, provide motivation to achieve desired results. The reports themselves need not be lengthy. However, they should include the key tasks planned for completion during the prior week, actual tasks completed, and highlights of the next steps to be taken.

Documenting Matters Discussed
and Conclusions Reached

Human as we are, we tend to forget what we talked about and what we decided. Accordingly, in the absence of documented details, the tendency is to rehash old matters before we address new matters. During weekly progress meetings, a record should be kept regarding matters discussed and conclusions reached. Furthermore, in the event of a nonperforming vendor, you will have documented evidence of that fact.

In all but the smallest organizations, a steering committee comprised of senior management should be formed. The steering committee should meet with the project team on a periodic basis (say monthly). In addition to reviewing progress to date, the agenda should include policy decisions and priorities. This will reaffirm the support of senior management and help eliminate management apathy.

INTEGRATING CONTROLS

Irrespective of whether you are computerizing accounting functions or functions such as administrative tasks, controls are necessary. What will vary under the circumstances is the extent of controls required. For example, controls over computerized administrative applications might simply consist of (1) adequate backup of programs and files, (2) restricting access to sensitive information, and (3) control totals (record counts, hash totals) over files to ascertain that all changes have been accurately processed and that the file remains intact. When it comes to computerized accounting functions, additional controls are necessary. In this regard, we need to consider the potential for both errors and irregularities. Our concerns are much broader since we are dealing with pervasive concepts such as safeguarding of assets, reliability of accounting records, and so on. The approach we will use in this section deals with accounting controls. To the extent that some of these are not necessary for other computerized applications, they can be eliminated. An understanding of where and when controls are needed, as well as control objectives, will help you to decide the extent of controls necessary in your environment.

Understanding Where and
When Controls Are Needed

The flow of transactions through the system is the key to understanding where and when controls are needed. In this regard, controls are needed whenever:

- Assets are exchanged (e.g., shipment of goods or delivery of services in exchange for a receivable).
- Liabilities are incurred (e.g., liability arising from receipt of raw materials or services rendered).
- Accounting information is transferred or summarized.

To illustrate these concepts, let's follow the flow of transactions for shipments in a computerized environment. Figure 17.3 illustrates the flow. The shipping transaction commences in the warehouse when the customer's order is filled. The goods are forwarded to the shipping dock for delivery to the customer. After the goods are shipped, the information on the picking ticket is key entered into the shipping department terminal and transmitted to the computer. Using the transmitted information and the price masterfile, the computer prepares the sales invoice and posts the sales information to a sales transaction file. Each week, the accumulated sales and cash receipts transactions are used to update the accounts receivable file, prepare the sales and cash receipts registers, produce an accounts receivable aging, and post the totals to the general ledger account.

Using this flow of transactions concept, let's review the points at which controls are needed:

Point	Type	Information requiring control
1. Shipment	Exchange of assets	(a), (b), (c), (d)
2. Transmittal of shipping information	Transfer of information	(a), (b), (c), (d)
3. Price changes entered	Transfer of information	(c), (e)
4. Preparation of sales invoice	Transfer of information	(a), (b), (c), (d), (e)
5. Update weekly sales transaction file	Transfer of information	(a), (b), (c), (d), (e), (f), (g)
6. Update accounts receivable	Transfer of information	(a), (f), (g), (h)
7. Print invoice register and accounts receivable aging	Transfer of information	(a), (f), (g), (h)
8. Update general ledger	Summarize information	(i)

(a) Customer ID	(b) Quantity shipped	(c) Description of goods
(d) Unit of measure	(e) Unit price	(f) Invoice number
(g) Invoice amount	(h) Invoice date*	(i) Register totals

---

*For discussion purposes, assumed to be the same as the shipping date.

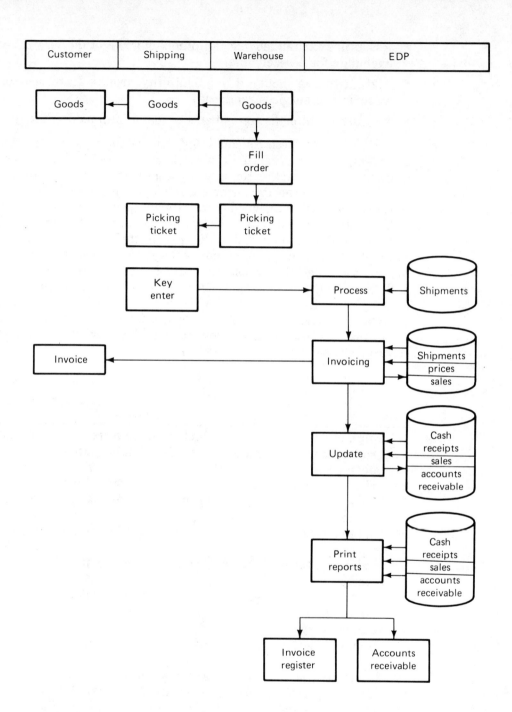

FIGURE 17.3
Flow of transactions.

Let's explore the reasons that controls are needed at each and every one of these points:

Point	Examples of what can go wrong	Results
1. Shipment	Errors: picking ticket not in agreement with goods shipped	Incorrect billings or unbilled shipments
	Irregularities: additional goods shipped	Unbilled shipments
2. Transmittal of shipping information to EDP	Errors: information not entered or incorrectly entered	Incorrect billings or unbilled shipments
	Irregularities: picking ticket information changed	Same
3. Price changes entered	Errors and irregularities: some not entered, some entered in error, wrong file updated	Incorrect billing
4. Preparation of sales invoice	Errors: wrong transaction file used; invoicing program not run	Incorrect billings Unbilled shipments
	Irregularities: price file altered; unauthorized program changes	Incorrect or unbilled shipments
5. Update weekly sales transactions file	Errors: wrong file updated; information lost	Erroneously recorded or unrecorded transactions
	Irregularities: unauthorized program changes	Same as above

(Continued on following page)

Point	Examples of what can go wrong	Results
6. Update accounts receivable	Errors: wrong file used, wrong account updated	Customer accounts updated twice or not updated at all
	Irregularities: unauthorized program changes	Customer accounts not updated or updated incorrectly
7. Print invoice register	Errors: wrong file used	Invalid transactions recorded twice and valid transactions not recorded
	Erroneous programming changes	Aging incorrect
8. Update general ledger	Errors: wrong file used	Wrong general ledger account updated
	Irregularities: account balances modified	General ledger not updated

Having reviewed the philosophy of where and when controls are needed as well as what can go wrong, let's move on to the types of accounting controls necessary in a computerized environment.

Understanding EDP Accounting Controls

The discussion that follows has been structured with the assumption that you have few, if any, data-processing employees. In the vast majority of micro and mini environments, that assumption will be valid. Accordingly, the materials that follow exclude the highly technical matters (control software, database administration, production cataloging controls and on-line programming controls, etc.) applicable to larger EDP departments. With that background then, there are two categories of EDP accounting controls:

- General controls
- Application controls

General Controls. General controls comprise the framework within which application controls function. In this regard, they have a pervasive effect on all applications. While general controls can be categorized in a number of different ways, for our purposes we will categorize them as follows:

- Segregation of duties
- Access controls
- Application development and acquisition controls
- Application maintenance controls

Segregation of Duties. As is the case with a manual environment, the purpose of segregation of duties in a computerized environment is to minimize the possibility of any individual being in a position to perpetrate and conceal errors or irregularities. EDP functions that are incompatible are programming, computer operations, and data control. One purpose of computerization is to eliminate much of the clerical activity associated with manual environments. In so doing, the result is to centralize record-keeping functions within EDP. A programmer who also operates the computer has everything needed to commit irregularities:

1. The programs (which could be modified as desired).
2. The resources (the computer).
3. The records (the data files).

Even if you don't have any EDP employees, you still have computer operators—the users. The key consideration here is to segregate the data-control function (logging batch totals, reconciling input with output, etc). In this regard, take steps to limit exposures in this area such as using the receivables clerk to perform data-control functions for payables, and vice versa.

Access Controls. While segregation of duties is important both as to errors and irregularities, the purpose of access controls is to minimize the risk of irregularities and provide a reasonable level of physical security over the resources themselves. In this regard, access should be restricted to programs, data files, documentation, terminals, and the computer itself. Techniques include:

- Physical access (lock and key, all resources).
- Passwords (terminals, data files, and programs).
- Librarian functions (data files, programs, and documentation).

A common deficiency is to place the computer right in the middle of the accounting department. After all, doesn't this facilitate its use? The answer is yes, but that extends an invitation to everyone to attempt to do whatever they want with the computer. In this day and age, when modular construction is fairly inexpensive, at least put a lockable partition around the computer and purchase some lockable filing cabinets to which keys are thoughtfully made available.

Application Development and Acquisition. This category deals with the overall management approach to adding applications. Experience shows that it is the least understood and most poorly implemented of all the general control areas. One reason for the apparent misunderstanding deals with documentation. While documentation is obviously important, the focus on standards for documentation is totally misdirected. The formalization of the standards is not the important issue; rather, it is the quality of the management approach and the degree to which management supports and enforces it. Whether original programming will be done in-house or by a third-party vendor, the considerations consist of:

1. **User involvement**: As noted during the discussion of project team responsibilities, it is the responsibility of the user to implement applications. The user is no less responsible for the other critical phases, including approval of (a) project commencement, (b) design specifications, and (c) acceptance testing. While formal sign-offs evidence the approvals, it is not the sign-offs that are critical. What is critical is the quality of the involvement.

2. **Adequacy of testing**: The major deficiency in this area is that the design-testing criteria are frequently delegated totally to programmers and vendors. Don't misunderstand this observation. This is not to say that EDP involvement in testing is not important. To the contrary, programmers are critical to the overall test plan. However, programmers cannot be left in a vacuum to determine all the test criteria. It is the user who lives with the day-to-day issues and understands the recurring exceptions and problems. It is also the user's responsibility to take a major role in designing the test criteria.

Application Maintenance. Making revisions is a hazard in and of itself. Changes require a "cold" look at what has been done to date in order to implement revisions. It was tough enough to implement the original system. Given the pressures of a live system, changes are frequently made under duress without the management techniques employed during the application development phase. Each technique employed during the application development phase should be rigidly enforced. A typical weak link is the absence of thorough testing of program changes. In this regard, a frequently used and deficient approach is to use a copy of a live file for testing purposes. If the same results are achieved, the modification is assumed to be adequately tested. The flaw here is the testing procedure. The file used was a file of *accepted* transactions. In other words, none of the critical edit and validation procedures were tested. Whenever changes are made, all the original testing procedures should again be applied to determine that the program continues to function as intended.

Application Controls. Application controls represent the control procedures used in specific applications (such as accounts payable, inventory, etc.). From an accountant's viewpoint, a computerized application can be thought of as being comprised of four separate functions. Using our earlier shipments example, these four functions are depicted in Figure 17.4. The four application functions shown consist of input, files, processing, and output.

1. **Input.** In addition to source transactions, input includes the edit reports produced by the system. The edit reports are included with input because they are the source for correcting input errors.

2. **Files.** To be processed by the application, input transactions must be converted to machine-readable form. In the example, shipping and cash receipts transactions are converted to machine readable transaction files. Using the price masterfile, shipments are converted to

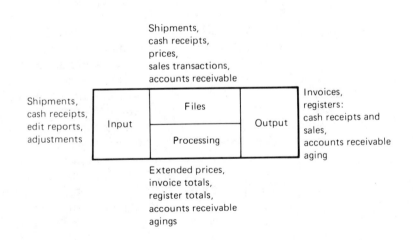

FIGURE 17.4
Accountant's view diagram.

sales transactions to produce invoices. The transaction files can then be used to update customer balances on the accounts receivable masterfile.

3. **Processing.** The principal accounting activity in the processing function is the creation of new data. In the example, the computer is used to calculate invoice extensions and totals, weekly transaction totals, and age the accounts receivable open items.

4. **Output.** Application output represents what the system is designed to produce. In the example, the application is designed to produce customer invoices, transaction registers, and an aged accounts receivable listing.

Using these four application functions, let's review the related control objectives and examples of controls designed to accomplish those objectives.

Function	Control objectives	Examples of control procedures
Input	Authorized	Approvals on transmittal documents, terminal passwords
	Complete (none missing)	Document counts, numeric sequence checks
	Accurate	Comparison of control totals on key fields (dollars, hash totals)
Files	Correct version	Internal and external label checking, control totals
	Changes are: Authorized	Approvals on transmittal documents, terminal passwords
	Complete and accurate	Document counts, review of printouts showing changes, control totals
	Data remain authorized	Detailed review of masterfile contents, control totals, passwords
Processing	Accurate	Testing of new application programs and changes thereto, independent recalculations (detailed, key items, or random samples), access controls
Output	Complete and accurate	Control totals, testing of new application programs and changes thereto, numeric sequence checks
	Valuable forms (e.g., checks) safeguarded	Blank stock locked up, logs of forms issued, used, and voided

Before concluding our discussion on controls, we need to focus on control strategies. For this purpose, it is helpful to reconsider how controls function in a manual environment. For example, consider the preceding shipments example. Person A receives the shipping documents, prepares the sales invoices, lists them in the sales journal, posts the accounts receivable cards, totals the sales journal, and prepares a journal voucher for posting the general ledger. Controls consist of total redundancy. In other words, person B checks that person A has accounted for all shipping documents, has prepared invoices for all shippers, has used the authorized selling prices, has calculated invoice extensions and footings correctly, has listed all invoices in the sales journal and listed them only once, has posted all receivables cards correctly, and that the sales journal total is mathematically correct and in agreement with the journal voucher. In our computerized example, person A disappears. The shipping department enters the shipping information and the computer does the rest (and more—maintains the price list and so on). The question to be asked is, "Are person B's functions still applicable and, if so, why?" The answer is "yes" and the reason is as follows. While the computer is performing the processing, the nature of the processing is represented by the computer programs. Do the original programs function as intended? When authorized changes are made, do the programs continue to function as intended? Have unauthorized changes been made? Have programs been used to perform unauthorized processing? Do masterfiles contain current data (pay rates, selling prices, etc.)? Have unauthorized changes been made to masterfiles? Are the correct versions of files and programs used during the updating process? And so on. The answer to these questions is, "You don't know!" And, since you don't know, you need controls.

The preceding materials regarding control objectives, control examples, and where controls are needed (flow of transactions) should help you to design and implement effective control procedures. From a strategy standpoint, in a micro or mini environment, I suggest consideration of the following:

1. **Detecting errors.** Provided that you perform the following steps, rely on programmed controls (edit and validations, detecting out of balance conditions, numeric sequence checks) to detect errors. In this regard, during your low-volume and parallel testing, ascertain the extent and functionality of programmed controls. To the extent they are effective, rely on them. Then, whenever any changes are made, rerun *all* test criteria to ascertain that the programs still function as intended. Ascertain that the correct version is being used. In other words, your rerunning the test criteria constitutes the control.

2. **Detecting irregularities.** As a practical matter, don't rely on any programmed controls to detect irregularities. The rationale is as follows. In a micro or mini environment in which there are few, if any, data-processing employees, it is impractical to implement an adequate segregation of duties and effectively restrict access to programs, data

files, documentation, and computer resources. The associated costs are prohibitive. Accordingly, assume that, if motivated, personnel could make unauthorized program changes to circumvent programmed controls or perform unauthorized processing. Programming languages can easily and quickly be learned. Don't assume ignorance on anyone's part. Do assume that data on masterfiles might be changed—it's easy to do. By all means, take steps to minimize your risks; however, don't count on these to be sufficient to detect irregularities. In this regard, design manual procedures for this purpose. Many of person B's control functions are still necessary. Consider what could go wrong at each point in the flow of transactions. Determine whether you have responsive control procedures at each point. If not, implement more manual controls until they are sufficient. The appropriate time to implement controls (be they manual or programmed) is during the low-volume and parallel-run phases. Once you go live, it's too late (or too costly). Integrate controls on a timely basis. With that in mind, only one more task remains.

PERFORMING POSTIMPLEMENTATION EVALUATION

Once you're up and running, there is a tendency not to look backward. After all, there are new challenges to be met. Don't make the mistake of not taking the time to look backward. It's important for you to perform a postimplementation evaluation. Why? Believe it or not, the likelihood is that in another three or four years (or even sooner), you will go through another major conversion. More cost-effective solutions will be available. It will be extremely difficult for you to remember the details that at the moment are fresh in your mind. Accordingly, do the following:

- Review your documentation journal.
- Reassemble the project team for a postimplementation evaluation.

Review Your Documentation Journal

Review your documentation journal. Are some items unclear? If so, clarify them. Based on your review, make a list of problems that were encountered. What went wrong? Review the implementation checklists. Which tasks were not completed on schedule? Which tasks took more time than anticipated? Jot these down on paper or make notes on the checklists.

Reassemble the Project Team

Meet with the project team one more time. Review the problem areas you noted. Ask for their suggestions. What else could have been done? How might problems have been anticipated? How might tasks have been done better? Document suggestions. These will save you time and grief the next time around. Also discuss what was accomplished. Congratulate the group for the successes achieved. They have been through a lot and deserve some praise.

We've come a long way together, you and I. It's been a lot of hard work for both of us, but I have certainly enjoyed it. Congratulations for your successes and hard work. Now that you are up and running, it's time for you to move on to those new challenges. The same is true for me. Best of luck!

appendices

A Glossary

B Checklists

    1. Identifying Requirements

    2. Vendor Evaluation and Selection: Larger Micros and Minis

    3. Vendor Evaluation and Selection: Desktop Micros

    4. Implementation Checklists and Reports

Absolute address   The binary number that is assigned as the address of a physical memory storage location.

Access time   The interval between the instant at which data are required from or for a storage device and the instant at which the data actually begin moving to or from the device.

Address   A label, name, or number that designates a location in memory where information is stored.

Algorithm   A prescribed set of well-defined rules or processes for the solution of a problem in a finite number of steps.

Alphanumeric   Referring to the subset of ASCII characters that includes the 26 alphabetic characters and the 10 numeric characters.

ANSI   American National Standards Institute.

Application program (or **package**)   A program that performs a function specific to a particular end-user's (or class of end-users') needs. An application program can be any program that is not part of the basic operating system.

Array   An ordered arrangement of subscripted variables.

ASCII   The American Standard Code for Information Interchange; a standard code using a coded character set consisting of 8-bit coded characters for upper- and lowercase letters, numbers, punctuation and special communication control characters.

Assembler   A program that translates symbolic source code into machine instructions by replacing symbolic operation codes with binary operation codes and symbolic addresses with absolute or relocatable addresses.

Assembly language   A symbolic programming language that normally can be translated directly into machine-language instructions and is, therefore, specific to a given computing system.

Asynchronous   Pertaining to an event triggered by the occurrence of an unrelated event rather than "synchronous" or related operations scheduled by time intervals.

Backup file   A copy of a file created for protection in case the primary file is unintentionally lost or destroyed.

Bandwidth   The range of frequencies that can be passed by a piece of electronic equipment without undue distortion.

Base address   An address used as the basis for computing the value of some other relative address; the address of the first location of a program or data area.

BASIC (Beginner's All-Purpose Symbolic Instruction Code) An interactive, "algebraic" type of computer language that combines English words and decimal numbers. It is a widely available, standardized, simple beginner's language capable of handling industry and business applications.

Batch processing A processing method in which programs are run consecutively without operator intervention.

Baud A unit of signaling speed corresponding to the number of discrete conditions or signal elements per second. If each signal event represents one bit of information, "baud" is equal to "bits per second." When a signal event represents other than one bit (e.g., in some types of phase-shift modulation), "baud" does not equal "bits per second."

BCD Binary coded decimal is a 6-bit alphanumeric character set code.

Binary The number system with a base of 2 used by internal logic of all digital computers.

Binary code A code that uses two distinct characters, usually the numbers 0 and 1.

Bit A binary digit. The smallest unit of information in a binary system of notation. It corresponds to a 1 or 0 and one digit position in a physical memory word.

Block A group of physically adjacent words or bytes of a specified size that is peculiar to a device. The smallest system-addressable segment on a mass-storage device in reference to I/O.

Bootstrap A technique or routine whose first instructions are sufficient to load the remainder of itself and start a complex system of programs.

Buffer A storage area used to temporarily hold information being transferred between two devices or between a device and memory. A buffer is often a special register or a designated area of memory.

Bug A flaw in the design or implementation of a program that may cause erroneous results.

Bus A circuit used as a power supply or data-exchange line between two or more devices.

Byte The smallest memory-addressable unit of information.

Call A transfer from one part of a program to another with the ability to return to the original program at the point of the call.

Central processing unit (CPU) A unit of a computer that includes the circuits controlling the interpretation and execution of instructions.

Character   A single letter, numeral, or symbol used to represent information.

Clock   A device that generates regular periodic signals for synchronization.

COBOL   Common Business-Oriented Language.

Coding   To write instructions for a computer using symbols meaningful to the computer itself or to an assembler, compiler, or other language processor.

Command   A word, mnemonic, or character that, by virtue of its syntax in a line of input, causes a computer system to perform a predefined operation.

Compile   To produce binary code from symbolic instructions written in a high-level source language.

Compiler   A program that translates a high-level source language into a language suitable for a particular machine.

Computer   A machine that can be programmed to execute a repertoire of instructions. Programs must be stored in the machine before they can be executed.

Computer program   A plan or routine for solving a problem on a computer.

Computer system   A data-processing system that consists of hardware devices, software programs, and documentation that describes the operation of the system.

Configuration   A particular selection of hardware devices or software routines or programs that function together.

Console terminal   A keyboard terminal that acts as the primary interface between the computer operator and the computer system. It is used to initiate and direct overall system operation through software running on the computer.

Constant   A value that remains the same throughout a distinct operation. (Compare with *variable*.)

Control character   A character whose presence in a particular context causes a control operation to occur, e.g., a carriage return character causing a terminal carriage return to occur.

Conversational   See *interactive processing*.

CPU   See *central processing unit*.

Crash   A hardware crash is the complete failure of a particular device, sometimes affecting the operation of an entire computer system. A software crash is the complete failure of an operating system, usually characterized by some failure in the system's protection mechanisms or flaw in the executing software.

Create   To open, write data to, and close a file for the first time. (See *file*.)

Cross-reference listing   A printed listing that identifies all references in a program to each specific symbol in a program. It includes a list of all symbols used in a source program and the statements where they are defined or used.

Data   A term used to denote any or all facts, numbers, letters, and symbols. Basic elements of information that can be processed by a computer.

Database   An organized collection of interrelated data items that allows one or more applications to process the items without regard to physical storage locations.

Data collection   The act of bringing data from one or more points to a central point for eventual processing.

Debug   To detect, locate, and correct coding or logic errors in a computer program.

Define   To assign a value to a variable or constant.

Delimiter   A character that separates, terminates, or organizes elements of a character string, statement, or program.

Device   A hardware unit such as an I/O peripheral, magnetic tape drive, or card reader.

Device control unit   A hardware unit that electronically supervises one or more of the same type of devices. It acts as the link between the computer and the I/O devices.

Device independence   The ability to program I/O operations independently of the device for which the I/O is intended.

Diagnostics   Pertaining to a set of procedures for the detection and isolation of a malfunction or mistake.

Digit   A character used to represent one of the nonnegative integers smaller than the radix (e.g., in decimal notation, one of the characters 0 to 9; in octal notation, one of the characters 0 to 7; in binary notation, one of the characters 0 and 1).

Direct access   See *random access*.

Directory   A table that contains the names of and pointers to files on a mass-storage volume.

Disk device   An auxiliary storage device on which information can be read or written.

Display   A peripheral device used to portray data graphically (normally refers to some type of cathode-ray tube system).

DMA   Direct memory access. A process whereby information can be transferred to main memory from a peripheral device without central processor intervention.

Downtime   The time interval during which a device or system is inoperative.

EBCDIC   Extended binary coded decimal interchange code. An 8-bit alphanumeric character set representation, used primarily on IBM equipment.

Edit   To arrange and/or modify the format of data (e.g., to insert or delete characters).

Editor   A program that interacts with the user to enter text into the computer and edit it. Editors are language dependent and will edit anything in character representation.

EIA interface   A standardized set of signal characteristics (time duration, voltage, and current) specified by the Electronic Industries Association. Most commonly refers to EIA recommendation RS-232C.

Emulator   A hardware device that permits a program written for a specific computer system to be run on a different type of computer system.

Error   Any discrepancy between a computed, observed, or measured quantity and the true, specified, or theoretically correct value or condition.

Error-correcting code   A code incorporating sufficient additional signal elements so as to both detect and correct errors in a data stream at the receiving end.

Execute   To carry out an instruction or run a program on the computer.

Executive   See *supervisory programs*.

Expression   A combination of operands and operators that can be evaluated to a distinct result by a computing system.

Extension   Historically used synonym for file type. Often used to imply nonstandard language features.

External storage   A storage medium other than main memory, e.g., a disk or tape.

Field   A specified area of a record used for a particular category of data.

FIFO (first in/first out)   A data manipulation method in which the first item stored is the first item processed.

File   A logical collection of data treated as a unit, which occupies one or more blocks on a mass-storage volume such as disk or magtape, and has an associated file name (and file type).

File maintenance   The activity of keeping a mass-storage volume and its directory up to date by adding, changing, or deleting files.

File name   The alphanumeric character string assigned by a user to identify a file. It can be read by both an operating system and a user. A file name has a fixed maximum length that is system dependent.

File specification   A name that uniquely identifies a file maintained in any operating system. A file specification generally consists of at least three components: a device name identifying the volume on which the file is stored, a file name, and a file type.

File-structured device   A device on which data are organized into files. The device usually contains a directory of the files stored on the volume. (For example, a disk is a file-structured device, but a line printer is not.)

Floating point   A number system in which the position of the radix point is indicated by the exponent part and another part represents the significant digits or fractional part (e.g., 5.39×10^8 for decimal; 137.3×8^4 for octal; 101.10×2^{13} for binary).

Flow chart   A graphical representation for the definition, analysis, or solution of a problem, in which symbols are used to present operations, data, flow, and equipment.

FORTRAN (FORmula TRANslation)   A problem-oriented language designed to permit scientists and engineers to express mathematical operations in a form with which they are familiar. It is also used in a variety of applications, including process control, information retrieval, and commercial data processing.

Full duplex   In communication, pertaining to a simultaneous, two-way independent transmission.

Function   An algorithm accessible by name and contained in the system software that performs commonly used operations. For example, the square root calculation function.

Half-duplex   Pertaining to a communication system in which two-way communication is possible, but only one way at a time.

Handler   See *device control unit*.

Hardware   The physical equipment components of a computer system.

Hardware bootstrap   A bootstrap that is inherent in the hardware and need only be activated by specifying the appropriate load and start address.

High-level language   A programming language whose statements are typically translated into more than one machine-language instruction. Examples are BASIC, FORTRAN, and COBOL.

Image mode   Refers to a mode of data transfer in which each byte of data is transferred without any interpretation or data changes.

Indirect address   An address that specifies a storage location containing either a direct (effective) address or another indirect (pointer) address.

Industry standard   A condition, format, or definition that is accepted as the norm by the majority of the (computer) industry.

Initialize   To set counters, switches, or addresses to starting values at prescribed points in the execution of a program, particularly in preparation for reexecution of a sequence of code. To format a volume in a particular file-structured format in preparation for use by an operating system.

Input   The data to be processed; the process of transferring data from external storage into internal storage.

Input/output device   A device attached to a computer that makes it possible to bring information into the computer or get information out.

Instruction   A coded command that tells the computer what to do and where to find the values it is to work with. A symbolic instruction looks more like ordinary language and is easier for people to deal with. Symbolic instructions must, however, be changed into machine instructions (usually by another program) before they can be executed by the computer.

Intelligent terminal   A terminal that is programmable and can perform a certain amount of processing on its messages, such as validity checking or editing.

Interactive processing   A technique of user/system communication in which the operating system immediately acknowledges and acts upon requests entered by the user at a terminal. Compare with *batch processing.*

Interface   A shared boundary. An interface might be a hardware component to link two devices or it might be a portion of storage or registers accessed by two or more computer programs or systems.

Internal storage   The storage facilities forming an integral physical part of the computer and directly controlled by the computer, e.g., the registers of the machine and main memory.

Interpreter   A computer program that translates, then executes a source language statement before translating (and executing) the next statement.

Interrupt   A signal that, when activated, causes a transfer of control to a specific location in memory, thereby breaking the normal flow of control of the routine being executed.

Interrupt driven Pertaining to software that uses the interrupt facility of a computer to handle I/O and respond to user requests.

Iteration Repetition of a group of instructions.

Job A group of data and control statements that does a unit of work, e.g., a program and all of its related subroutines, data, and control statements; also, a batch control file.

Kluge A crude, makeshift solution to a problem.

Label One or more characters used to identify a source language statement or line.

Language A set of representations, conventions, and rules used to convey information.

Latency The time from initiation of a transfer operation to the beginning of actual transfer, i.e., verification plus search time. The delay while waiting for a rotating memory to reach a given location.

Library A file containing one or more macro definitions or one or more relocatable object modules that are routines that can be incorporated into other programs.

LIFO (last in/first out) A data-manipulation method in which the last item stored is the first item processed; a push-down stack.

Light pen A device resembling a pencil or stylus that can detect a fluorescent CRT screen. Used to input information to a CRT display system.

Linkage In programming, code that connects two separately coded routines and passes values and/or control between them.

Linked file A file whose blocks are joined together by references rather than consecutive locations.

Listing The printed copy generated by a line printer or terminal.

Load To store a program or data in memory. To place a file on a device unit and put the unit on-line.

Location An address in storage or memory where a unit of data or an instruction can be stored.

Logical device name An alphanumeric name assigned by the user to represent a physical device. The name can then be used synonymously with the physical device name in all references to the device. Logical device names are used in device-independent systems to enable a program to refer to a logical device name that can be assigned to a physical device at run time.

Loop   A sequence of instructions that is executed repeatedly until a terminal condition prevails.

Machine instruction   An instruction that a machine can recognize and execute.

Machine language   The actual language used by the computer when performing operations.

Macro   An instruction in a source language that is equivalent to a specified sequence of assembler instructions, or a command in a command language that is equivalent to a specified sequence of commands.

Main program   The module of a program that contains the instructions at which program execution begins. Normally, the main program exercises primary control over the operations performed and calls subroutines or subprograms to perform specific functions.

Manual input   The entry of data by hand into a device at the time of processing.

Mass storage   Pertaining to a device that can store large amounts of data readily accessible to the computer.

Matrix   A rectangular array of elements. Any matrix can be considered an array.

Memory   Any form of data storage, including main memory and mass storage, in which data can be read and written. In the strict sense, memory refers to main memory.

MICR   Magnetic ink character recognition.

Microfiche   A sheet of microfilm capable of containing microimages in a grid pattern, usually containing a title that can be read without magnification.

Microfilm   A high-resolution film for recording microimages. To record microimages on film.

Microprogram.   A sequence of elementary instructions that corresponds to a computer operation, that is maintained in special storage, and whose execution is initiated by the introduction of a computer instruction into an instruction register of a computer.

Microprogramming   The preparation or use of microprograms.

MIS   Management information system.

Mnemonic   An alphabetic representation of a function or machine instruction.

Monitor   The master control program that observes, supervises, controls, or verifies the operation of a computer system. The collection of routines that controls the operation of user and system programs, schedules operations, allocates resources, performs I/O, etc.

MTBF   Mean time before failures. The average time for which a system or system component operates without fault.

Multiprocessing   Simultaneous execution of two or more computer programs by a computer that contains more than one central processor.

Multiprogramming   A processing method in which more than one task is in an executable state at any one time, even with one CPU.

Multitasking   See *multiprogramming*.

Multithreading   Concurrent processing of more than one request by a computer program.

Nondirectory structured   Refers to a storage volume that is sequential in structure and therefore had no volume directory at its beginning. File information (file name, file type, length, and date of creation) is provided with each file on the volume. Such volumes include magtape and cassette.

Nonfile-structured device   A device, such as paper tape, line printer, or terminal, in which data cannot be organized as multiple files.

Object code   Relocatable machine-language code.

Octal   Pertaining to the number system with a radix of eight; for example, octal 100 is decimal 64.

Off line   Pertaining to equipment or devices not currently under direct control of the computer.

Offset   The difference between a base location and the location of an element related to the base location. The number of locations relative to the base of an array, string, or block.

On line   Pertaining to equipment or devices directly connected to and under control of the computer.

Op-code (operation code)   The part of a machine-language instruction that identifies the operation the instruction will ask the CPU to perform.

Operand   That which is operated upon. An operand is usually identified by an address part of an instruction.

Operating system   The collection of programs, including a monitor or executive and system programs, that organizes a central processor and peripheral devices into a working unit for the development and execution of application programs.

Operation   The act specified by a single computer instruction. A program step undertaken or executed by a computer, e.g., addition, multiplication, comparison. The operation is usually specified by the operator part of an instruction.

Operation code See *op-code*.

Operator's console The set of switches and display lights used by an operator or a programmer to determine the status of and to start the operation of the computer system.

Option An element of a command or command string that enables the user to select from among several alternatives associated with the command.

Output The result of a process; the transferring of data from internal storage to external storage.

Overflow A condition that occurs when a mathematical operation yields a result whose magnitude is larger than the program is capable of handling.

Overlay segment A section of code treated as a unit that can overlay code already in memory and be overlaid by other overlay segments when called from the root segment or another resident overlay segment.

Overlay structure A program overlay system consisting of a root segment and optionally one or more overlay segments.

Parameter A variable that is given a constant value for a specific purpose or process.

Parity A binary digit appended to an array of binary digits to make the sum of all bits always odd or always even.

Patch To modify a routine in a rough or expedient way, usually by modifying the binary code rather than reassembling it.

Peripheral device Any device distinct from the computer that can provide input and/or accept output from the computer.

Physical device An I/O or peripheral storage device connected to or associated with a computer.

Priority A number associated with a task that determines the preference it receives for service requests from the monitor, relative to other tasks requesting service.

Process A set of related procedures and data undergoing execution and manipulation by a computer.

Processor In hardware, a data processor. In software, a computer program that includes the compiling, assembling, translating, and related functions for a specific programming language.

Program A set of machine instructions or symbolic statements combined to perform some task.

Program development The process of writing, entering, translating, and debugging source programs.

Program section   A named, contiguous unit of code (instructions or data) that is considered an entity and that can be relocated separately without destroying the logic of the program.

Programmed request   A set of instructions (available only to programs) that is used to invoke a monitor service.

Protocol   A formal set of conventions governing the format and relative timing of information exchange between two communicating processes.

Queue   Any dynamic list of items; for example, items waiting to be scheduled or processed according to system- or user-assigned priorities.

Radix   The base of a number system; the number of digit symbols required by a number system.

RAM (random access memory)   See *random access*.

Random access   Access to data in which the next location from which data are to be obtained is not dependent on the location of the previously obtained data. Contrast *sequential access*.

Read-only memory (ROM)   Memory whose contents are not alterable by computer instructions.

Real-time processing   Computation performed while a related or controlled physical activity is occurring so that the results of the computation can be used in guiding the process.

Record   A collection of related items of data treated as a unit; for example, a line of source code or a person's name, rank, and serial number.

Recursive   A repetitive process in which the result of each process is dependent upon the result of the previous one.

Reentrant   Pertaining to a program composed of a shareable segment of pure code and a nonshareable segment that is the data area.

Relative address   The number that specifies the difference between the actual address and a base address.

Relocate   In programming, to move a routine from one portion of storage to another and to adjust the necessary address references so that the routine, in its new location, can be executed.

Resident   Pertaining to data or instructions that are normally permanently located in main memory.

Resource   Any means available to users, such as computational power, programs, data files, storage capacity, or a combination of these.

Response time   The time a system takes to provide a response to a user request.

Restart   To resume execution of a program.

RO   Receive only. Used in reference to terminals that may be used for printed or displayed output only and have no input capability.

ROM   See *read-only memory.*

Routine   A set of instructions arranged in proper sequence to cause a computer to perform a desired operation.

Run   A single, continuous execution of a program.

Sector   A physical portion of a mass-storage device.

Segment   See *overlay segment.*

Sequential access   Access to data in which the next location from which data are to be obtained sequentially follows the location of the previously obtained data. Contrast *random access.*

Simulate   To represent certain features of the behavior of a physical or abstract system by the behavior of another system, e.g., to represent a physical phenomenon by means of operations performed by a computer or to represent the operations of a computer by those of another computer. To imitate one system with another, primarily by software, so that the initiating system accepts the same data, executes the same computer programs, and achieves the same results as the imitated system. Contrast *emulate.*

Simulator   A device, data-processing system, or computer program that represents certain features of the behavior of a physical or abstract system.

Software   The collection of programs and routines associated with a computer (e.g., compilers, library routines).

Software bootstrap   A bootstrap that is activated by manually loading the instructions of the bootstrap and specifying the appropriate load and start address.

Source code   Text, usually in the form of an ASCII format file, that represents a program. Such a file can be processed by an appropriate system program.

Source language   The system of symbols and syntax easily understood by people that is used to describe a procedure that a computer can execute.

Spooling   The technique by which I/O with slow devices is placed on mass-storage devices to await processing.

Storage   Pertaining to a device into which data can be entered, in which it can be held, and from which it can be retrieved at a later time.

String   A connected sequence of entities such as a line of characters.

Subprogram   A program or a sequence of instructions that can be called to perform the same task (though perhaps on different data) at different points in a program, or even in different programs.

Subroutine See *subprogram.*

Subscript A numeric valued expression or expression element that is appended to a variable name to uniquely identify specific elements of an array. Subscripts are enclosed in parentheses. There is a subscript for each dimension of an array. Multiple subscripts must be separated by commas. For example, a two-dimensional subscript might be (2, 5).

Supervisory programs Computer programs that have the primary function of scheduling, allocating, and controlling system resources rather than processing data to produce results.

Swapping The process of moving data from memory to a mass-storage device, temporarily using the evacuated memory area for another purpose, and then restoring the original data to memory.

Synchronous Pertaining to related events where all changes occur simultaneously or in definite timed intervals.

Syntax The structure of expressions in a language and the rules governing the structure of a language.

System program A program that performs system-level functions. Any program that is part of or supplied with the basic operating system (e.g., a system utility program).

System volume The volume on which the operating system is stored.

Table A collection of data into a well-defined list.

Terminal An I/O device that includes a keyboard and a display mechanism.

Time sharing A method of allocating resources to multiple users so that the computer, in effect, processes a number of programs concurrently. A mode of operation that provides for the interleaving of two or more independent processes on one functional unit. Pertaining to the interleaved use of time on a computing system that enables two or more users to execute computer programs concurrently.

Translate To convert from one language to another.

Trap A conditional jump to a known memory location performed automatically by hardware as a side effect of executing a processor instruction. The address location from which the jump occurs is recorded. It is distinguished from an interrupt, which is caused by an external event.

Truncation The reduction of precision by ignoring one or more of the least significant digits; e.g., 3.141597 truncated to four decimal digits is 3.141.

Turing machine A mathematical model of a device that changes its internal state and reads from, writes on, and moves a potentially infinite tape, all in accordance with its present state, thereby constituting a model for computerlike behavior.

Turnaround time The elapsed time between submission of a job and the return of complete results.

Turnkey Pertaining to a computer system sold in a ready-to-use state.

Two's complement A number used to represent the negative of a given value in many computers. This number is formed from the given binary value by changing all 1's to 0's and all 0's to 1's, and then adding 1.

User program An application program.

Utility program Any general-purpose program included in an operating system to perform common functions.

Variable The symbolic representation of a logical storage location that can contain a value that changes during a processing operation.

Virtual storage The notion of space on storage devices that may be regarded as main storage by the user of a computing system, in which virtual addresses are mapped into real addresses. The size of the virtual storage is limited only by the addressing scheme of the computing system and by the amount of auxiliary storage available, rather than by the actual number of main storage locations.

appendix B
CHECKLISTS

1. Identifying Requirements
2. Vendor Evaluation and Selection: Larger Micros and Minis
3. Vendor Evaluation and Selection: Desktop Micros
4. Implementation Checklists and Reports
   a. Implementation Checklists
      - Planning
      - Data-File Conversion
      - Training
      - Testing
      - Supporting Documentation
   b. Other Forms
      - Report/Output Review
      - Program Modification Log
      - File Conversion
      - Application Procedure Description
      - Low-Volume Test Plan

IDENTIFYING REQUIREMENTS
STEPS TO TAKE BEFORE COMMUNICATING WITH VENDORS

		Date	
		Target	Actual
1.	Define goals	_____	_____
2.	Define present systems		
	a. Gather sample input documents	_____	_____
	b. Gather sample reports and generated documents	_____	_____
	c. Prepare flow charts of present systems	_____	_____
	d. Prepare work sheets		
	i. Input fields and volumes	_____	_____
	ii. Output fields and volumes	_____	_____
	iii. Calculate clerical time	_____	_____
3.	Identify and document information requirements		
	a. Prepare outline of requirements	_____	_____
	b. Prepare report layouts	_____	_____
4.	Identify and document systems for automation		
	a. Prepare systems summary schedule	_____	_____
	b. Select systems for automation		
	i. Calculate cost savings	_____	_____
	ii. Document intangible benefits	_____	_____
	iii. Select systems	_____	_____
	c. Specify system relationships and summarize key features	_____	_____
	d. Document file requirements	_____	_____
	e. Summarize volume requirements		
	i. Input	_____	_____
	ii. Files	_____	_____
	iii. Output	_____	_____

5. Identify and evaluate alternatives
   a. Identify alternatives   ———————   ———————

   b. Evaluate alternatives

      i. Perform research   ———————   ———————

      ii. Calculate present value of investment   ———————   ———————

      iii. Perform cost/benefit analysis   ———————   ———————

VENDOR EVALUATION AND SELECTION
LARGER MICROS AND MINIS

		Date	
		Target	Actual
1.	Draft Request for Proposal (RFP)	_____	_____
2.	Determine evaluation criteria		
	a. Cost limit	_____	_____
	b. Overall rating approach	_____	_____
3.	Finalize RFP	_____	_____
4.	Identify vendor candidates	_____	_____
5.	Contact vendor candidates	_____	_____
6.	Mail RFPs	_____	_____
7.	Screen RFP candidates	_____	_____
8.	Summarize evaluation results	_____	_____
9.	Select vendor finalists	_____	_____
10.	Check vendor references and revise evaluations as necessary	_____	_____
11.	Attend demonstrations	_____	_____
12.	Perform final evaluation	_____	_____
13.	Negotiate vendor contract	_____	_____

VENDOR EVALUATION AND SELECTION
DESKTOP MICROS

	Date	
	Target	*Actual*

1. Identify vendor candidates
   a. Review current literature for industry leaders _____ _____

   b. Locate dealers _____ _____

2. Screen vendor candidates
   a. Visit dealers and tour facilities _____ _____

   b. Determine maintenance capability _____ _____

   c. Determine whether dealer has application software for all your applications _____ _____

   d. Eliminate unsatisfactory dealers _____ _____

   e. Obtain product brochures _____ _____

   f. Schedule demonstration appointment _____ _____

3. Attend demonstrations and evaluate vendors
   a. Complete Software Demonstration Checklist _____ _____

   b. Complete Hardware Demonstration Checklist _____ _____

   c. Obtain Vendor Price Quotation _____ _____

4. Select the best alternative _____ _____

IMPLEMENTATION CHECKLIST
PLANNING

Task identification	Company personnel			Vendor Level	Completion date	
	Name	Level	Hours		Target	Actual
Assess needs and skills	_____	_____	_____	_____	_____	_____
Assemble project team	_____	_____	_____	_____	_____	_____
Inventory available and unavailable time	_____	_____	_____	_____	_____	_____
Commence documentation journal	_____	_____	_____	_____	_____	_____
Review vendor implementation plan	_____	_____	_____	_____	_____	_____
Review detailed systems design	_____	_____	_____	_____	_____	_____
Prepare implementation check-lists and summarize time requirements	_____	_____	_____	_____	_____	_____
Assign responsibilities	_____	_____	_____	_____	_____	_____
Arrange for temporary assistance as necessary	_____	_____	_____	_____	_____	_____
Schedule project team meetings and milestone reviews	_____	_____	_____	_____	_____	_____
Perform postimplementation evaluation	_____	_____	_____	_____	_____	_____

NOTE: "Level" = Review, perform, and so forth.

IMPLEMENTATION CHECKLIST
DATA FILE CONVERSION

Task identification	Company personnel			Vendor Level	Completion date	
	Name	Level	Hours		Target	Actual
Define requirements	_____	_____	_____	_____	_____	_____
Determine key dates	_____	_____	_____	_____	_____	_____
Define conversion techniques Presently computerized files	_____	_____	_____	_____	_____	_____
Noncomputerized files	_____	_____	_____	_____	_____	_____
Establish conversion schedule	_____	_____	_____	_____	_____	_____
Specify test criteria for files to be converted (to determine that conversion is complete and accurate)	_____	_____	_____	_____	_____	_____
Perform testing of converted files	_____	_____	_____	_____	_____	_____
Document test results	_____	_____	_____	_____	_____	_____
Status report	_____	_____	_____	_____	_____	_____

IMPLEMENTATION CHECKLIST
TRAINING

Task identification	Company personnel			Vendor Level	Completion date	
	Name	Level	Hours		Target	Actual
Assess training requirements	_____	_____	_____	_____	_____	_____
Assign training responsibilities	_____	_____	_____	_____	_____	_____
Develop training schedule	_____	_____	_____	_____	_____	_____
Review plan with management	_____	_____	_____	_____	_____	_____
Obtain training materials	_____	_____	_____	_____	_____	_____
Schedule training	_____	_____	_____	_____	_____	_____
Rehearse in-house briefings and trainings	_____	_____	_____	_____	_____	_____
Conduct training sessions	_____	_____	_____	_____	_____	_____
Monitor outside training	_____	_____	_____	_____	_____	_____

IMPLEMENTATION CHECKLIST
TESTING

Task identification	Company personnel			Vendor Level	Completion date	
	Name	Level	Hours		Target	Actual
Assess overall requirements and prepare plan	——	——	——	——	——	——
Review site requirements and prepare plan	——	——	——	——	——	——
User review of plan	——	——	——	——	——	——
Schedule activities	——	——	——	——	——	——
Review vendor test plan	——	——	——	——	——	——
Draft input and output control forms	——	——	——	——	——	——
Prepare detailed low-volume test plan	——	——	——	——	——	——
Review test results	——	——	——	——	——	——
Initiate modifications	——	——	——	——	——	——
Retest and review results	——	——	——	——	——	——
Perform parallel runs	——	——	——	——	——	——
Document results	——	——	——	——	——	——
Management acceptance	——	——	——	——	——	——

IMPLEMENTATION CHECKLIST
SUPPORTING DOCUMENTATION

Task identification	Company personnel			Vendor Level	Completion date	
	Name	Level	Hours		Target	Actual
Assign responsibilities	_____	_____	_____	_____	_____	_____
Prepare documentation standards	_____	_____	_____	_____	_____	_____
Document input and output formats	_____	_____	_____	_____	_____	_____
Review vendor manuals	_____	_____	_____	_____	_____	_____
Develop error recovery procedures	_____	_____	_____	_____	_____	_____
Develop DP operations manual (incorporate vendor materials as applicable)	_____	_____	_____	_____	_____	_____
Approve DP operations manual	_____	_____	_____	_____	_____	_____
Prepare system controls plan	_____	_____	_____	_____	_____	_____
Detail general and application controls	_____	_____	_____	_____	_____	_____
Prepare contingency plan	_____	_____	_____	_____	_____	_____
Approve standard operating procedures manual	_____	_____	_____	_____	_____	_____

REPORT/OUTPUT REVIEW

Application _____   Page _____ of _____

                                           Date _____

Prepared by _____ Reviewed by _____

Report name _____ Format _____

                                           (Hard copy, CRT, etc.)

Current report equivalent _____

Frequency of preparation _____

Distribution _____

Adequacy of:
    Headings _____ If not adequate, suggest any changes _____

                                    _____

                                      _____

    Formats _____ If not adequate, suggest any changes _____

                                      _____

                                      _____

Any missing elements _____ If so, describe _____

                                      _____

                                      _____

Program/module identification   _____

Change description _____

_____

Completed _____ Verified _____

PROGRAM MODIFICATION LOG

	Name	Date
Prepared by	_____	_____
Approved by	_____	_____
Page _____ of _____		

System _____

Application _____

Modification narrative _____

_____

_____

_____

_____

_____

Program/module identification _____

Change description _____

_____

_____

_____

_____

_____

_____

FILE CONVERSION

Date ____/____/____ Prepared by _____ Review date ____/____/____

1. MASTER FILES

File identification	*Transfer ready date*	*Proposed transfer method*
_____	_____	_____
		_____
		_____
_____	_____	_____
		_____
		_____
_____	_____	_____
		_____
		_____
_____	_____	_____
		_____

2. TRANSACTION FILES

_____	_____	_____
		_____
		_____
_____	_____	_____
		_____
		_____
_____	_____	_____
		_____
		_____
_____	_____	_____

APPLICATION PROCEDURE DESCRIPTION

Name   Date

Prepared by _____   _____

Approved by _____   _____

Page _____ of _____

Procedure name _____

Purpose _____

_____

Performed by _____

Input source(s) _____

Output disposition _____

Entry edit rules _____

_____

_____

Instructions _____

Normal results _____

Description	Error message source	Suggested recovery
_____	_____	_____
_____	_____	_____
_____	_____	_____
_____	_____	_____
_____	_____	_____

Handling of exceptions _____

_____

_____

References for help _____

_____